Vienna and the Young Hitler

Vienna AND
THE YOUNG HITLER

By WILLIAM A. JENKS

Columbia University Press   New York   1960

TO JANE

Preface

WHILE it is dubious that Adolf Hitler ever will receive the attention which has been lavished upon Napoleon Bonaparte, there are increasing indications that Hitler's rise and fall continue to interest the generations which suffered from the forces he represented.

My study adds nothing to the biographical data previously collected. It attempts rather to re-create the Vienna in which Hitler spent six aimless but intensely important years. Granted that a reading of *Mein Kampf* calls for great caution, there still emerges from its early chapters a conviction that practically all of the future dictator's disreputable ideas were conceived or stimulated while he sojourned in the Habsburg capital. At times my text inevitably will wander from the picture of young Adolf in Vienna to the larger tableau of the city itself, for he left no explicit diary of all of the events or tendencies which aroused his attention.

Konrad Heiden's *Der Fuehrer* represents the first admirable work done in tracking down the outlines of the "Vienna period." Since the crash of the Nazi empire two of Hitler's friends of the Viennese days have recorded their impressions. Josef Greiner's *Das Ende des Hitler-Mythos* depicts the truly miserable vagrant-dreamer, and, though some of his episodes severely strain one's imagination, he gives an excellent atmospheric touch. August Kubizek's *Adolf Hitler: Mein Jugendfreund*, available in English under the title *The Young Hitler I Knew*, is an extremely valuable and credible memoir whose worth is attested by H. R. Trevor-Roper's introduction to the English version. Here we have fine descriptions of the last years in Linz and part of the first year spent in Vienna. This Hitler, of course, has yet to develop to the full his venom and frustrated hates, and it is rewarding to contrast Greiner's characterization with Kubizek's. In 1956 Franz Jetzinger published *Hitlers Jugend*, in which he attempts to discredit Kubizek's intimate knowledge of the Hitler family. More convincing are his praiseworthy efforts to bring order into the chronological confusion that inevitably surrounds these earlier years and his interesting account of Hitler's return to Salzburg in February, 1914, to face the question of his military service.

Save for the very recent English version of Jetzinger's volume, I have employed for the general reader the English translations of works originally published in German. Some excellent authorities on the Dual Monarchy will regret my use of the term "Christian Socialists" in place of "Christian Socials." Since usage permits "Utopian Socialists" and "National Socialists," I have kept to the less awkward version.

I am very much indebted to Professor William W. Pusey, III, of Washington and Lee University for his helpful advice on most of the manuscript. I also have profited greatly from the suggestions of my editor, Mr. William F. Bernhardt. Mr. Henry E. Coleman, Jr. and Miss Martha R. Cullipher of the McCormick Library of Washington and Lee University have been constantly generous with their time and skill, while the personnel of the Library of the University of Vienna never failed to evidence efficiency and kindness.

My research was made possible by a grant-in-aid from funds given to Washington and Lee University by the Carnegie Foundation for the Advancement of Teaching and by a Fulbright Award to Austria in 1955. The Glenn Grant Publications Fund of Washington and Lee University made a considerable contribution toward the cost of publication.

WILLIAM A. JENKS

Lexington, Virginia

Contents

Vienna and the Young Hitler

But Vienna was and remained for me the hardest, but also the most thorough, school of my life. I had once entered this city when still half a boy and I left it as a man who had become quiet and serious. In that city I received the basis of a view of life in general and a political way of looking at things in particular which later on I had only to supplement in single instances, but which never again deserted me. But it is only today that I am able to appreciate fully the real value of those years of learning.

This is the reason why I have dealt with this period more fully, as it gave me the first object lessons in those very questions which formed part of the fundamental principles of the party which, rising from the smallest beginnings, is in the course of hardly five years on the way to develop into a great mass movement. I do not know what my attitude towards Judaism, Social Democracy, or better Marxism, social problems, etc., would be today if the basic stock of personal opinions had not been formed at so early a time under the pressure of fate and of my own learning.

ADOLF HITLER, *Mein Kampf*, 1924

Introduction

THE DEVELOPMENT of one of the truly catastrophic cases
of totalitarian nationalism in a city that was for centuries noted
for internationalism is one of the supreme ironies of our era.
The House of Habsburg, with its anchor in Vienna, was the
living relic of Western man's long-standing belief that Christen-
dom required a commonwealth to complement the spiritual
authority of the Church. The rise of national states, the religious
revolution of the sixteenth century, and the thrust of Bona-
partism had shattered the always insubstantial foundations of the
Holy Roman Empire, but the Habsburgs and Vienna never
ceased to seek fresh energies from a multitude of sources. To
eliminate the enigmatic Wallenstein during the Thirty Years'
War, the instruments of imperial polity were a General Pic-
colomini from Pisa, a Father Taaffe from Ireland, a Captain
Devereux from England. To follow up Vienna's salvation by
the Polish Sobieski in 1683, the Parisian Eugene of Savoy, whose
mother was of the Mazarin clan, first destroyed Turks by the
thousands and then contemptuously rolled back the armies of
Louis XIV, the Sun King who once had tried to thwart his
military ambitions. In the eighteenth century a Kaunitz, whose
family had only recently Germanized its Moravian Slavic origins, restored Habsburg diplomatic prestige, if not fair Silesia.
The Rhinelanders Stadion and Metternich, "mediatized" by the
triumphant march of liberty, equality, and fraternity, volun-
teered the Habsburgs their enthusiasm and intelligence in the
struggle against Napoleon.

The good folk of Vienna make jokes over their varied antecedents. The guide who beguiles a busload of weekend vacation-

ers during the last dull miles with his burlesque of a Viennese Czech's command of German knows that half his audience have a Czech grandparent and will laugh with the rest. The handsome woman who is Octavian in *Der Rosenkavalier* at the Staatsoper makes a wry face over the lines that concern Croatia, her father's land, but her actual performance is always described in "Viennese" as *charmant*. The menu one faces in a superior hotel is as much of a linguistic hurdle for a Westphalian as for someone from Wisconsin and largely accounts for the Berliner's absolute impatience with Vienna.

Yet this was the city in which Hitler, on his own testimony, learned his basic lessons in ideology. This was the city, if one trusts Konrad Adenauer's bitter jab, which more rapturously than any other German city applauded the triumphal entry of its onetime sojourner.

The dynasty's internationalism during Hitler's formative years was not simply shored up by Vienna's increasingly varied population. During the 1860s and 1870s a distinguished group of intellectuals, aristocrats, bureaucrats, and army officers gave allegiance to the tenets of Liberalism, and they had dreams of seeing the day when the similarly minded Crown Prince Rudolph would mount the throne and repel the forces of "darkness." Closely allied with the world of industry, business, and press, these German Liberals of Austria sympathized fully with their spiritual brothers in England, France, the German Empire, Italy, and other countries where ecumenical Liberalism had sizeable bodies of supporters. Their "internationalism" embraced a fervent belief in freedom of economic activity, speech, and press, in parliamentary immunity and control of state budgets, and in rigid separation of church and state. Their stand on suffrage, however, was conditioned by their honest conviction that the more literate Germans of Austria should continue to preponderate over less well-educated (and probably poorer) Slavs, Rumanians, and Italians.

Vienna was their earthly paradise. Here their ties with the moneyed and talented stimulated a lively salon and literary activity in which some landed aristocrats, many ennobled financiers, and a substantial number of successful Jews intermingled. But it was the bureaucracy which gave Liberalism its momentary strength and patina. Recruited primarily from the legal graduates of Austrian universities, the new civil servants combined the doggedness which the old-time traditions demanded with a doctrinaire assertiveness that steadily widened the gap between their party comrades and the peasantry, the workers, the devout Roman Catholics, and, most tragic of all, Liberal-minded Czech, Slovene, Italian, and Ruthene leaders. In the process younger Liberals drifted into the more uncompromising German Nationalist movement or discerned a greater challenge to serve all of humanity in the still uncongealed and raucous "Democracy" and "Christian Socialism" of the more disaffected Viennese wards. Also appealing to some of the secessionists was Marxian Socialism, though adherence to this creed was often a risk in the 1880s, when anarchism and socialism were identical in the minds of polite society.

German Liberals dominated Austrian political life, save for a brief interlude, from 1867 to 1879, when Francis Joseph tired of their internal disagreements and their less than united support of the occupation of Bosnia-Herzegovina. Thereafter the scene belonged to increasingly vociferous non-German politicians and to German Nationalists, to radical and conservative German Catholic factions, and to a Marxian Socialism that divested itself of an ultraviolent wing to secure a greater degree of toleration from cabinet and police. These developments were the inevitable concomitants of the rapidly changing social and economic scene, for Austria was catching up with more industrialized areas and the problems industrialization creates without in any way escaping a deterioration of her farmers' situation.

Some of the tension which affected pre-1914 Europe and Austria had its origin in the painful readjustment agriculture had to make in response to the technical revolutions of the nineteenth century. The increasing use of machinery on fertile North and South American plains, plus speedier modes of ocean transportation, brought on real distress in lands such as Austria where farming had been small-scale and relatively easy-going.

The German Empire's Agrarian League had its counterparts in every European country whose farmers raged over American tinned beef and disastrously competitive Canadian and Russian wheat. The tillers of the soil are notoriously reticent about full participation in politics, but they had numerous champions in the party-life of the day. In France it might be a lawyer of their market-town whom they sent to the Chamber of Deputies, while in Austria it might be an aristocrat who could not quite abide belching smokestacks and the moral laxity of urban slums. These champions tirelessly depicted in their speeches the pleasant virtues of the unblemished countryside, always as the antithesis of the corrupt and alien-ridden city. Austrian farmers liked politicians who manifested keen distrust of big business, of anticlericalism, and of the Jews, whether the last-named were accused of fomenting assassinations of emperors or of rigging stock markets. The peasant's grim-visaged resentment of his precarious situation colored the political life of all of the Western and Central countries of the Continent, and it was the farmer whose vote did much to cut down laisser-faire Liberalism and to restrain Marxian Socialism in Austria.

Social and economic tensions likewise affected life in the urban areas. Probably no Continental country suffered the rigors of early industrialism as much as England had, but long hours, low pay, depressing and unsafe factories, and submarginal housing were the lot of thousands of Europeans. Where the worker was a recent migrant from the country, his disgruntlement was usually softened by the bustle and tinsel of his new surroundings. At the lowest level he found it easier to be free of the moral restrictions he knew on farms or in villages. On a different level he had increased chances to immerse himself in political movements or to absorb the pat information ladled out by cheap journal, self-help club, or neighborhood "folk-protection" group. His partner in the crowded factory might be far less hypnotized by the city's glamor, for thousands of the new proletariat were descended from the once-flourishing artisan class, whose skill with simply manipulated machines had been overwhelmed by the swift motion and efficiency of newer industrial devices. Acutely conscious of a descent to a lower social stratum, such displaced handicraftsmen were as avid as the irate peasantry for an explanation, a scapegoat, and speedy rehabilitation. With the hard-pressed shopkeeper and businessman, who alternately denounced mammoth enterprise and misleading peddlers, the artisan-turned-proletarian was a natural convert to any program which stressed a return to the "good old times" and a regard for the dignity of the laborer and his individual product.

Especially tailor-made for such anguished "victims" of big industry were the Catholic confessional parties, whose social consciousness distinctly antedated Leo XIII's proclamation of a Catholic labor policy in 1891. Most effective of these organizations was the German Empire's Center Party, which attracted peasants, businessmen, artisans, and factory workers alike. Its stalwart opposition to Bismarck's more reactionary moves enhanced its standing with Catholic intellectuals, and its generally cool attitude to *Weltpolitik* in William II's reign garnered non-Catholic votes as well. With well-organized trade-union and youth movements, it was a pivotal force in German politics. In Austria the Christian Social movement, similarly attuned to the aspirations of the dispossessed or threatened classes, built up an expert propaganda and effected noteworthy changes in Vienna before losing its attractiveness to the "little man" there. Thereafter it found replacements in the rural areas of German Austria, whose inhabitants were ripe for the leadership which town-dwellers nearly always have furnished their country relatives.

The Christian Social movement's precipitate decline in Vienna after 1910 and the less than noteworthy advance of avowed Catholic parties in France and Italy point to the increasing vogue of Marxian Socialism among those laborers who were convinced that proletarian solidarity was worth more than a reconstruction of capitalistic society. Roman Catholic activism, first inspired by revulsion against reckless laisser faire, gradually awakened to the threat of Marxism, but it never substantially undercut the allurements which millions of voters in Western and Central Europe found in economic determinism. Many workers were suspicious of a party which enrolled employers as well as laborers, while thousands more demonstrated their "progressivism" and "modernity" by rejecting a political affiliation honestly based on religious precepts.

After devastating factional quarrels in the 1880s, international Socialism entered upon an era of comparative harmony after 1890 that was ruffled but never seriously menaced by the rise of revisionists who were willing to forego a rigorous belief in all of the Marxist gospel in favor of admittedly opportunist deals which would ease the proletariat's lot then rather than later. The Second International absorbed this danger to doctrinal conformity rather astutely, and in actuality the member parties often practiced a revisionism which brought applause and support from nonproletarians while clinging formally to the corpus of Marxian analysis and prediction.

Otherwise it would be almost impossible to explain the amazing number of ballots that went to Socialists between 1890 and 1914, most conspicuously in the German Empire, France, and Belgium. When restrictions on universal suffrage were temporarily or permanently relaxed, as in Austria, Russia, and Italy, Marxian parties always profited. Some adherents were seekers of bloody revolution, and many of this sort had their chance in the chaotic days of 1917–18. But a vast number, whether they had heard of Eduard Bernstein's revisionism or not, simply believed with him that Socialism was not intent upon destroying bourgeois society. "Rather, it labors incessantly at lifting the worker from the social position of a proletarian to that of a 'bourgeois' and thus to make 'bourgeoisie'—or citizenship—universal." [1]

If party leaders denounced Bernstein while acting very much on his principles, amateur students of Marxism were sometimes understandably convinced that Socialists were enemies of tradition, of nationality, of order, and of decency. The countess in the baroque *Palais* in Vienna had her confreres in the student who desperately wanted a post in the government or in the ill-prepared lower middle-class lad who abhorred the prospects of a life spent in a mill or carrying bricks. In the kaleidoscopic political arena that was Europe on the eve of war in 1914, it was impossible to know how many men were Socialists for principle's sake or how many were anti-Socialist for desperation's sake. Young Hitler was among the latter, and it is not surprising that he admired a most persuasive Catholic activist while never moving very far from a sturdy German nationalism in his own recoil from Marxism.

A steady round of international Socialist meetings never failed to grapple with nationalism as the greatest obstacle to the fulfillment of Utopia. War and its evils were never far from the conferees' minds, and hours beyond number were spent denouncing the armaments race, the delusions of jingoism, and the procedures all good Marxists must follow should the "imperialist" war break out. The emphasis was proper, for the European states abounded in a hopeless variety of nationalistic impulses, most of which deserved the later appellation of "totalitarian."

French intellectuals, stung by the defeat of 1870-71, preached traditionalism, or regionalism, or even a cult of ancestor-veneration as ripostes to concepts of individualism and popular sovereignty. In Germany Treitschke wrote of war "as an institution ordained of God," praised the Germans as the creative and masculine element in modern history, and vented his contempt upon complacently prosperous neighbors such as Switzerland, Belgium, and the Netherlands. The Russian Danilevsky saw only rottenness and senility in the West, with whom his people inevitably would fight. In the end a victorious Russia would synthesize the Hebrew gift for religion, the Greek aptitude for art, the Roman talent for politics, and the European competence for securing economic supremacy.

It is unfair to single out three European states in a brief attempt to recall the ethnocentric absurdities of an age which agreed only that the white man was a chosen vessel of God or the logical instrument of an evolutionary and mechanistic fate. Italy had her dreams of a revived Rome, England cheerfully shouldered her task of leading the world, while less fearsome

Magyars, Serbs, Irish, and Czechs, to name but a few, recklessly worked out their schemes of national protection or aggrandizement.

If the intelligentsia uttered the boastful words which were refashioned by the comparatively new popular newspapers to fit the levels of the literacy of the day, the statesmen, the diplomats, and the parliamentarians kept up their loyalties to monarch and native land by regularly falling into nasty international crises from which they extricated themselves with growing difficulty. Rumelia, Siam, Afghanistan, Port Arthur, Morocco, Bosnia—the foci of collisions were as exotic as the adventure serials of the day, and the bored laborer, with his *Petit Parisien* and his carafe of *rouge*, could get a genuine thrill from his government's manful decision to stay where the troops had been sent. In England it might be the impoverished miner who took some satisfaction from the final reckoning with Sudanese or Boer, and in Vienna the zealous Sudeten student might feel his spirits rise when the imperial ministers steadfastly declined to revoke the annexation of Bosnia-Herzegovina.

When national egoism suffered a rebuff, then the recriminations against ally and the choked anger against opponent reached unhappy proportions. Often it was enough to cavil at "English selfishness," "Italian duplicity," or "German obtuseness." In areas, however, where there was painful remembrance of recent physical defeat or where class and income differences were especially marked, there was a traditional quarry to be subjected to abuse—the Jew. In England, the German Empire, and Italy antisemites existed, but down to 1914 their influence was slight. In France, Austria, Russia, and Rumania antisemitism was the order of the day, vigorously contested only where representative government had some established roots.

Hitler's homeland had more than its share of European antisemitism, as the following study hopes to indicate. But Vienna and Austria were not alone in giving welcome to this stubborn prejudice, and it might be remembered that young Adolf's supposedly first encounter with Jews involved refugees from tsarist persecution. The pogroms of Bessarabia and other lands of the

Jewish Pale in Russia were the worst examples of Christian inhumanity to Jew. In the West there sometimes was a rather sour legalistic insistence that one's antisemitism was merely religious, or economic, and not "racial." Such distinctions were especially commanded of Catholic activist parties, if not absolutely followed in the sometimes rough electioneering. Liberals and Marxists in all lands vigorously censured manifestations of "racial" and religious prejudice, often, it must be admitted, to defend the Jews who had naturally gravitated to their organizations. It should be remembered, however, that it was their championing of toleration and equality which first made them attractive to many Jews, whether rich or impoverished.

The outspoken antisemite who built his entire system upon hatred of the Jew was abetted considerably by the apologists for specific nationalisms. In France Taine was a protagonist of the Aryan cult because he was sure that the "Aryans" were superior to Semitic and Chinese "races." Barrès castigated internationalism as a Jewish "trick" created to protect Jewish investments and credit in all lands and to allow the Jews to continue to feast upon the blood of "good" Frenchmen. If Taine and Barrès had enough prestige as writers to counterbalance somewhat their unpleasant notions, Édouard Drumont, the ace Jew-baiter of the period, was more typical of the irresponsible journalist common to antisemitic circles in Central Europe. He ranted about a "Jewish system" that held France in chains and that destroyed her will to fight. No lie was too crude for the columns of his newspaper, *La Libre Parole*, and his monotonous and reckless tirades were eagerly reprinted or imitated in "racialist" organs outside of France.

Treitschke, the highly respected German professor, was responsible for saying, "The Jews are our misfortune," though actually he desired the assimilation of those already in the Reich. His implicit repudiation of racialism was echoed by the far more sensational Adolf Stöcker, whose antisemitism was honestly economic. Though the latter went beyond accusations of Jewish frivolity and fraud to demands that Jews be limited in the number of judgeships and teaching positions they could fill, he heartily praised the Jew whom he deemed to be industrious, patriotic, and upright. The parties he led had little real success at the polls, however. The germs had to be incubated for some years before Germany would rival Austria, France, and Russia in succumbing to the more feverish stage of the disease.

In the Russia of Alexander III and Nicholas II there was little need for intellectualized or journalistic apologia for antisemitism. The implacable court figures, Pobedonostsev and Plehve, offered firm juristic and police support for persecutions that generally outraged the West. Antisemites in Western Europe were quick to argue that Russian policy was proof that Jews were troublesome and dangerous, and their asseverations lost nothing in volume when Jewish refugees began escaping from tsardom. The Habsburg monarchy was particularly the haven for many of the unfortunate, and the course of antisemitism in Vienna clearly was influenced by this fact. But such prejudice was never a Viennese monopoly. In an era of vast economic change it appeared wherever other resentments obtained, and, as it had for centuries, it rallied its devotees primarily among the poor, the demoralized, and the thoughtless.

Hitler's generation was subject to growing religious indifference as well as to the dislocations of a rapidly expanding world economy and the thrills and dangers of nationalism and its offshoots. Urbanization was increasingly productive of apathy among nominal church members, for the second half of the nineteenth century witnessed far fewer examples of laborers who found comfort in the Christian hereafter rather than in the "here." There were new allegiances, more modern, seemingly more dynamic, sometimes more "practical." Socialism taught an earthly millennium that went well with the materialistic ethos of the times. Nationalism brought a man out of himself as pilgrimages and hymn-singing once had done. Pure self-indulgence had its own rewards, and it was downright simple to escape moral condemnation in the cities. The famous skirmish between science and religion often reinforced the convictions already induced by Socialism, or nationalism, or simple hedonism, but it is dubious that it primarily or conclusively stirred many of the masses.

The figures were sometimes shockingly revealing. In Berlin in the 1880s, 26 percent of the births, 59 percent of the marriages, and 80 percent of the burials dispensed with religious accompaniment of any kind. In Russia subservience to the state, ignorance, and inertia characterized the Orthodox Church. Leo XIII set Roman Catholicism on a new social and economic course that was as praiseworthy as it was imperative, but the tide of ingrown anticlericalism in Italy, France, Austria, and the German Empire moved back imperceptibly. The emancipated Western Jew proudly integrated himself with a particular European nationality, often embracing Christianity or "neutrality," though his Eastern cousins of the unyielding Orthodox persuasion offered what was an impressive example in an epoch of fluctuating allegiances of loyalty to spiritual heritage.

Certainly there was nothing peculiar to Vienna and German Austria that made inevitable the production of an Adolf Hitler. Paris, Berlin, London, Rome, and the rest of the great cities knew overpopulation, poverty, the restlessness and impatience which come from a marked disequilibrium in the sharing of the world's goods. The individual nations and empires ran neck-and-neck in their nationalistic egoism and in their daring quest for new areas to exploit. From the Neva to the Tagus young men rejected established standards and treasured credos, most often giving their support to programs that reflected the era's staunch faith in man's capacity to aid man. Some became disillusioned before the Great War of 1914–18 broke out, and more were shocked into a tougher frame of mind by its horrifying course. A dozen cities or milieus could have produced fifty Hitlers from the generation that reached manhood by 1914. The making of a particular Hitler in a particular milieu is the theme of what follows.

Voices of Spring: Vienna, 1906

ADOLF HITLER's fateful encounter with enchanting and implacable Vienna began early in May, 1906. Our best source for his adolescent days, August Kubizek, does not spell out the reasons which prompted this first visit, but it seems reasonably clear that young Adolf was merely another provincial who wanted to inspect the wonders of Francis Joseph's glittering capital. His interests, to be sure, ran to the fine arts, and his postcards to Kubizek mentioned trips to the opera and the theater. When the latter wrote his invaluable recollections in after years, he noted that Hitler had significantly picked cards illustrating buildings—the rather startling Karlskirche, the imposing Musikvereinssaal, the exterior and interior of the Imperial Opera, and the stately Parliament Building. Kubizek also remembered that the sojourn of May and June, 1906, was sufficiently exciting to make Hitler enthusiastic for "everything that had especially attracted him . . . but not long enough to observe the distress and misery which were concealed by the magnificent façade of the city." [1]

At seventeen Adolf was ready to succumb to the lures of the sparkling capital. Born in 1889 in Braunau, along the frontier with the German Empire, he was the third child begotten of Alois and Klara Hitler. His father was a customs official and his mother, twenty-three years younger, had come from placid peasant stock. In primary school their boy made excellent marks, but his work in the Linz Realschule, a technical school which he entered in 1900, was vastly disappointing to his father, by that time retired from his job of searching for smugglers.

Bitter scenes between father and youngster ended only with Alois Hitler's sudden death in 1903. The widow moved to Urfahr, a suburb of Linz, and Adolf continued to mark time in secondary school. In September, 1905, he finally quit the Realschule in Steyr, to which he had been consigned by the disgusted teachers of Linz, with a record that revealed excellent marks only in gymnastics. His simultaneous development of a lung ailment convinced his mother that further attendance at school might kill her beloved, and so he had freedom to dream and to draw, to hike and gossip with his friend Kubizek, and to fight all suggestions that he try for the civil service or for any vocation unworthy of an artistic temperament.[2] It is not hard to imagine his wheedling from his mother the funds necessary for a junket to the heart of Habsburg glory.

The Vienna which survived two crushing defeats in the twentieth century has consistently demonstrated an ability to serve the interests of culture despite inflation and occupation, near-starvation and intimidation. What young Hitler had a chance to see and hear in the spring of 1906 was but a happier season's manifestation of the love which the Viennese have for the arts. Above all else, the visitor of pre-World War I days could enjoy the admirable productions of the Imperial Opera, whose director was the fearsomely gifted Gustav Mahler. Hitler, already a fervent Wagnerian, wrote back to Linz that he would attend a performance of *Tristan and Isolde* on May 8 and *The Flying Dutchman* on May 9. The singers he heard were among the brightest of the day. Anna von Mildenburg and Erik Schmedes portrayed the hapless mortals betrayed by a love potion in the former music-drama, aided by the youthful Richard Mayr as King Marke and by Friedrich Weidemann as Kurwenal. On the next evening Leopold Demuth's impressive Dutchman was supported by Frau Bland as the dreamy Senta and by the versatile basso Hesch as Daland. During his four weeks' visit Adolf also saw *Lohengrin*, with Schmedes in the title role and Mayr as the medieval King Henry. Since it is not clear which of the two performances given during his stay he actually attended, it is possible that he again heard Anna von

Mildenburg as Ortrud and, for the first time, the greatly admired Lucy Weidt as the blameless Elsa.[3]

The reverent attention which the Bayreuth master's works received did not preclude equally careful preparation of the other items of the repertory. Between May 1 and June 9, 1906, the probable period of Hitler's stay, Mozart was represented by *The Marriage of Figaro, The Abduction from the Seraglio,* and *The Magic Flute.* The French style was generously displayed by performances of *Manon, The Tales of Hoffmann, Carmen, Werther, Mignon, The Jewess, The Huguenots,* and *Faust,* which was called *Margarete* because of what had been done by the librettists to Goethe's tale. The Italian composers, whom Hitler never really learned to like, were represented by Donizetti's *Lucia di Lammermoor,* Verdi's *Il Trovatore, A Masked Ball,* and *Aïda,* and by Puccini's *La Bohème.* Bolstering the German repertory, in addition to the Wagnerian dramas already mentioned, were Weber's *Der Freischütz,* Kienzl's *Der Evangelimann,* Nicolai's *The Merry Wives of Windsor,* and Johann Strauss's *Die Fledermaus,* plus Wagner's *Rienzi* and *Tannhäuser.* A nod to the Slavic elements of the empire was evidenced by productions of Smetana's *The Bartered Bride* and of Tchaikovsky's *Queen of Spades.* This recital of the contents of the repertory for forty days should be proof enough of Mahler's wide-ranging interests; his singing artists, needless to say, were among the best in the Western world. The most superficial sampling of the programs of the spring of 1906 would turn up such names as Selma Kurz, Leo Slezak, and Mme. Charles Cahier. A close check of the casts indicates that there were no second-rate performances even when indisposition forced changes.[4]

In addition to the Wagnerian events mentioned above, Hitler also wrote that he was attending the Jubilee City Theater, more generally known then and now as the Volksoper. This theater, whose architectural lines he learned in time to detest, was host to nothing less than Franz Lehár's *The Merry Widow;* a servitor of Adolf's days of glory recalled that the Chancellor loved to whistle Lehár's gay tunes or to listen to recordings of them.[5]

Vienna was proverbially gay, sometimes risqué, and Lehár's worldliness was matched by other lighthearted shows. The Raimund Theater advertised a musical burlesque, *A Czech in America,* whose last three scenes were enterprisingly entitled "At the Slave Market," "In the Courtroom," and "The Land of Gold." At the Carl Theater a less than lasting operetta called *Hug Dietrich's Wedding Trip* boasted of a score by the promising young Oskar Straus. Early in June the Lustspiel Theater offered a "première" of three one-act operettas by Offenbach, the best known of which was *Marriage by Lantern Light.*

Drama was perhaps directed more toward tragedy and the classic authors than toward frivolous comedy. The Hofburg Theater fulfilled its task of offering the best of the German literary past by producing masterpieces by Lessing, Goethe, and Schiller. Aeschylus and Shakespeare were called upon to re-create the enduring human problems of the past, while stagings of plays by Ibsen and Sudermann memorialized the equally involved human struggles of more recent decades.

Like Gustav Mahler's operatic troupe, the players at the Hofburg Theater had cause to regard themselves as among the best in the dramatic world. The men overshadowed the women, for a magnificent male tradition was represented in Vienna in the spring of 1906 by Adolf Sonnenthal, who celebrated his fiftieth jubilee on May 31 as Lessing's Nathan the Wise, and by Josef Kainz, who had just unveiled a Torquato Tasso in Goethe's play of the same name which is unrivaled even today on German stages. Sonnenthal, once a great Hamlet and Mortimer in Schiller's *Maria Stuart,* had surrendered such parts to Kainz, contenting himself with character or paternal roles. Their efforts were almost equalled by the third great actor of the day, Max Devrient, who, as Philip II, was a properly forbidding foil to Kainz's Don Carlos in Schiller's classic tragedy. Watching over several of the productions was the *régisseur* Hugo Thimig, later to embark upon a most fruitful collaboration with Max Reinhardt, whom his gifted daughter married. The dignity and effectiveness of the Hofburg Theater's offerings were in full consonance with the splendid building in which the company had its residence, a building whose lines always filled Hitler with unalloyed pleasure.

For those Viennese who wanted more easily digested fare, a French actor named Le Bargy and described as "the man of supreme elegance, the darling of the ladies, France's own sweetheart" offered *Le Demi-Monde* by Alexandre Dumas the Younger, a proved master of inculcating morality via titillation. Even more successful was a detective comedy based on Conan Doyle's immortal Sherlock Holmes. Most exotic of all of the intellectually slight extravaganzas was Buffalo Bill's Wild West show, booked for only three weeks, with 500 horses and, almost as an afterthought, 800 human performers. The première attracted a most fashionable audience, for even the imperial family was represented by enchanted archducal youngsters in the court box.

The resident players of the Hofburg Theater also were given some stiff competition by guest performances of the Berlin Lessing Theater company, whose outstanding star was Albert Bassermann, particularly esteemed for his portrayals of Ibsen characters. The Berliners diplomatically staged as their first event Arthur Schnitzler's one-act study, *The Puppeteer*, and *Elga*, by Gerhart Hauptmann, which was based on one of Grillparzer's short stories. Such bows to the distinguished past and present of Austrian belles-lettres were but a prelude to frankly competitive presentations of some major Ibsen problem plays.

Just before the curtain went up on Bassermann as Hjalmar Ekdal in *The Wild Duck* on May 23, news reached the cast that Ibsen had died in Oslo. The audience gathered at the lovely Theater an der Wien was informed of the popular dramatist's passing by the director of the company, who spoke impressively of the Norwegian's contributions.

The Berliners further honored Schnitzler by staging his *The Lonely Way*. If this author could not yet claim sympathetic approval of all that he wrote, particularly among the directors of the official theater's programs, he could at least smile whimsically over the fact that his *Green Cockatoo* was chosen to follow the Volkstheater's production of Oscar Wilde's *Salome*, a sensational little tidbit interpreted by one who called herself Lili Marberg.

Apart from the abundance of dramatic and musical entertainment, there were the usual social and military events which accompanied the cadenced tread of the Habsburg dynasty. It could be argued that Francis Joseph never had been young, as his contemporary Edward VII had so definitely been, and the social life revolving about the court ostensibly was ultra-dignified; at least the etiquette was spartan. When the important persons of society appeared before the populace, there was the usual respect for gravity. Not even the joyous appearance of spring was allowed to get out of bounds by respectable ladies and gentlemen; its arrival was celebrated decorously by the May Corso, a lovely procession of elegant personages driving along the Ringstrasse and in the Prater, Vienna's then incomparable park. Did our curious tourist from Linz stand with the great crowds along the side lines, gawking at the empire's elect? His later seizures of rage over the unproductive existence of the Viennese "haves" merely tell us that the showy parades of the wealthy were not novel to him.

If he did witness the Corso of 1906, he likely shared the fate of most visitors to Vienna in May—he was rained upon during the first part of the afternoon. Possibly because of the weather, the Emperor did not take part in the traditional affair; more courageous were the ladies, with bright vernal toilettes to exhibit, who retired within their carriages while the rain lasted, imperiously ordering the tops down again when gray sky gave way to blue.

Their frills and ruffs, as decreed by the latest Pierette mode, were set off by tiny flowered hats or by larger bonnets trimmed with the ever-fashionable heron feathers. In an age and in an empire which believed wholeheartedly in the paraphernalia of armed might, if not always in its substance, more than a few of the gentlemen wore marine and hussar uniforms to rival their ladies. The *Neue Freie Presse*, Vienna's most influential newspaper, courteously mentioned first of all the Emperor's guest, Duke Karl Eduard of Coburg-Gotha, in his blue German regalia. At about the same time that he appeared in the Prater, the Heir-Apparent Francis Ferdinand was seen driving with his pleasant but embarrassingly nonroyal consort, Princess Hohenberg, whose white hat trimmed with red roses was dimmed a bit by the sensible but undistinguished wrap she wore in case of another downpour.

Reciting the titles and names of the rest of the gracious participants would be an exercise in the history of the development of Habsburg power. Memories of the unforgettable defense of Vienna against the Turks jostled the painful reminiscences of the losses in fair Italy as the society editor went down the list of notables. Archdukes and archduchesses were flanked or followed by a Schwarzenberg and a Pallavicini, by a Clam-Gallas and a Potocka. The Chinese ambassador competed with the French, the carriage of the antisemitic mayor of Vienna was easily passed by Baron Alfons Rothschild's sensational electric automobile. Biliński, whose reputation for financial wizardry had contributed to the Emperor's acquiescence in a continuing Polish domination of Galicia, found himself nodding to Wassilkó, a Ruthene deputy renowned for his manful pleas against Polish oppression of his people in Galicia. The presence of Princess Montenuovo reminded the knowing gossips, however, that Habsburg gratitude and remembrance could be short-lived with peoples and with persons. Her husband's ancestor had been Marie Louise, easily solaced by a one-legged roué when Napoleon was shipped off to St. Helena.

The crowds were respectful in the presence of the dour Heir-Apparent and smiled indiscriminately at the children of the houses of Habsburg, Parma, or even ridiculous little Montenegro. Their real love and applause went out to a veritable institution, Princess Pauline Metternich-Sandor, whose colossal ugliness of face was matched only by her indomitable championship of unpopular causes. The little people of Vienna had been taught to vote for the antisemites, but they never questioned Princess Pauline's friendship with Jews. Decades before, while her husband was ambassador to Napoleon III's curious court, she had been unable to cajole the riotous Jockey Club of Paris into a

modicum of respect for Wagner's *Tannhäuser;* that she had
failed to persuade such arrogant worldlings of the worth of the
latest German cultural hero was but the beginning of her legend
among the Viennese. With a shrewd eye for the perpetuation
of the legend, she appeared with her married daughter in one of
the most dazzlingly decorated of the carriages; lovely sprigs of
laburnum enhanced the woodcarver's and enameler's cunning.
The carriage was closed, for it was not proper to compete
overmuch with archduchesses. It would have been easier, of
course, to camouflage the Emperor himself.

While Francis Joseph might spare his seventy-six years a social
promenade during threatening weather, his incredible sense of
duty kept him from acknowledging the shower that greeted the
Spring Parade on May 30. Another wearisome tiff with the
Magyars had already forced one postponement. Rain or no, he
rode out from the main entry of Schönbrunn at the appointed
time, surrounded by a swarm of resplendent equerries. For the
courtiers, military attachés, and thousands of spectators a charming scene was enacted that was veritable manna for the news-
hawks of the day. The Emperor's granddaughter, Princess
Elisabeth Windischgrätz, curtsied low as the imperial party
emerged from the palace, expertly snapping her kodak at the
same time with her right hand. Her children meanwhile waved
to their great-grandfather from the palace's windows, wafting
kisses in his direction.

The troops passed in review, with the Emperor stationed at
the obelisk so as not to miss a single flaw in the lines. It was
easy to forget that the soldiers might someday have to march
into real battle, that the Russian military attaché was something
more than a cultivated cosmopolitan, that the name Windischgrätz was identified with the cruel bombardments of Prague
and Vienna of less than sixty years before. The tulips at Schönbrunn and the roses along the Ring proclaimed that spring
was not the time for disagreeable thoughts. Adolf Hitler himself, in mysterious code, wrote his friend in Linz that he hoped
to see the girl he worshiped from afar.[6]

We cannot know whether or not Hitler witnessed the May

Corso or the Spring Parade. They were logical sights for the
curious who had free time and who might not yet be totally
immune to the dynasty's glamor. Almost certainly the adolescent visitor must have avoided the Health Exhibit of May, 1906.
Ironically, here were exhibited those hints of the life of the
underdog in Vienna which he later was to know catastrophically
well.

What might the well-fed habitué of the cafés read in his
favorite paper on May 19? Simply that the conscientious lord
of the land had moved slowly and politely through almost endless proofs of the misery of his capital, as artistically arranged in
the exhibit's booths. He was particularly drawn to a collection
of daring photographs of bums and vagrants who hid by night
in the sewers, in foul flophouses, or, if the weather was warm
enough, in the grass of the Prater. He solemnly declared that
this was a frightening picture of poverty and woe. Why did
these men hide from society? What did they do by day to secure
the bare sustenance to keep them alive? To the photographer,
a court secretary named Dr. Hermann Drawe, he expressed his
appreciation: "Your pictures have interested me very much."

As he progressed, the officials of the Association for the
Shelter of the Homeless thanked him for his gracious acceptance
of the honorary presidency of the association. In turn, he was
glad to hear that they were taking care of 500 persons a day
and hopeful they would have more abundant funds in the future.

Even more cordial was his conference with the directors of
the Vienna Association for Warming Rooms and Welfare. In
this society titled ladies worked with journalists, surgeons, and
bureaucrats to soften the agonies of the poor wretches, often
whole families, who had only the vicious Viennese wind to keep
them company on the deserted wintry streets. Compliments
poured from the Emperor, who was particularly pleased to find
a familiar ministerial secretary much involved in the activities.

Young tourists and aged emperors are likely to show only the
most conventional interest in the eternally present poor, and
Kubizek has written that Hitler indubitably failed to see Vienna's
shocking miseries on his first trip. It was later that hunger be-

came his faithful guard and pitiless friend, later that his contempt
for the Habsburg state turned to consuming hate.

Later, too, that a near-morbid interest in the politics centering at Vienna became a maddening substitute for a decent lunch,
that normal bargaining among self-confessed politicians always
became corruption and chicanery in young fanatic eyes. In
May and June, 1906, the postcards to Linz were totally unconcerned with dull maneuvering in cabinet and parliament.
One minister-president resigned as Hitler arrived, and his successor's successor was getting a cabinet together when Hitler went
home. The momentary resemblance to France was superficial.
It was simply a matter of shuffling ministers a bit to placate the
Magyars while pushing ahead with the bill for universal manhood suffrage in the Austrian half of the empire.

While it was not at all clear who might emerge as the Emperor's new minister-president in Austria, the unconcerned
permanent bureaucrats set in motion the nationalization of one
of the last of the private railroads, the once enormously profitable Nordbahn. The government's refusal to take such a step
twenty years before had been the occasion for vociferous attacks
upon the Rothschilds and all Jews in general. Now the issue was
quite lifeless; the Nordbahn for two decades had been rigidly
restrained from making undue profits. As will be made clear
later on, the foes of the Jews had not been silenced thereby,
for the attack could be mounted from a multitude of false
positions.

Adolf most likely was a convinced antisemite long before
seeing Vienna, and in naughty schoolroom tantrums he also had
already evinced well-nigh traitorous adoration of the tremendously impressive Hohenzollern Empire and some distaste for
the dynasty shakily entrenched in Vienna. Love of the German
Empire and contempt for the "Jew-ridden" Habsburg domain
was a constant theme peddled by the Pan-Germans in Austria.
That these Pan-Germans had been properly ignored by Bismarck and William II alike never seemed to diminish their
ardor. If it was easy to ignore cabinet problems and the Health
Exhibit, every young Pan-German must have thrilled to the

announcement that the Berlin Kaiser would come to Vienna in June, preceded by Graf Helmut von Moltke, chief of staff, who would confer with his Austro-Hungarian counterpart. Moltke arrived on May 22, put up at Frau Sacher's renowned hotel, and interrupted his conferences with his Austro-Hungarian allies only to pay a courtesy call upon the Emperor in the small Lower Austrian town of Bruck. The young Kaiser's arrival on June 6 meant a drenching for the well-wishers who went to the station. Having received certain selected callers, William II betook himself to the Capuchin Crypt, where the dust of Rudolph and Elisabeth waited for the still living Francis Joseph. Any café philosopher would have argued, of course, that Elisabeth's restless spirit was at peace, for her scheme to provide her prosy husband with a lively and devoted friend was still crowned with success. Among "the representatives of the arts" who attended the Whitmonday Derby the day before William II moved into the rococo splendors of Schönbrunn was this very friend, Katharina Schratt, ex-actress, who did much to keep the aging Emperor from exploding with bewilderment over a world which did not function as it should have.

The Hohenzollern visit must have forced all other news into the unconscious recesses of Hitler's retentive mind. In Russia the new representative government was suffering from sudden ministerial changes just as the Duma met. Rumors were current that a certain Izvolsky would become the new Russian foreign minister. Only crystal-gazers could have predicted that he would live to be accused by some German publicists of being the instigator of World War I.

The French were having general elections while their bishops were mulling over the new law separating church and state. Republican vengeance upon the devout French Roman Catholics was underlined by the announcement that the Court of Cassation was going to review the Dreyfus case. In the United States President Theodore Roosevelt expressed less than full admiration for the business methods of the Standard Oil Company in a message to Congress. In Madrid dashing Alfonso XIII and his bride were almost eliminated as representatives of the monarchical principle by an unsentimental anarchist bomb-thrower on their second wedding day.

Such were the seemingly important events of spring, 1906.[7] Who could know or care that an unsettled and unpromising fellow from dreary Linz had come to Vienna and had been thoroughly seduced by the city's charms? Tragically for himself and for uncounted millions, he could not resist the temptation to return to make his mark. If Vienna did not originally inspire his hatred for "inferior races" and his insensate fear of being pushed into the grubbing proletariat, it at least fixed and intensified his unholy complexes. The Hitler who returned to Vienna in 1907 was not wholly twisted or evil, one gathers from Kubizek's undoubtedly sincere memoirs. The Hitler who left for Munich in 1913 is not truly known to us save through the pages of *Mein Kampf*. There the outlines of the frustrations and sufferings are clear. What might Vienna have contributed to the production of the arch-nihilist of our day?

"The Most Miserable Time

of My Life"

BETWEEN the spring of 1906 and the autumn of 1907 Adolf Hitler mooned for the girl he never dared speak to, studied and read as the mood struck him, and in general suffered the torments of a young man who could not or would not find a niche in society. He matched his mother's worried looks with spells of depression and with romantic wanderings through the woods surrounding Linz. Kubizek, equally unhappy over his apprenticeship in upholstery, summed up these months of his friend's maturing pains as follows:

Vienna was calling. That city had a thousand possibilities for an eager young man like Adolf, opportunities which might lead to the most sublime heights or to the most sombre depths. . . . She demanded the highest stakes from everyone who pledged himself to her. And that is what Adolf wanted.[1]

What Adolf wanted, his bewildered and ever-loving mother dared not deny. Before the leaves fell in 1907 he had deserted the unexciting town of Linz for the haughty showplace of the empire. His first objective was the Academy of Fine Arts, to which he submitted a portfolio of drawings as proof that he should be permitted to enter the classes in painting. According to the account in *Mein Kampf*, he was rejected but advised to apply for work in architecture. Without a diploma from his secondary school in Linz, he was utterly unable to follow the advice.[2]

The first cut of the lash of frustration had been applied to his back. He could only wait for the examinations of the following year, resolutely refusing to let Linz know of his disaster.

So far the future hero of the German folk had experienced what thousands, if not millions, of young persons had endured in that vast phenomenon of migration from country or small town to teeming metropolis. No societal commentator on the effects of industrialization and urbanization dares omit mention of the problem of those whom Maurice Barrès called the *déracinés*, the uprooted who flee the familiar and ofttimes banal scenes of childhood and early youth for the glitter and potential profit of the big city. In the city there is almost complete anonymity, if that be desired, anonymity that can be a source of either anguish or relief. If the would-be superman fails to impress his pedestrian contemporaries, there need be no chorus of half-sympathetic, half-contemptuous neighbors and relatives to comment on the fiasco. If failure results in hunger and lack of shelter, somewhere in the city there are impersonal agents to whom one gaunt face is the same as another.

After weeks of silence Hitler finally sent his address in Vienna to his friend in Linz. The location meant nothing to Kubizek until he joined Adolf in February, 1908; then, as a new arrival, he began to realize the difference between a comfortable home and a miserable room in a noisy alien city.

Adolf's first home in Vienna was a tiny room on the second floor of a dingy house on the Stumpergasse. This area was close to the busy Westbahnhof, which accommodated the fast trains from Munich and Paris, and it was dominated by the bustling Mariahilferstrasse, a haven for lower middle-class shoppers and so a center of many "bargain counter" establishments. The more glamorous Vienna was downtown amid the monumental piles of the Ringstrasse or garlanded about the Imperial Palace; Adolf and later his friend Kubizek were forced to measure their space in centimeters and to treasure the few rays of sunshine which flickered over the bricks of a neighboring house.

After his friend went back to Linz, Adolf reportedly moved to another room on the Felberstrasse, still in the vicinity of the

Westbahnhof, but further removed from the sparkling Inner City. When Kubizek returned to look for his friend in November, 1908, their landlady informed him that Herr Hitler had departed without leaving an address. There seems little reason to doubt the tradition that Hitler by this time had settled in the Home for Men on the Meldemannstrasse.[3]

This "hotel" for men who were alone in the world and who did not make more than 1,500 kronen (373.75 1909 dollars) a year had been completed in October, 1905. It was the fourth project sponsored by the Emperor Francis Joseph I Jubilee Foundation for Citizens' Housing and Welfare Institutions, which had been created in 1896 to tackle the miserable living conditions of the less well-paid Viennese. The first three investments in better housing stressed homes for families, with a few buildings added to take care of unattached males and females. The Home for Men of 1905, with living quarters for 544 persons, was something of an expensive experiment, but one which was especially needed in a city which attracted thousands of hopeful young men who would not go home short of starvation.

A description of Hitler's most regular abode in Vienna will vary with the witness being questioned. The official prospectus published by the Foundation would bear out the stories that sober middle-class citizens were shocked by its "luxuriousness." The account left by Josef Greiner, another of Hitler's very few friends of the dismal Vienna era, is a necessary corrective, if only in its depiction of some of the home's guests.[4] Between the two sources, a reasonably clear picture begins to emerge.

The administration of the home was simplified from the beginning by two basic rules. First, there were special sleeping areas set aside for men engaged in night work. Secondly, the sleeping areas furnished the regular day laborers were cordoned off during the day. If the laborer happened to have a holiday or be between jobs, he was free to use the dayrooms and self-help rooms which were available.

The raw provincial who was directed by a policeman to the home would undoubtedly have been impressed by the well-lighted and well-ventilated lounges, reading room, and writing room on the first floor. The dining room had accommodations for 352 men, and one of the two kitchens was reserved for those guests who wanted or had to prepare their own food.

The sleeping quarters were arranged so that each man had four meters of floor space and "breathing space" of twelve meters. He slept in an iron bed covered with the traditional three-sectioned mattress and rested his head on a bolster filled with horsehair. Two sheets, a bolster cover, and a double blanket enhanced the blessings of the central heating. There was a clothes-rail and the inevitable chamber pot.

Cleanliness was ensured by adequate washrooms, showers, tubs, and footbath troughs. Outside of the shower and tub rooms was a disinfecting chamber, where the bather's clothes were left for treatment while he removed the dirt and possibly the lice from his own body.

In charge of the establishment from its opening until another home was opened in 1910 was Johann Kanya, aided by Dr. Joseph Winterberg, house physician. Certain rooms were reserved for guests who had to be under the doctor's supervision, including a small kitchen where tea and light nourishment were prepared. Winterberg and his successors always had the right to order ailing tenants into this quarantine, on pain of expulsion.

The impecunious Hitler was up against a large number of additional regulations in this rather sought-after refuge. In the first place Director Kanya was empowered to refuse any prospective roomer without citing a single reason therefore. He was bound to turn down any lad under fourteen, and he was supposed to see that none of his charges made more than 1,500 kronen a year in wages. With Hitler the problem never arose.

Games and singing which became too noisy were forbidden, as were all actions that might cause fire or lead to immoral conduct. No spirits were to be consumed on the premises; if a man showed signs of drunkenness, he was to be forbidden beer and wine as well. Chess, checkers, and dominoes were the only approved games, and loud arguments over certain plays could lead to expulsion from the home. The property of the home was to be treated considerately: no standing on beds and no expectoration save in the spittoons provided.

Rules and regulations reached a climax with regard to bathing facilities. They were available between 6:30 and 9:30 every night and between 6:30 and 11:30 in the morning on Sundays and holidays. The footbaths always were gratis, but limited to fifteen minutes. To shower, the guest had to pay ten heller (two and one-half cents) for a bath towel and bathing "apron," for walking around in the shower rooms totally unclad was forbidden. For twenty-five heller (six cents) one could soak for half an hour in a tub, with soap and towel supplied; only one person in a tub at a time, however, warned the regulations.[5]

The extremely moderate rates charged by the home made up for some of the rigidity of the rules. Lodging for one night cost less than fifteen cents. A weekly card was sold for two kronen fifty heller, that is, sixty cents.

Emil Kläger's sensational description of the needy and criminal elements in Vienna, published in 1908,[6] was almost rapturous over the elegance and reasonableness of the Home for Men on the Meldemannstrasse. The genuine bums whose reserve he finally was able to pierce repeated endlessly the marvels of the establishment as they swallowed their tea and soup at charitable institutions. The home indubitably stood out proudly in its neighborhood of dumpy dwellings and naked factory buildings. Kläger approved of its arc-lighted dining room whose walls were tiled halfway up with a warm shade of green. He was intrigued by the system of paying for food; automatic machines dispensed tokens in return for regular currency, and these had to be proffered by the diners when their dishes appeared at the serving window. The victuals were tempting in price and in taste, he reported. An admirable serving of roast pork with a vegetable cost only nineteen kreuzer, a complete midday meal only twenty-three kreuzer.[7] A good bowl of soup was offered for four kreuzer, while tea or coffee went for five kreuzer. The pretty library was well stocked with newspapers, light romances, and quasi-scientific journals.[8]

When Josef Greiner, the other major witness of these years,

met Hitler at the home in the autumn of 1908, the future Führer was in sad shape. A half year before, Adolf had met Kubizek in a most presentable outfit and even sporting an ivory-handled walking stick. Now he was practically a tattered bum who could not have had much desire to see anyone from Linz.

Though the chill of September was painfully apparent when Greiner took up residence on the Meldemannstrasse, he soon learned that his new friend Hitler had neither shirt nor under-drawers. They simply had worn out. The coat Adolf wore was an old-fashioned salon model, a gift from one Neumann, who peddled the future dictator's dreary little water colors. Its sleeves were raveling and the lining was but a fragment of its original self. Grease and dirt were ground into the fabric, harmonizing with the gray trousers and the disintegrating shoes. Only the young man's cultivated voice, said Greiner, offset the dubious impression he made with his sunken and pale cheeks, his hurried manner, and his dirty rags.[9]

Hitler's wretched appearance finally passed the limits of Director Kanya's patience. Using his unquestioned authority to accept or reject guests as he so willed, Kanya refused to issue the frustrated artist another weekly card. According to Greiner, Kanya feared that inevitably Hitler's clothes would fall apart, leaving him stark naked. The young man's unsociable habits and his penchant for arousing violent political strife were two more black marks. The men in the home, overwhelmingly Social Democratic in their sympathies, were fed up with "re-actionary harangues." They had expressly requested Kanya to expel Hitler. Where might he go? To the Refuge for the "Roofless" in the Meidling district, which he already knew from even more desperate days, according to Greiner. The latter asserted that he intervened with Kanya, pointing out that the refuge in Meidling took in the homeless only for the night. How and where could Hitler paint his little scenes during the daylight hours? The director was sorry, but his edict was not changed; Hitler was allowed to stay only when Greiner borrowed fifty kronen, interest-free, from the far from heartless administrator, who held Greiner's watch as collateral. The loan was to be used to provide Vienna's future tyrant with some decent clothes, which Greiner easily and reasonably obtained from the professional panhandlers who made up part of the home's clientele. Adolf wept when presented with a pair of shoes, striped trousers, another unfashionable salon coat, and a stiff melon-shaped hat. His friend remembered there was even enough money left over to pay for a warm bath and the weekly room card.[10]

Hitler not only desperately needed the home's dayrooms for working on his illustrations; he also used the kitchen facilities almost daily. When he was totally out of funds he prepared a watery soup. When there were kronen to spend, he cooked a big platter of rice and milk, liberally doused with sugar and grated chocolate.[11] These relative luxuries alternated with dark periods of absolute want which probably no one will ever be able to document convincingly. Greiner left Vienna at the behest of an uncle who was willing to pay for his studies in Germany, and he returned only for short visits. Though he later argued that he found Hitler in the new and more capacious Home for Men on the Wurlitzergasse in 1911, his remembrance is challenged by a *Meldezettel* (or residence record) which Jetzinger has uncovered. This document definitely places Hitler in the home on the Meldemannstrasse from June 26, 1910, to May 24, 1913.[12]

Before Greiner and Hitler ever met, the latter had stretched his slender frame over the park benches in the Prater when the night closed in on his misery. He learned, in case of rain, to take refuge under the arches of the Rotunda, using his coat for a pillow and the unyielding ground for a bed. When the autumnal frosts began, he swallowed what pride was left and stood in line for a place in the refuge in Meidling.[13] Thus he became part of the welfare statistics, of even lower caste than the proletariat he professed to lecture. In the Home for Men he brushed shoulders with a count, a baron, and more than one businessman who had lost everything at the race tracks. Here he argued with hefty Socialist laborers, measured his talents with those of struggling young artists, and learned to sneer at the Jewish traders and peddlers who also rented rooms.[14] In the parks, flophouses, and

warming rooms of imperial Vienna he was but one face in a
crowd of defeated men.

The society which helped keep Hitler alive during his tough-
est bouts with hunger was the Association for the Shelter of the
Homeless, which enjoyed the gracious protection of Francis
Joseph himself. It endeavored to nourish the hungry with soup
and bread and to give shelter to those who had no place to
sleep. At the beginning of this century it operated a refuge
which, when remodeled in 1903, could handle 420 wretches per
night. In the year of its remodeling it welcomed 46,000 men,
more than 10,000 women, and 3,000 children. Undoubtedly
these figures do not indicate 46,000 *different* men; names never
were asked for, and it is extremely likely that there were hundreds of "repeaters." No person could stay in the refuge more
than five nights in a row, but one wonders how the permanent
staff of six persons ever enforced such a rule. Between December 1 and March 15, the months of agonizing cold, a *Massen-
quartier* also was operated. As the German indicates, the over-
flow of men was simply crowded into a structure which at best
kept them from freezing in the streets. In these three and a half
winter months, such primitive accommodations had to take care
of another 42,000 men.

On November 21, 1908, the asylum for homeless men was
transferred to the Meidling district, and it was here that Hitler
went when the Prater became unendurably cold. Whether or
not he was galled by the fact that the Meidling home was
largely made possible by the endowment of the wealthy Jewish
Epstein family, we know not. Thanks to their generosity, and to
the benevolence of others, the new home was serving in 1911
approximately 710,000 portions of soup and bread to the unfortunate and sheltering 226,000 men, 50,000 boys, 61,000
women, and 46,000 children.[15]

This private group's contribution, albeit an impressive one,
was but part of the charitable program. The city maintained a
refuge for the homeless in which further thousands were allowed
to find a spot in which to sleep. In 1911 this asylum handled
94,000 persons, of whom 63,000 were men and 12,000 were

women, the rest being children up to fourteen years of age. Tax funds provided three meals a day for these persons. Ten years before, an average of 284 persons per day were being cared for either by the private society or by the city. In 1911 the figure had increased to 2,403 persons per day who were being fed and given sleeping quarters by both agencies. It should be remembered as well that both men's homes were opened in this ten-year period.[16]

Another society which tried to meet the misery of the homeless was the Viennese Soup and Tea Institute, which sold soup and tea and bread at cost to anyone. This program not only proposed to give the poorer classes a "tasty and energy-building nourishment"; it hoped as well to prevent the "damnable consumption of spirits." At the beginning of this century it was disposing of roughly 2,200,000 portions yearly, of which more than 100,000 went gratis to the indigent.[17]

When Emil Kläger began his investigation of the moral and physical miseries of the capital city, he dressed like a tramp and made his way to the Soup and Tea Institute's permanent center on the Tiefer Graben. Pushing open the glass door, he entered a large, decently lighted room, filled with mean but neat wooden tables and extremely primitive armchairs, nearly all filled with guests. He was surprised to find most of the "boarders" comparatively well dressed. Many were the servitors of large business firms whose names were blazoned on their caps. These customers picked up their soup, bread, and tea from the serving table and then searched for an empty spot, carrying their victuals as if they were fragile gems. They sat down slowly, almost dully, and then plunged their faces into the steaming vapor of the soup. In seconds they were greedily gobbling down what they had purchased with their paltry coppers.[18]

Infinitely more horrible were the warming rooms of Vienna, which Hitler may well have experienced when there was no money for rooms and too cold a wind to chance the Prater. These establishments were operated by a private charitable society, the Vienna Association for Warming Rooms and Welfare, which boasted of the protection of the Archduchess Marie Valerie. During 1901 six warming rooms scattered about the city had taken in 368,000 men, 228,000 women, and 583,000 children. Each person sheltered received a piece of bread and a serving of soup.[19] A decade later these rooms were besieged by 421,000 men and 200,000 women who desired shelter from the bitter cold. Again it should be stressed that "repeaters" were the order of the day; even so, it is a shock to add to the above statistics the 597,000 acts of charity which this society vouchsafed the innocent poor children of Vienna during 1911. Here, as with the Meidling shelter, Jewish funds had been abundantly contributed. The well-known warming room on the Erdbergstrasse was wholly endowed by Baron Moritz Königswarter, to mention but one example.[20]

On a freezing December night at about the time that Hitler was beginning to feel at home in glamorous Vienna, Kläger continued his research into the life of the wretched by applying for entry to the warming room in the dismal Brigittenau district. This newest of Viennese developments was its grimmest. Max Winter, a caustic Socialist journalist of the day, said it would be hard to outdo this district's absentee building owners, whose unabashed and usurious rent-racking ranked with the cold profit-seeking of the contractors who had long flourished there.[21]

Horror was Kläger's first reaction as he caught sight of the tightly packed human beings. There was not an inch for the slightest bodily movement, save for the jerking of weary heads when sleepiness became overpowering. The recipients of this shelter had to remain seated at the tables all night long; it was impossible to tell if they were sleeping or not. When a newcomer arrived, the overseer jabbed his elbow into one of the dozers to secure somehow a bit of sitting room. No talking and no smoking were allowed. Coughers and snorers were disciplined at once. Here sat the lowly on hard wooden benches, tortured and mute, glad to get insipid soup and a slice of bread to deaden the bite of their empty bellies. In the rear was a corner for

women and the floor for their children. That the latter were
allowed to sleep thereupon was, remarked Kläger, to be expected in a century devoted to child welfare.

The warming rooms, for all of their fetid disagreeableness,
were free and as decent morally as charity usually demands.
The police often directed the hopeless and the lost to their
doors, but there were hundreds of shadowy figures who were
wary of the police and fearful of coming to a warming room.
These were the unemployed who had police records or else
outlanders who had been ordered by the Viennese authorities
to go back to their native province or village. As long as they
had the tiniest bit of cash left, they walked the streets by day
and sought out the foulest of refuges by night, the privately run,
illegal flophouses.

Kläger, again, and his friend, a judicial official named Hermann Drawe, drew unforgettable sketches of the flophouses of
Hitler's youthful Viennese days. Ordinarily these places were
called *Massenquartiere* (mass quarters), and their operators were
eager to justify the title. Drawe secured entry to one by dress-
ing appropriately, noting that the owner and his old woman
confederate asked no questions after the forty heller were paid.
Forty persons were jammed into two rooms, some on divans, a
few on straw cushions, the rest on the floor. Not the slightest
effort was made to segregate the sexes or the obviously con-
sumptive. An argument ended with the flash of sharp knives,
and only the operator's threat to call the police quelled the hotheads, who were disputing the ownership of a shirt. A drunk
who argued about the nature of the accommodations was
kicked to the floor. A teen-age boy sneaked in to whisper to a
"buddy" the latest developments of a burglary which friends
seemingly were perpetrating.[22]

Dozens of illegal holes operated in the Leopoldstadt, whose
winding alleys went back to the days when the ghetto existed.
Grasping tenants of old, half-decayed houses sublet three to four
rooms every night, often to eighteen and more persons of both
sexes. At times their hapless guests were left only the window
sill on which to curl up. Kläger wrote of one house in which an

old man and a young girl shared a bed; the politeness of their verbal intercourse indicated that accident alone made them bed-mates. In the same room, of course, were other "boarders," including two children sleeping on wooden planks. They had been completely undressed, and only the rags which had been piled on top of them kept them from shivering in their sleep.

Another establishment sandwiched fifty persons into one diminutive hallway and a small room adjoining. Here shreds of blankets and sheets served as cover, and one needs little imagination to evoke the stench of such a hell. Some of the vagrants whom Kläger met swore that they walked the streets for three or four days in order to be sufficiently exhausted to endure the dreadful atmosphere of such flophouses. Filth, disease, agony of spirit, and degradation of body were the most obvious by-products of these supremely ugly habitations. Needless to say, they were much frequented by "amateur" prostitutes, who often seemed willing to sell themselves just for the cost of the night's lodging, that is, for twenty to thirty heller. The rest of the flophouse's customers seemed to care not at all that the sale was consummated in their presence. The mumblings of a drunk were far more likely to arouse protest.[23]

Could a man sink further? That depended upon one's taste, for the bums who could not stomach these hovels might possibly find out how to get to the sewers which ran parallel to the Danube Canal and the Wien River. The favored spots were near the Stephanie and Ferdinand bridges, where it was not too difficult to force open the iron doors leading to the sewage canals and find some room for sleeping and even for wood fires. Kläger remembered old experienced tramps asleep on planks, with their heads pillowed in straw, their arms and legs spread-eagled so as to give their muscles the maximum relaxation possible. The prized locations were those closest to the corridor that led to the actual sewage canals, for there the moist, warm vapor cut the sharpness of the wintry temperatures. In some of these less than stylish anterooms the stench was incredibly loathsome, and only men truly fearful of the police forced themselves to hide here.

Along the Wien River there were numerous kiosks which were plastered with announcements of lectures, the programs of the state theaters, etc., and one of them, named for Pestalozzi, the Swiss educational reformer, was an entry to the most heavily populated of the sewer areas. The attraction was the amount of space available, not the atmosphere, which was sickeningly noisome. Men made beds of stones to escape unexpected floodings as they slept, or else they took refuge in tremendous sewage pipes temporarily not being utilized. The area was subject to a sort of group law, at least in that one old-timer acted as *Hausmeister* or overseer. It was his job to pick out certain spots for cooking and to limit the number of guests. Most popular of all the grottoes of this extensive sewage development was the *"Zwingburg,"* separated from snooping eyes by deep water and by slanting rooflike constructions. Little did the average Viennese know, or probably care, that the tattered vagrant who suddenly seemed to merge imperceptibly with a kiosk on the Karlsplatz was scurrying like a rat to the sewage canal below.[24] The police occasionally raided these retreats but with little real vigor. In the Vienna of Hitler's youth, there had to be flophouses and sewers to augment the work of the soup kitchens and warming rooms. Vienna, like the rest of the Western European cities, was plagued by an unending shortage of housing.

Young Adolf probably spent more time in furnished rooms than in illegal "mass quarters," to say nothing of sewers. He told Greiner, it should be remembered, that he knew quite well from personal acquaintance what other vagrants called "our green bedmate," that is, the park in the Prater; he also slept in the home in Meidling. Greiner is authority as well for the rather amusing report of the researcher who tracked down all of the sixteen addresses Hitler had during the lean years in the hope that Der Führer would allow the Party to erect marble tablets celebrating his old residences. This act of piety was not only unrewarded—further research and talk of printing a brochure were brusquely prohibited by the Nazi dictator. Greiner speaks of sixteen *Privathäuser*, that is, private houses; when not in Meidling or in the Home for Men, Hitler was most likely a *Bettgeher*, that is, one who rented a bed or couch in another's home.[25]

It was no wonder that Hitler wrote in *Mein Kampf:* "There was hardly any other German city where social questions could have been studied better than in Vienna." He never forgot the unemployed and homeless who sought shelter "in the twilight and the mud of the canals." [26] The bitter fight for living space in the Habsburg capital was well launched when Hitler was born. In 1890, 44 percent of the dwellings in Vienna were one- or two-room affairs which had to accommodate more than one-third of the total population. By 1900, 43 percent of the population had to live in one- or two-room flats. The vast majority of quarters in the workers' districts consisted of room and kitchen or even one room which had to serve all purposes. One observer found a house, admittedly the worst he had seen, which sheltered 276 persons distributed among 31 flats. In the eight districts heavily populated by the workers, a flat ordinarily absorbed 4 to 5.2 persons. The smallness of the rooms and often their lack of any ventilation intensified the workers' dissatisfaction and partially explained their shift from Christian Socialism to Social Democracy. These slum areas were saturated with the odors of popular dishes, while sanitary facilities were practically always communal and inadequate.

Protagonists of housing reform were especially disheartened by the fact that the most overcrowded flats were the very ones which had to take boarders or subtenants. In the eight working-class districts, two to three of every five flats had to take in extra persons. The worst crowding was in the desperately poor district of Brigittenau. Here the more intimate privacies of family life had to be sacrificed to the job of meeting the rent. In this raw new suburb 17 percent of the population lived as roomers or as subtenants.

Rentals for two-room apartments ran from twenty-two to twenty-eight kronen per month in the laboring districts, depending upon the closeness to the street. A mere roomer paid two to two and one-half kronen per week for his right to sleep in such cramped quarters. The subtenant, who had cooking rights, had to pay appreciably more. One roomer, in a year's time, would pay enough to meet 40 percent of the total rent, for even the poor tended to gouge the poor. Friedrich Funder, the young editor of the *Reichspost* after the turn of the century, estimated that there were 80,000 to 100,000 of these roomers in Vienna. Every twentieth person in the city had no place to go save a bed at night in a virtual stranger's house, a bed which, if lucky, he shared with only one other unfortunate. In those wards which were the most crowded the death rate was highest, especially among children. In middle-class Wieden the ratio was only 4.1 per 10,000 persons in 1899. Proletarian Ottakring's mortality rate was 15.4, Favoriten's, 16.4. Tenements in the last-named areas were expected to return 6 to 8 percent on the mortgages floated to build them, and often there might be "third mortgages" calling for 10 percent interest. And yet 4,000 of the 27,000 dwelling-units in Favoriten did not possess kitchens.[27]

Was Vienna worse off than other great cities in her housing situation? There are no thoroughly satisfactory statistics, for decent housing depends not only upon square feet of area per person but also on the number of windows, the number of flights of stairs to be negotiated, and other obvious factors. A table of comparisons for the year 1900, however, was worked out by a writer who clearly was anxious to praise the Viennese scene. Some of his figures were favorable, for fewer persons lived per square kilometer in Lueger's city than in Paris, Berlin, or London. The same was true of "houses," an admittedly ambiguous word. There were far fewer per square kilometer in Vienna than in the other three capitals named. How many human beings lived in each house in these cities? On this count Vienna had nothing to crow about. Her conditions forced fifty-one persons into each house, whereas Berlin counted only thirty-one per house, Paris thirty, and London eight. Even Budapest had only forty-five persons per house. Vienna's population had gone up 259 percent between 1860 and 1900, surpassed in this respect only by Berlin, with an increase of 281 percent. Paris had 60 percent more residents in 1900 than in 1860, very close to

London's record of a 62 percent increase. Other population statistics for 1900 pointed to the obvious situation which had developed; of 1,674,957 persons resident in Vienna, only 46.4 percent were natives.[28]

This veritable flood of new citizens was severely straining the housing which existed and constantly made new demands upon all charitable organizations. Building did not keep pace with demand, and it was not hard to find reasons for the lag. Labor and material costs were rising, and much of the land available for new housing was in the hands of speculators who could afford to wait for the best possible occasion to sell or to build. One observer who denounced these heartless profiteers claimed that the weight of property taxes was discouraging.[29] The socialization of Vienna by Lueger had cost sums which basically had to be repaid by increased tax revenues, to be sure, but the fundamental reason for misery and overcrowding was to be found in the too-rapid increase in residents. It was no wonder that the police constantly were ordering the unemployed to go back to their villages.

There are no indications that Hitler ever was ordered back to Linz, that he slept in sewers, or even in "mass quarters." A man who knew what it was to sleep on benches in the Prater and at the home in Meidling was perilously close, however, to the lowest of the vagrants. He must have brushed shoulders with them constantly after his first winter in Vienna, and their looks of misery and apathy may well have stirred in him a desire to settle the "social question." Hitler's Vienna was not the Vienna of decadent archdukes, well-fed party hacks, and international businessmen. He hated all such persons with the loathing that failure, hunger, and filthy rags alone can instill in a human soul. "Even now I shudder when I think of those pitiful dens, the shelters and lodging houses, those sinister pictures of dirt and repugnant filth, and worse still." [30]

Lueger and the Common Man

THE FRUSTRATIONS and miseries of the Viennese years never completely erased Hitler's admiration for two Austrian political figures, Burgomaster Karl Lueger of Vienna and Georg von Schönerer, the leader of the Pan-Germans. Of the former Hitler wrote in 1924:

> Therefore he put the weight of his political activity on winning over those classes the existence of which was threatened, and this, therefore, became a stimulant rather than an impediment of the will to fight. In the same way he was inclined to use all the instruments of power already existing, and to gain the favor of influential institutions, in order to be able to draw the greatest possible advantage for his own movement from such old-established sources of power.
>
> So he based his party primarily on the middle classes which were threatened with extinction, and so assured himself a group of followers almost impossible to unnerve, filled with a readiness for sacrifice as well as with a tough fighting strength.

. . . .

> Had Doktor Karl Lueger lived in Germany, he would have been placed in the ranks of the great figures of our nation; that he had labored in this impossible State was the misfortune of his work as well as his own.[1]

Lueger, of course, never admitted that his beloved homeland was an "impossible State," however much the Magyars might arouse his distrust and anger. He lived long enough to be recognized as Francis Ferdinand's first choice for the minister-presidency of Austria, and he ever scorned the Pan-German dreams of *Anschluss*.[2]

This last great vital defender of the Habsburg monarchy was born in Vienna of most humble parentage in 1844. His father, whose ancestors had been simple peasants, was employed as a janitor at the Polytechnical Institute, rising later to the position of caretaker in one of the laboratories. His mother was a native Viennese, the daughter of a cabinetmaker. As a child Karl Lueger could not speak until his fourth year. Later he liked to joke about his ample correction of his early silence. Despite his plain origins, he entered after primary school the highly reputed Theresianum Gymnasium, from which he was graduated with honors in 1862. Merely remaining in school was no small task for the son of a petty civil servant, and the strain on his family was inordinately increased by his ambitious attendance of classes given by the Faculty of Jurisprudence of the University of Vienna. Karl's father died during this epic struggle for an education and a career, leaving Frau Lueger almost penniless. Thanks to her son's energy she was able to open a small tobacco shop which barely provided for her necessities. In 1866 the formal law studies were completed, and the embryonic lawyer, who was not to receive his doctorate in law until 1870, threw himself heartily into the blossoming political life of the day.

The defeat at Sadowa forced a complete reorganization of political patterns in the Danubian empire. The most striking development was the closing of a bargain with the Magyars, the celebrated *Ausgleich* of 1867, which left Hungary almost completely in the hands of the dominant Magyar national leaders. To gain support for this compromise among the influential Germans of Austria proper, the Emperor's chief minister, Beust, promised that full constitutional government would be restored in those lands not included in the kingdom of Hungary. Despite the outraged cries of the Czechs, who envied the Magyars their new freedom, a "constitution" of five fundamental laws was eventually approved by the German majority in the Reichsrat late in 1867.

The second fundamental law provided for a bicameral parliament in which rank, wealth, and tradition heavily outweighed democratic aspirations. The House of Lords was a glittering assembly of princes of the blood, patricians of the realm, clergy-men of episcopal rank, former ministers who no longer were of any real use to the empire, and a scattering of "safe" exponents of the arts. The House of Representatives, or Lower House, at first was chosen by the diets of the various crownlands and provinces. These diets were in turn elected by a most narrow and incongruous system which time and again favored the rich, the aristocratic, and, most of all, the Germans.

Such a system necessarily irritated the non-Germans of Austria and provoked the disfranchised Germans themselves to strenuous politicking that is reminiscent of the excitement and enthusiasm of the idealists of 1848. Vienna was the center of a mushroomlike development of unions and clubs whose chief animus was directed, often confusedly, against the reigning laisser-faire Liberal tendencies of the well-to-do.

Young Karl Lueger at first attached himself to a "German Democratic Union," but its seeming futility propelled him directly into the circles of the powerful Liberals. Having caught the eye of their vice-mayor of Vienna, he was elected to the Municipal Council in 1875 and reelected for a three-year term in 1876. Yet his cooperation did not necessarily denote a total repudiation of his earliest beliefs or a blind acceptance of Liberal leadership. Almost as soon as he was reelected he began to consort with Ignaz Mandl, an old Jewish friend of "radical" tendencies who also was on the Council, and between them they denounced the heartlessness, "corruption," and apathy of the opulent merchants, manufacturers, physicians, architects, editors, and enterprisers in real estate who made up the overwhelming bulk of the Council's membership.[3] In the autumn of 1876 Lueger suddenly resigned his post to devote more time to building up the following he now undoubtedly attracted and to work harder at his law practice, which had included all too many charity cases. A series of sensational cases kept him in the public eye, and by 1878 he was returned to the Council just as Burgomaster Kajetan Felder was retiring to avoid the increasing clamor of the disfranchised Viennese, whose complaints interfered with his gentlemanly hobby of catching butterflies.

For the next ten years Lueger flirted with several political tendencies in an attempt to secure his future, but at least he was consistent in demanding political and economic guarantees for those craftsmen and small businessmen who hated and feared the increasing competition of Liberal big business interests. Antisemitism of an unbridled type often was utilized by the would-be leaders of these dissatisfied classes in Vienna in the 1880s, but Lueger joined in their diatribes only gradually and always with qualifications.

Membership in the Municipal Council was valuable in the development of a political career, but greater renown was to be had on the floor of the Lower House of parliament itself. There a man could beard the imperial ministers and have his remarks carried the next day to all parts of the empire by the rapidly growing press. Since 1879 the German Liberals had been replaced as ministers by a group of experts under Count Taaffe, who relied generally on clerical, conservative, and even Slavic votes. To maintain the once-influential Liberals in their impotence and to meet some of the democratic pressure, Taaffe had agreed to an electoral reform in 1882 which would enfranchise any male citizen paying five gulden or more in direct taxes.[4] When parliamentary elections came in 1885, Lueger ruthlessly placed his name in competition with a fellow "democrat" and won.

For fifteen years the new deputy had been involved in tricky and often disappointing maneuvering. Popular with thousands, he still had no firm hold over any significant group. Vastly superior to most of the demagogues in oratory, he had wasted too much time in trying to reconcile their differences. He needed a ready-made political apparatus which could be transformed into a fighting party, for it was obvious that denunciations of "Manchesterisms" and calls for a return to the "true" liberalism of 1848 were failing to galvanize the strength implicit in the simmering bitterness of the insecure lower middle classes. Where could he find his potential cohorts? What issue transcending mere economic distress could promise a solid framework for the party of the "little fellow"?

Christianity often had served as a framework for purposes
other than spiritual, and Karl Lueger had always been a devout
son of the Roman Catholic Church, save for a youthful seizure
of despairing doubt. Much of his early disillusionment with
Liberalism had stemmed from his distaste for that movement's
small-scale "war" on the Church in the 1870s, and he also
tended to identify the "obscenity" of the Viennese theater and
press with Liberal freethinking. Was it possible somehow to
fuse the general devotion of the common man to Roman Catholicism with his incessant demand that he be saved from economic
destruction?

The Center Party in Bismarck's German Empire had effected
such a fusion with most gratifying results, and there were men
in Austria who were tentatively searching for a similar formula.
Their leader was Baron Karl von Vogelsang, a Prussian con-
verted from Lutheranism to Roman Catholicism in 1850, who
had left what was to become the German Empire for Austria in
1864. In his new environment Vogelsang naturally won adherents to his anti-Liberal ideas among Catholic aristocrats who
found no Christian justice in a pure laisser-faire system and who
feared for their future should such a system completely enrage
the put-upon masses. In 1875 Vogelsang was appointed editor
of the leading Catholic journal, *Das Vaterland*, whose columns
he enriched with his economic and social arguments until his
death in 1890. He and his patrician friends, especially Prince
Alfred and Prince Alois Liechtenstein, were in the van of the
battle for social legislation in Austria in the 1880s. The resultant
compulsory insurance against accidents and sickness took care of
2,372,213 workers by 1890.[5] In good time, he and Lueger learned
to appreciate what each had to offer in rousing the Catholic
masses against both outrageous capitalism and materialistic
socialism.

Vogelsang always argued that social and economic life could
only be based on the Christian moral code, which had been set
forth most clearly by the medieval scholastics in their discussions
of ethics and natural law.[6] The guild life of the medieval period
might not be restored easily to modern industrial society, but

at least its ideals were eternally worthy. Man is God's glorious creation, to be protected from the unrestrained selfishness of his more predatory brothers by the erection of powerful vocational associations. If every Christian worker were assured membership in such an association, competitive capitalistic battles would cease and voracious individualism would be succeeded by a more Christian spirit of common cooperation. Enormous accumulations of property must be brought to an end, the impoverished peasants and handicraftsmen must be saved by protective legislation, interest must be abolished, women and children must be spared the horrors of factory life, the old and sick must be insured against starvation and ruin. All of these reforms were to be accomplished by cooperation between state authority and the new vocational associations. Vogelsang had no intention of exchanging impersonal laisser faire for state-controlled welfare. In regard to the Jews of Austria, Vogelsang wrote editorials and accepted articles in *Das Vaterland* which inevitably stimulated the active antisemitism of the 1880s.[7]

Lueger was only one of many attracted by these editorials and articles. Princes and counts, fanatical journalists, Dominican fathers, and master mechanics sooner or later gathered to agree with or dispute Vogelsang's theories. Earlier, the former Prussian Protestant had been employed as a tutor in the palace of the Liechtenstein family; now his greatest friend and follower was Prince Alois Liechtenstein. Theoretically the work of converting the higher aristocracy to a renewed consciousness of Christian economic idealism was the responsibility of Rudolf Meyer, a restless German who loved fighting much more than gentle persuasion. Meyer had run afoul of Bismarck in the German Empire and sometimes in his new Viennese environment lost more patrician support than was necessary by expressing open admiration for Karl Marx.[8] At first Vogelsang and Meyer met their friends and future disciples at a simple inn in the heart of Vienna. Later, no less a person than Countess Melanie Zichy, the youngest daughter of Princess Metternich, opened her villa in Hietzing to the increasingly prominent company. A Christian Social *Verein* had been founded in 1887 to further Vogelsang's

ideas, and Lueger shrewdly noted its growing influence over
many Viennese. At the beginning of 1888 Lueger began to meet
regularly with Vogelsang and his coterie and spoke constantly
of the need for a union of all Christians to combat "Liberal
Jewish materialism." His formal commitment to the new *Verein*
came in 1889, the year of Hitler's birth, during the celebration
of the Austrian Catholic Day.

Actually Lueger was committing himself only to those portions of the Christian Social program which were politically
vendible. During the Catholic Day sessions devoted to social
problems, he adroitly sidetracked a definite decision on the question of interest; was it not likely that even the poorer Catholics
might own interest-bearing paper of some sort? [9] Though the
leaders of the meeting voted to hold regular weekly conferences
to make decisions on social and political affairs in the future,
Lueger was soon recognized as the most potent deviser of
strategy. Vogelsang's death in the latter part of 1890 removed
the one man who might have softened the blunt appeal to the
Catholic masses. From 1890 until 1910 Christian Socialism was
virtually the contented prisoner of one Karl Lueger.

The party's ideals and program were first fully enunciated
by Prince Alois Liechtenstein in 1891 in the Reichsrat. The
peasants were to be saved from usury, mortgages, and excessive
taxation, while the craftsmen were to be allowed their own
associations and granted favorable tax measures. All industrial
labor should be organized into vocational associations which
could then demand a share in the profits of big business. The
workday's duration should be decreased; labor by women and
children was to be abolished. The social insurance schemes
recently adopted were to be revised for greater protection of
the sick and those suffering from accidents. Lueger's new ally
took pains to refute statements that the group believed in religious and racial antisemitism. There was a Jewish "problem,"
he was quick to say, but the Jews, in their desire to make profits,
were merely following the normal Liberal way of life. Eliminate
the poisons of complete economic freedom and the Jewish
"problem," he implied, would end.[10]

There was good reason for a scion of one of the most distinguished of Germanic families to attempt to define the Christian Social program. Lueger's solid gifts for inflaming a crowd, plus the rank unpleasantness of the tone employed by the *Deutsches Volksblatt,* a daily which sometimes patronizingly, sometimes fawningly, identified itself with Christian Social activity, had outraged most of the powerful ecclesiastics of the empire. Though Vogelsang prior to his death had warmly greeted Lueger as the dynamic element needed for Christian-directed reform, the great aristocrats and bishops who underwrote *Das Vaterland*'s steady deficits were appalled by the violence of the passion he seemed to provoke. More to their credit was their definite repugnance for the antisemitic diatribes which both Lueger and Ernst Vergani, the editor of the *Deutsches Volksblatt,* indulged in.

In 1894 Dr. Franz Schindler, Professor of Moral Theology at the University of Vienna and one of Lueger's devoted admirers and co-workers, was unofficially informed that Cardinal Franz Schönborn, Prince-Bishop of Prague, was preparing a bill of complaints against the Christian Social movement which he intended laying before Pope Leo XIII. The original suggestion for such an unusual step came from within the cabinet presided over by Prince Windischgrätz, whose Liberal supporters were notably eager to scotch Lueger as soon as possible. Schindler, Lueger, and Liechtenstein quickly conferred with their chief lieutenants and decided that a very precise statement had to be devised and rushed to Rome before the high-powered Cardinal of Prague made his representations. The program was put into final form by Schindler and relayed to Cardinal Rampolla, the Papal Secretary of State, by way of Agliardi, the Papal Nuncio in Vienna, whose own energetic nature led him to sympathize with the "activists."

Schindler's summary of Christian Social objectives candidly reviewed the party's attitude toward the Jews. Some of its members did call themselves antisemites, he admitted, primarily to express their loathing for ruthless capitalism and atheistic materialism, which they felt the Jews particularly favored and ad-

vanced. Basically the Catholics in the movement still were aware
of the injunction to love all men, and their occasional failure to
remember it could only be ascribed to the seriousness and duration of the struggle in which they were involved. Somewhat
weakly Schindler also suggested that some of the Christian Socialists were recruited but recently from Liberalism and so had
not yet acclimated themselves to the mild spirit of Catholicism.
Rampolla sent back to Schindler a flatteringly lengthy commen-
tary on the program, raising a few points in a manner that might
hint at light reproof but generally praising what had been
proposed. In July Cardinal Schönborn received a message from
the Pope, and the press pithily noted that the Christian Socialists
still escaped censure.

Early in 1895 a more or less authorized disclosure by a
Redemptorist professor accented the curia's high regard for
the noisy agitators in Vienna. The episcopacy had been ordered
to desist from any anti-Christian Social pronouncement. More,
it had been directed to uphold the party in every possible manner. Thoroughly aggrieved by such an indelicate undermining
of their position, Schönborn, the Bishop of Brünn, and the chief
adviser of the Cardinal Prince-Bishop of Vienna undertook a
trip to Rome to brief the curia authoritatively on the menace
posed by Lueger's partisans. In their audience they accused the
movement of sheltering individuals and tendencies that were not
Catholic but revolutionary and socialistic. The sincere Catholics
in the movement would end up as dupes of calculating
demagogues. The party acted independently and even contrary
to the wishes of the bishops in Austria and stirred up insubor-
dination among the lower clergy. It preached class warfare and
the reversal of the existing social order. Immoderate in oratory
and in print, these zealots openly embraced antisemitism.

Rampolla obligingly had this vigorous protest transmitted by
the Papal Nuncio to Schindler for rebuttal. The defense was
worthy of the man who came closest to being Vogelsang's successor as the party's theorist. Again there was admission that
some Christian Socialists acted too impulsively and too intemperately. But had not men like Alois Liechtenstein and Vogel-

sang, impeccably acceptable and coolheaded, thrown in with Lueger? Did not this Christian band follow Leo XIII's *Rerum novarum?* The prelate-professor made no effort to deny the party's antisemitic overtones. He did categorically assert that it did not share in the racial antisemitism of the day. Not long thereafter Leo XIII graciously received Schindler in Rome and expressed appreciation of what Lueger was doing. His blessing went to the lively Viennese politician, plus his "full understanding" of certain difficulties which would be overcome. The denouement was rapid. On May 16, 1895, at a festive party gathering Liechtenstein exulted over the Pope's wisdom and firmness in repudiating the anti-Christian Social maneuver spearheaded by "our diplomats in Rome and the entire European Liberal press." Wisely the ever-correct Prince left Schönborn and the other discomfited bishops out of the picture.[11]

With the ultraconservative Catholics on the defensive, Lueger stepped up his campaign to capture the allegiance of the common man wherever he might be found among the Germans of Austria. In the Municipal Council, in the Reichsrat, and in the Diet of Lower Austria after 1890, handsome Karl was constantly on his feet, fighting to build his party's strength among the masses. Unlike the later years of real power and achievement, these years were unmistakably scarred by Lueger's unabashed employment of antisemitic propaganda.

In May, 1887, Lueger had made shockingly clear his attitude toward the Jewish "question" by supporting the German Nationalist bill to prohibit all future Jewish immigration into Austria.[12] Never again did he come so close to the true fanaticism of Schönerer and his bullies, though his public utterances continued to flay those Jews who, in his opinion, economically oppressed good Christians. In a speech given two years later he declared that only fat Jews could survive the murderous competition of economic freedom. Christian folk had to be protected from insatiable capitalism. "Antisemitism is not an explosion of brutality, but the cry of the oppressed Christian people for help from church and state." [13] In the Reichsrat of 1890 Lueger was painfully explicit about the "oppressions" visited upon his co-

religionists by the Jews. After accusing the Jews of an un-
quenchable lust for vengeance upon anyone who questioned
their activities, he point-blank likened his foes to wolves, lions,
panthers, and leopards in the habiliments of human beings. The
gallery hissed his extravagance, a demonstration which only fed
his ardor. Limiting himself strictly to the economic position of
the Jews, he averred that they controlled the grain trade, money-
lending and speculation in land, the sale of ready-made clothing,
shoe factories, peddling, and even the Viennese law and medical
practices. What could Christian peasants, bakers, tailors, and
cobblers do in the face of such inexorable competition? Need
one search very far for an explanation of the rise of antisemitic
sentiment? Even if one could stomach Jewish economic power,
how could a good Catholic endure the teaching of his children
by a Jew, who had the right to prohibit their making the sign
of the cross lest Jewish student sensibilities be wounded? But,
emphasized Lueger, his followers did not hate the poor Jew or
the little Jew; his group hated stifling big business which was
controlled by certain Jews. As for Jews who wished to assimi-
late themselves into another nationality, Vienna's rising politico
denied their ability to shed their cultural heritage so easily.
Centuries of tradition and what one feels in one's heart—such
are the true symbols of nationality, not superficial fluency in a
particular language. Toward the end of his speech, Lueger dis-
gustingly recounted with no sign of disapproval the remedy his
friend Ernst Schneider had prescribed for the Jewish "problem." Schneider, one of the wildest of the antisemites, would
have liked placing all of the Jews upon a large ship, to be sunk
on the high seas with the loss of all aboard, as a great service
to the world.[14]

Here, of course, is the ghastly prefiguration of the gas chambers of the 1940s. Once Lueger attained the supreme goal of the
mayoralty of Vienna, he rarely reverted to quotations from
Schneider, who as late as 1901 anticipated the worst Nazi ab-
normalities by declaring:

The Jewish question is a racial question, a question of blood, a
question of culture, which can only be solved by blood and iron,

as hundreds and thousands of years of ancient history have taught not only our people, but all peoples, and you will not escape this truth. I do not engage in any discussion of Jewish baptism, I only say this: If I should have to baptize Jews, then I might act in accordance with St. John's system, though somewhat improved; he held them under the water for baptism, but I would immerse them for five minutes' duration.[15]

Before reaching his final office, however, Lueger was never backward about blaming the Jews for assorted evils. He claimed that they controlled the Liberal Party and its merciless ideology,[16] that their newspapers incited all of the troubles between Czechs and Germans,[17] and that they even dominated, through their powerful financial network, the conduct of Hungarian policy.[18] As Christian Socialism increased its strength in Vienna, Lueger used antisemitism less and less as a vote-getting weapon. In the crucial year of 1895, when he first reached for the insignia of the mayoralty, he delivered what proved to be his last important parliamentary statement on the "threat" of Judaism. Coupled with the old bromide that Jewish capital was wrecking Christian farmers and artisans was the accusation that crooked Austrian Jewish capitalists in the Balkans were turning the Balkan peoples against all Austrian penetration. At home Judaism labored mightily to dissolve the empire by stirring up nascent nationalism, while abroad it supported its fellow "conspirators" in such affairs as the Panama Canal scandal and the Dreyfus case. Almost as if delivering a swan song, Lueger concluded:

We fight against these dangers, and perhaps if an historian in the future busies himself about us, then he will write: There was a party which recognized the danger and the real foe of the monarchy and even combated it; but the ministers of the state were stricken with blindness and raged against the truest friends of the fatherland.[19]

In *Mein Kampf*, Hitler was of the opinion that Christian Socialism "was wrong in its fight against Judaism and had no idea of the power of the national idea." [20] He did not mean that the antisemitic campaigns were morally wrong, of course. He felt rather that antisemitism not based primarily on "racism" was ineffective. There can be no doubt that the Christian Social leaders active during his abode in Vienna were far less turbulent and much more the esteemed friends of the dynasty than they had been at the inception of their movement. Their antisemitism had always been pretty clearly economic in inspiration, and Lueger himself could never really please Hitler as an exponent of the true Germanic national idea. For instance, in the 1890s he distrusted the alliance with William II's Germany and sometimes grew wrathful over the gratuitous remarks of the German press and suspicious of German intrigues against Russia which might involve the Habsburgs.[21] He railed against Italian irredentism and Magyar intransigence, to be sure, but his apostrophe to the "genius of the German nationality" was more than overbalanced by his insistence upon equal rights for all nationalities and by his proud refusal to reject Austrianism merely to identify himself totally with Germanism. The German renaissance Hitler had in mind was indeed an unclear conception with Lueger.

Though the party and its spokesmen might wriggle uncomfortably over loyalty to everything German, there was no such indecision in regard to the campaign to seize control of the capital city. Every year after 1890 witnessed noisier street demonstrations that underlined the growing Liberal weakness in Vienna, and the elections of April, 1895, returned a slight anti-Liberal majority. On May 14 Lueger was elected first vice-mayor, whereupon the Liberal mayor resigned and the administration fell into Karl's eager hands. On May 29 Lueger succeeded in obtaining a paltry majority in his fight to become mayor. Disappointed, he refused to accept office under such conditions, and on May 30 the Austrian cabinet dissolved the Municipal Council. New elections were scheduled for September, and, after a feverish campaign, Lueger's party won command of the Council and reelected him as mayor. The Hungarian Minister-President, well aware of Lueger's blistering comments on Magyar egoism and greed, besought the Emperor to refuse his approval of the election. Fearful Jews added to the pressure, while Badeni, the Austrian Minister-President, surrendered momentarily to German Liberal protests and added his launched a vitriolic campaign against Badeni and his reforms, and there was open talk of the need of a rescue operation headed by the Hohenzollerns.

Even among more moderate Germans there was dismay and honest anger. Lueger found himself in a most perilous position, for Vienna was increasingly threatened with mass disorder and Christian Socialism was brutally challenged on the basic issue of the German position in Austria. Personally, the new mayor had complete contempt for Badeni's failure to consult the Reichsrat while simultaneously he saw some need for a language law that would advance Czech opportunities in the controversial crownlands. Lueger begged the Emperor to work for a parliamentary inquest into the dispute, fought valiantly to keep his party followers from aping the grossest excesses of the ultra-nationalists, and even suffered at the hands of fellow Germans the disgrace of being mocked and kept from speaking in the Reichsrat itself.[23]

As governor of Galicia, Badeni had not been accustomed to noisy and annoying interruptions of his decisions. He had been called to Vienna to take a strong hand, and, faced with unprecedented obstruction in the Reichsrat, he decided to take draconic measures late in November, 1897. One of his supporters recommended new rules of parliamentary procedure, which would permit the president of the Lower House to exclude an unruly member from the House's deliberations for a period of three days. Should the House decide to discipline the disturber of orderly business, it might lengthen the term of exile to thirty days. The mere announcement of such a motion set off waves of uproar that made the resulting voting a farce. In the midst of the frightful din, the Polish president of the Lower House, Abrahamowicz, declared that the new restrictions had been accepted by the majority. Lueger could fight no more for possible compromise. He openly warned that his group would join most of the other German deputies in unyielding obstructive tactics.

The next day, November 26, saw the session chamber turned into a scene of riot and confusion. Marxian Socialists grabbed

pleas for nonapproval. The Emperor, afraid of con
in the renewal of the economic *Ausgleich* with Hu
fused confirmation. The Municipal Council defiantl
its hero for the third time and was sent home for

A new Council undertook the job of picking a
April, 1896, and came up with the now well-wor
Lueger, by a vote of 96–42. At court the Emperor w
that he should not trifle too much with the loyalty of
nese by snubbing Lueger again. Indeed, most of his
plainly recommended confirmation as a way of endir
turbing situation. Francis Joseph's solution was typi
limited thought processes. Lueger was favored with
audience and was induced to surrender the supreme l
party comrade while accepting for himself the offi
vice-mayor. No one was deluded by this arrange
believing that anyone save Lueger was in charge, an
peror confirmed Lueger's fifth election on April
Badeni, Austrian Minister-President, who was expec
like Bismarck, was in dire need of parliamentary su
hoped that Lueger was a gentleman who might return

It is ironic to note that Lueger's final victory of A
was almost wiped out and his prestige among Germ
destroyed by Badeni's experimentations. The new
elected in 1897 had as its chief task the approval of the
Ausgleich with Hungary, and the Austrian Ministe
definitely needed Czech votes. To please the Czechs
on April 5, 1897, two tremendously significant langua
tions which were to prevail in Bohemia and Moravia.
German were to be "equal" languages thereafter in
offices. As of July 1, 1901, every official in either crov
to be able to speak and write in both languages. Ever
that ambitious young Germans would suffer tremend
these rules, for young Czechs who wished bureaucra
perforce learned German at an early age. Germans
ditionally insulted by the realization that these chang
been considered by the Reichsrat. The more viol
Germans, especially Schönerer's German Nationalis

the presidential chairs and were ejected only by hastily summoned police. Their treatment was bitterly protested by the
German Nationalists (never did politics make for stranger bed-
fellows), who in turn were forcibly removed by the police.
Outside, university students shouted and jeered, alternating their
boisterous siege of the Parliament Building with forays in the
direction of City Hall and the Ministry of the Interior. Their
antics grew worse the following day; on November 28, a
Sunday, Vienna looked like an armed camp and Lueger abruptly informed the Emperor that he could no longer guarantee
order in the capital. The Emperor graciously accepted Badeni's
resignation. There were the usual quips about the Habsburgs,
ministers who had failed them, and the similitude of the latter
to squeezed oranges tossed through Hofburg windows.

The burgomaster had almost lost his political neck by mis-
judging for the only time in his life the temper of the Viennese.
That they could be roused to hatred of Czechs more effectively
than he and others had been able to turn them against the Jews
was astonishing. Now it was all important to rally himself to
the crowd's leadership. With a theatrical flourish, he announced
to the mob on the Rathausplatz that Badeni was finished. Com-
mandeering a carriage, he next pacified the demonstrators surg-
ing about the ramp of the Parliament Building with the same
welcome news. The police were cautioned to treat with care the
dispersing men and women, who soon read in newspaper extras
of a union of nearly all German deputies, pledged to obtain the
complete lifting of the offensive language ordinances. Conspicuously present in this united front were Lueger and the
Christian Socialists.

A new minister-president busied himself with plans to modify
the ordinances in a fair way but quit when the Czechs obdurately refused to step backward. In parliament Lueger paid
lip service to the cause of Germanism while actually finding
real dangers to the common man in the provisions of the proposed economic agreement with the Magyars. When Count Leo
Thun, the newest Minister-President, brushed off Lueger's wails
with disdain, the outraged mayor predicted Thun's speedy re-

turn to his home in Teschen. It took Thun a year to lose the Emperor's favor. In the interim Lueger had much to say about noble Poles who flayed the hides of hapless consumers of petroleum products, about the general immorality of indirect taxes, and about the failure of Austrian cabinets to beard the greedy Magyar economists.[24]

Was it politically wise to return to the defense of the common man and soft-pedal the agitation against the still-existent language ordinances? Unlike Schönerer and the German Nationalists at the end of the century, Lueger was convinced that economic panaceas and propaganda got more votes than did extreme utterances on nationalism. As long as he lived to direct his party, that party generally prospered on such a presupposition, while the German Nationalists before long dissolved into internecine chaos and futility. The party which finally snatched Vienna from the buoyant mayor's successors, moreover, was a party which also talked overwhelmingly of economics—the Marxian Social Democrats. By 1899, when the language decrees were finally withdrawn to the accompaniment of Czech groans and filibustering, Lueger was well embarked upon his most significant work, the revitalization of Vienna. All other problems became secondary.

Hitler analyzed Lueger as an Austrian patriot who had the "fundamentally correct idea" of reviving the dying body of the monarchy through a conquest and stimulation of its heart, the city of Vienna. As Lueger's unholy admirer put it in *Mein Kampf:*

What he achieved, as mayor of the city of Vienna, is immortal in the best sense of the word; however, he was not able to save the monarchy, it was too late. . . .

Doktor Lueger succeeded in everything he attacked practically; the result he had hoped for did not come.[25]

Much more than the renewal of Viennese spirit and energy was needed to save the empire, one can agree with Hitler. Lueger's foresight and his determination to make his city the talk of the world nevertheless command one's admiration even today. No one in Europe rivaled him in civic-mindedness, and

Hitler was not alone in feeling that Lueger's death was a tragedy.

The story of Karl Lueger's passion for his home city (it should be remembered that no mere woman ever figured as Vienna's rival in his heart) might logically begin with the last month of the year 1890. At that time the failing German Liberals at last recognized the demographic changes of the previous decades by incorporating various suburbs into Vienna proper, thereby sending the population figures from 700,000 to over 1,000,000. The nine older wards of the city had been separated from the newly annexed areas by Prince Eugene's defensive walls of 1704. By 1893 the demolition of these walls was slowly begun, perhaps the only tangible sign that integration might really come someday. Otherwise communication and transport between "Old" and "New" Vienna remained primitive, nor did the suburbs have cause to rejoice over the lighting and water systems now vouchsafed them.

Lueger vigorously protested the poor facilities offered his Viennese throughout his stay on the Municipal Council, with no results until his party and their allies captured the city's administration from the Liberals. There was much to protest, if not to laugh at. In the older wards the tramways were nothing more than horse-drawn vehicles, inadequate in size and number and most erratic in schedule. The challenge of a slight hill was met by adding teams of honest-to-goodness horsepower. Technically different from the tramways were the omnibuses, also pulled by horses. "These forlorn old vehicles, lumbering, dirty, musty, unspeakable, seem to be the dubious offspring of an alliance between a rural diligence and a decayed berlin." [26] The actual difference between tram and omnibus consisted in the near-anarchy of the omnibus schedules. Whenever patrons wished to get on or off, the omnibus obliged. No one could accuse the directors of the General-Omnibus-Gesellschaft of a hypocritical advocacy of the tenets of laisser faire! Since 1852 the illumination of the city and its homes and shops had been in the hands of an English-financed company, whose services to the Viennese had become increasingly costly and poor. Lovers might appreciate the wan reddish gleam of the English gas-

burners. Their no less poetic elders quipped that there was only
enough light furnished to see the dark. Actually dangerous was
the state of the Viennese water supply before Lueger assumed
power. The water itself, pumped in from mountain springs, was
clear and healthful. There simply was not enough of it when the
weather happened to be unpropitious.

A "new deal" had been promised the Viennese by the Christian Socialists, and it began as soon as Lueger was able to count
the necessary majority in the Rathaus sessions.[27] The first wicked
monster to be destroyed was the English company which controlled the gas supply. Its franchise was to run until October 31,
1899, and the doughty mayor coldly informed its owners to be
prepared to get out on that date. A municipal gas works would
be constructed to give the natives relief from the foreign blood-
suckers. To make good his program Lueger needed at least
60,000,000 gold kronen, engineers and laborers who could perform miracles, and an enormous amount of sheer luck. His
Liberal opponents, aghast over the possibility of a municipalization, even socialization, of a utility, struck back hard. Experts
in their camp ridiculed the proposed new system and predicted
that monstrous explosions would leave the capital in ruins. Austrian banks and consortia of capitalists were inexplicably uninterested in lending the necessary 60,000,000 gold kronen. It
would be difficult to prove that they poisoned the minds of
their fellow businessmen abroad against the city's new administration. Only after many curt refusals from sources of capital
in Germany, England, and Belgium, however, did Lueger secure
the loan from the Deutsche Bank of Berlin. The engineers and
laborers did perform miracles, the decisive winter of 1898–99
was relatively mild, and the triumphant mayor took over from
the chagrined private company on the appointed day. Everything was done to bring the wonders of gas lighting to the homes
of the poorest of citizens, while all of the inhabitants cheered
the introduction of truly incandescent illumination. The streets
of the city, uncomfortably close to medieval lighting before
Lueger had any authority, were gradually equipped with double-
flame lights which added greatly to the brilliance and safety of

Vienna's gala evenings. Ere long, of course, the most beautiful of the famous squares and streets were bathed in the light of electric arc lamps. The suburbs were not so fortunate, for the English company's contract there ran until 1911. It was perhaps just as well that the suburbs had to wait for socialized gas, for the strain on Lueger's plant grew rather than decreased with the years. The end of the franchise in the suburbs was anticipated, however, by the building of a second large gas works which went into operation in 1911.

Next came the municipalization of the electric system, a somewhat calmer operation since the three existing private companies simply were bought out. In January, 1900, a power plant to take care of the proposed electrification of all tramways was completed, and eleven months later Vienna could boast of a municipal plant which could handle the needs of governmental and private consumers. The moribund tramway companies bowed to the mayor's inexorable determination, and the trams, completely electrified by 1902, did four times the business of the pre-Lueger days. At last the helpless commuter was guaranteed accurate schedules and lower fares.

The problem of the water supply was tackled early in Lueger's administration, and a master plan which would bring a minimum of 200,000,000 liters of water to Vienna daily was approved on his recommendation in 1898. He surveyed possible sites in Styria, obtained possession of the sources, and a majority in the Municipal Council rubber-stamped his choice. The project was completed some months after its author died in 1910; he had often taken pleasure in watching the unrolling of its 170 kilometers of main line and 55 kilometers of branch lines. Vienna did not attain a population of 4,000,000 in 1940, as optimists at the first of the century predicted, but at least Lueger was getting ready for the bumper crop.

Quite interesting were educational trends in Vienna under Lueger. The devoutly Catholic burgomaster emphatically looked to the schoolteacher to provide religious and patriotic guidance along with the ordinary rudiments of learning, and over 100 public schools were added to the city's roster of schools during his term of office. Lueger was a bachelor who presumably had learned a great deal about child psychology before that subject became world-shaking in its importance, and he insisted upon schools which would invite rather than repel the reluctant scholar. The façades of the newer structures sported intriguing sculptured figures, while the interior rooms were spacious, almost dust-free, and rather well insulated from street noise. Classrooms for art work, for physical exercise and games, and for scientific experimentation all gave evidence of superior planning. The poorer the district, the more lavish the school—such seemed to be Lueger's dictum. For example, a school built in an impoverished area in 1907–8 was endowed with fifty-six lecture-rooms, two laboratories, four gymnasiums, and two dining rooms with kitchens attached.

Excellent classrooms did not begin to meet all of the problems of poor children, as Lueger well knew. To handle the children of the indigent, who sometimes numbered 80 percent of a school's rolls, a special society was formed under the mayor's active presidency. Books, writing materials, clothing, and free tickets to the municipal baths were doled out, while 10,000 received free meals at the schoolhouses. During one visit to a school dining room, Lueger did not fail to notice that some of the poor students had smuggled in their brothers and sisters who were too young to attend school. Other poor children were obviously trying to hide portions of their lunch so that persons at home might eat later. No man could eliminate all poverty, but Lueger did make use of this touching scene to work even harder for subventions for the poor.

When summer came, when even the newest of school buildings resembled a trap to its young occupants, a fine program of supervised play was begun. Every day 2,000 children were transported by electric tram to upland village areas to escape the heat and dust of the city. Should a poor child fall ill during winter or summer, it was extremely rare that he could not be accommodated in one of the many city hospitals whose space for children constantly grew. If the learned doctors prescribed a complete change of air, one could be sent to the city's hospice at Ischl (like a rich archduke or cattle baron) or to the seaside hospice near Rovigno. Special nurseries were municipally operated to care for children whose parents had to work outside of the home, orphanages were carefully inspected and made more appealing to their inmates, and homes for apprentices were established to prevent young people from succumbing to the easy temptations of city life.

Adults also came under the mayor's eagle eye, particularly if they were poor workers who might be seduced into godless materialism. In 1907 the Municipal Council took the first steps toward founding a mechanical and technical school for adults, and a similar move in 1908 paved the way for a school specializing in the training of electricians. Much earlier, in 1898, a municipal employment bureau had been created, with branches all over the city. While Lueger was mayor, more than 1,000,000 places were found for temporarily unemployed men and women. For the chronic poor, a reorganization of relief agencies was effected in 1901; in the new administration, the city had representation proportionate to the funds it contributed. For the aged, a most attractive retreat was erected next to the Lainzer Tiergarten, an imperial game preserve. In the midst of attractive gardens, 29 buildings resembling villas were located, capable of giving refuge to 4,000 weary veterans of the storms of life. Special pavilions were available for old married couples, and the Emperor himself attended the consecration ceremonies in 1904.

For the more fortunate citizens with less meager pocketbooks, Lueger's regime also had its appealing points. A magnificent new hospital, called the "Jubilee," was begun near the Lainzer Tiergarten, with all modern conveniences plus the cheerful green color and enchanting play of sunlight and shadow of the nearby Vienna Woods. There can be no doubt that Lueger was almost uniquely responsible for giving the Viennese their beautiful "lungs," the parks and woods of the city. Thanks to his dictatorial insistence, a girdle of meadow and woodland was left to surround the city he inherited from the Liberals. Here generations yet to come would gain refreshment from the fatigues of urban life. It is likely that the self-sufficient middle

class also learned to appreciate the fine new bathing establishments, where tubs and showers were available. Also aimed at
the middle class as well as the poor was the Central Savings Bank
of the City of Vienna, which opened early in 1907 and soon
attracted more than 100,000 depositors. Again, consumers in
general were aided by the addition of new slaughterhouses, a
great new market place, and a fish market along the Danube
Canal. The city authorities kept a sharp eye on unfair trade
practices and price gouging. Finally, since death was the common lot of rich and poor alike, Lueger's administration after
1907 offered municipal burial services which provided decent
yet inexpensive interment. The Central Cemetery was turned
into what purported to be a spendidly planned garden, with a
suitable church to memorialize the dead. From childhood to
death, the common man and woman of Vienna could thank
Lueger for consistently humane and sensible improvements.

Municipal socialism on the scale triumphantly secured by
Lueger naturally was bound to cost. Expenditures were more
than double those of the Liberal regime, while the number of
municipal employees increased from 4,760 to 25,151. In view
of the enormous changes made, the costs were reassuringly
moderate. Commentators less than completely taken with Lueger
and his work have pointed out that the real watchdogs in
budgetary affairs after 1899 were the Social Democrats, and it
is more than possible that their careful scrutiny did prevent too
much padding of the payrolls with Christian Social voters.

If one did secure a berth on the city payroll during Lueger's
ascendancy, the advantages were considerable. The Christian
Socialists had consistently pledged adequate protection of city
employees, and they kept their promises. After ten years of
uninterrupted service, the bureaucrat or laborer was assured that
he would be eligible for a pension in case his ability to work
should suddenly be brought to a close. Special municipal funds
to insure workers against sickness and accidents were created
to supplement imperial social security laws, and the expense of
their operation was met by proceeds from the various municipal
enterprises. To ease the housing problems, the city undertook

the construction of decently priced dwellings which were generally located close to the centers of municipal activity. Apologists for the party have maintained that the general level of bureaucratic efficiency was improved between 1897 and 1914. That there were more challenges thrust upon all of the employees during the period is obvious, and that the challenges were met is undeniable. An honest summary must also point out that the city employees achieved renown as most dependable centurions in the Christian Social political machine.

Lueger never forgot that his superb master plan for Vienna would be wasted draftsmanship without that power which only the voters could bestow. Mobilizing municipal employees was but part of a ceaseless endeavor to keep the capital a Christian Social fortress forever. In his famous will, dictated three years before he died, the iron-willed burgomaster meticulously enjoined the party to regard as its most important task the irreproachable continuation of the administration of the city of Vienna, and he named Dr. Richard Weiskirchner as the only man who had the competence to carry on as burgomaster in his own tradition.[28]

Politics to Lueger was a stern business, and he never underrated its unending demands upon its practitioners. Though Ernst Vergani's *Deutsches Volksblatt* became increasingly strident and annoying to the mass of party members, Lueger preferred to avoid breaking with his long-time confederate. He killed off the *Deutsche Zeitung*, a rather lame paper that served as the party's official organ, only when it had become totally inept in 1907. Remembering that the stiff-necked conservative Catholics always would revere *Das Vaterland*, he diplomatically put off recognizing the rival *Reichspost* as the leading Christian Social daily until 1908. Indeed, *Das Vaterland* survived anemically until 1911, when a gentleman's agreement merged it in a greater *Reichspost*.[29]

If Lueger was deft in his treatment of the extreme left and right wings of his army, he saved his full striking power for the persistent foe. In 1899 the Verwaltungsgerichtshof handed down a decision which would have crippled the Christian Social determination to give devout Viennese the churches needed in a rapidly growing metropolis. The court decreed that no municipal funds could be expended for projects which persons of all confessions could not enjoy or use. This meant no communal subvention to keep up St. Stephan's or the churches built where the old city-walls had once been, no underwriting of church music or of the electrical illumination of the city's religious buildings. Reinvigorated by an audience with Leo XIII, Lueger called his staff together in the Rathaus and together they worked out the details of his daring scheme to unleash a "storm" of popular assemblies against the court's verdict. In one day seventeen mass meetings were to be organized in all parts of the city, and the best haranguers on the party's roster were readied for action. Each received a list of what work or projects would be eliminated in the district in which he spoke. Lueger assigned himself four of the addresses, and Friedrich Funder remembered years later the assiduousness with which the commander-in-chief prepared these "impromptu remarks." The court did not officially bow to the popular tempest which the party successfully conjured up, but its subsequent review of individual appropriations was gratifyingly discreet.[30]

Entrusted with much of the tedious work of patronage and publicity was Albert Gessmann, an official in the Library of the University of Vienna by profession but a rather cynical and ruthless backstage political manager by preference. Soon after Lueger secured the mayoralty he created a bureau which could service provincial journals with information and articles from the capital. The news-hungry weeklies were grateful, while the party had increasingly close rapport with rural Austria. Lueger certainly was no exponent of the idea that the farming constituencies could be neglected, but it was Gessmann who first cultivated the areas where Christian Socialism finally found its surest base. When Lower Austria fell into the party's eager hands, Gessmann could not dismiss the hordes of public-school teachers who profoundly angered him with their anticlericalism, socialism, and freethinking. Before he had finished, however, half of the principals of these schools were from the Tyrol, a land noted for rock-bound piety. Though hardly a Louis XIV or a Princess von Werdenberg, the owlish Dr. Gessmann customarily met his party secretaries and his journalists at a levée in his home at seven in the morning, still in his underwear and snapping out his orders and advice for the day.[31]

Of such was the Christian Social realm compounded. When young Hitler first took up residence in Vienna, Lueger had attained something of the status of an elder statesman. His zeal for social reform was concretely illustrated by the changes wrought in Vienna, and there were only intermittent flashes of the old demagogic spirit in his public utterances. Well-founded rumor declared that the mayor and some of his closer party comrades had won the approval and confidence of the Heir-Apparent, Archduke Francis Ferdinand, and the appointment of Christian Socialists to the cabinet in November, 1907, did not destroy the force of the rumor. The anti-Magyar animus of the Christian Socialists fitted in well with Francis Ferdinand's tentative notion of a trialistic monarchy, for the creation of a third great unity under the crown, that of the South Slavs, would inevitably lessen the bargaining power of the Magyars.[32]

Lueger's last years and speeches were filled with concern over the future of dynasty and empire, and nearly always he found the Magyars to be the malcontents, if not the traitors. He energetically cheered Francis Joseph's peremptory refusal to allow changes in the army's flags, emblems, and language of command, as demanded by the more hotheaded Magyars,[33] and his party's electoral manifesto of 1907 bluntly declared that relations between Austria and Hungary had reduced the former to such servility that economic separation was inevitable. When Lueger ostentatiously visited Rumania to celebrate Carol I's jubilee, he brazenly avoided Magyar territory by traveling through Galicia and the Bukovina. In his speeches on his Rumanian experiences, he ranged himself on the side of the Rumanians who resented the treatment of their brothers in Hungary and exploded with exasperation over the anti-Habsburg feeling aroused everywhere in the Balkans by Magyarization excesses in Hungary. The ailing mayor's last chance to joust with the despised Magyars came in 1909, when the centennial of Haydn's death was being celebrated in the empire. The Viennese Municipal Council, captained by Lueger, visited Haydn's grave at Eisenstadt, then in Hungarian possession. It seemed likely that certain Magyar dignitaries would elbow the Viennese deputation out of honored position, so Lueger simply marched forward, put a wreath on the grave in the name of the "imperial capital and residence, Vienna," and apotheosized Haydn as a good German, a good Austrian, and the author of the patriotic *Kaiserlied*.[34]

Next to the constant irritation afforded by the Magyars, the Czech population of Vienna gave Lueger much to mull over in the last years of his life. Described much later as a "restless and industrious army" of tailors, shoemakers, fiddlers, cooks, furniture craftsmen, coachmen, house servants, and wet nurses,[35] the Czechs of Vienna could see no reason why their children were not able to go to schools where Czech was the language of instruction. In November, 1907, Lueger was able to prevent the authorization of an elementary school in which Czech would be the medium of communication, and it is quite clear that he was rigidly in favor of keeping Vienna, "built by German strength and courage," German in spirit forever.[36] Two years later, a pitiful figure, blind and ill, he again had opportunity to watch the incoming tide of Czech national sentiment, far from the accepted Czech homeland. The Diet of Lower Austria, mortally afraid that their sacred German traditions might be subjected to Czech subversion, voted under Lueger's chairmanship a law allowing German alone as the language of instruction. The Minister-President impassively informed the Diet that it was violating one of the fundamental laws of the realm by such a restrictive statute. Lueger visited the Emperor in hope of redress, but in vain.[37] Some days later the mayor spoke at what turned out to be his last meeting with Viennese voters. He begged his listeners to fight to keep the German language supreme in the very nucleus of the monarchy while urging them to remember that this vigilance did not in any way signify enmity toward other nationalities. The final peroration was true Lueger; one should strive always to be a good German, a good Austrian, a good Christian now and forever.[38]

The nephritis, the diabetes, the bouts of uremic poisoning could be delayed but not cured by the doctors. On March 10, 1910, Vienna was bereft of her celebrated son and master. Most witnesses of the impressive funeral ceremonies, like Hitler, felt that a man of great stature had passed on. Others, who never had forgiven Lueger for his narrow religiosity, his frightening hold over the masses, and his limited but damaging antisemitism, undoubtedly felt great relief. Typical of the second group was Felix Salten, the gifted writer of *feuilletons* for the *Neue Freie Presse*, a newspaper which always regarded Lueger as a menace. In 1909, Salten had published a description of the mayor which had some elements of devastating truth. Lueger has a fine appearance, with his height, broad shoulders, unruffled yet dedicated countenance, enthusiastic and kindly eyes, full beard, and well-formed, impudent little nose, said Salten, if one looks at him from afar. Close up, the eyes seem crafty and evasive. The beard hides a mocking mouth, and the seemingly straightforward countenance gleams with guile and counterfeit. People had said that the educated should rule. Lueger, with his degrees in law, with his university patina, "disintegrates the physicians, mangles the lawyers, insults the professors, jeers at learning." In his haste to capture the mob, he tosses away all restraints, so that the cobbler and the tailor, the coachman and the grocer exult and rave over the opening of a new era in which the poor in spirit will be the blessed.[39]

Was it not a kindness that poor Salten, lucky to die in exile from Nazism, could not know in 1909 that the master magician had an ardent admirer in the wings, ready to perfect in monstrous fashion the lessons already demonstrated with frustrated classes and individuals? Was it not equally fitting that Lueger, whatever his faults, died without premonition of the coming reversion of haughty "Österreich" to insignificant "Ostmark" at the hands of one who had learned to hate Vienna and the Viennese?

"*Deutschland, Deutschland*
über Alles"

"WHEN I came to Vienna, my sympathies were fully and wholly on the side of the Pan-German movement. . . . that the movement, after its first glorious rise, had sunk so deeply, this I could not understand." [1]

So testified Adolf Hitler in recalling his earliest political attitudes in the capital city. He also was of the opinion, retrospectively, that the most notorious Austrian Pan-German, Georg von Schönerer, was a "better and more thorough thinker in fundamental problems" than was Karl Lueger, who seemed to be so much more successful in practical politics. [2] What had been the history of modern Pan-Germanism in Austria prior to Hitler's arrival in Vienna? Why had the Germans of Austria lost interest in Schönerer and his ideology?

Hitler was basically correct in analyzing the decline of the movement in terms of Schönerer's own attitudes and activities. Just as the history of Christian Socialism was inextricably linked with Lueger and his personality, Pan-Germanism, at least for the exciting last two decades of the nineteenth century, was a state of mind gradually evolved from Schönerer's own political experience and his generous borrowing of the thoughts of others.

Born in 1842, Schönerer was a generation or so removed from those Germans of the Habsburg monarchy who had developed a distinct consciousness of nationality in the struggle against Napoleon in the first decade of the nineteenth century. Nurtured by the imperial house and its platoon of expert publicists, this new sentiment helped arouse the citizenry to valiant though ultimately fruitless deeds in 1809 and gave them hope until Leipzig and Waterloo had demonstrated the vulnerability of Bonaparte's system.[3] The years of watchful diplomacy between 1809 and 1815 were supervised by Clemens von Metternich, who scrutinized the movement for German unity as warily as he calculated the strength of Russian and French divisions. Quite sure that cosmopolitan Austria would die if a truly united Germany were created, he kept close check on the lands beyond the Inn, confederated after 1815 with portions of his master's domain, and coerced the good German Austrians into accepting a regime of fairly comfortable obscurantism until 1848. Then the winds of liberty and fraternity swept him into exile and retirement, and the German Austrians once again joined with their western brothers in an attempt to unify Germandom.

The idealism and enthusiasm of 1848 were insufficient to overawe the entrenched interests which would have lost prestige if unity had been achieved or to settle the half-dozen ticklish problems occasioned by the march of Germandom to the east and by the existence of two regnant houses which had claim to German leadership. Before the tumultuous year was out, Vienna fell to a victorious army of reaction, and the stripling Francis Joseph was enthroned there so that the promises of his predecessor could be ignored.

Neo-absolutism triumphed in the persons of the young Emperor's advisers, Schwarzenberg and Bach, and their exaltation of the German language in Habsburg lands was simply a reversion to the eighteenth-century utilization of that medium as an instrument of centralization. Francis Joseph was well briefed on the dangers of German nationalism, and he participated most perfunctorily in any ceremony that might give rise to the slightest degree of fervor. His police maintained close surveillance over all potentially subversive activity, and only the Austrian defeats in Italy in 1859 forced a relaxation of the controls which had restrained young German Austrians from organizing societies whose innocent charters poorly disguised the political ferment that existed among their members. Fraternities in the universities came to life as accompaniment to the constitutional experimentation that ensued after the loss of Lombardy, and a lively reminder of the great days against Bonaparte appeared in the form of rejuvenated *Turnvereinen,* whose athleticism was suspected of being dangerously democratic by grumpy bureaucrats not yet acclimated to the Emperor's "new course." [4]

Prior to the German civil war of 1866, several solutions to the "German problem" were debated in middle-class, army, and student circles in Austria. The *grossdeutsch* faction wanted German unity without any infringement upon the integrity of the Austrian state. Austria, always enjoying a position superior to Prussia's, simply would have the closest possible ties with the rest of the German states. Another segment, heir to the democratic heritage of 1848–49 and strenuously anticlerical, was willing to let Austria die in return for the union of all Austrian Germans in a great new German fatherland. Distinctly republican in sympathy, this *deutsch-national* fringe obviously had no love for the Prussian "Junker-state" and marked distaste for the centralized Habsburg monarchy. Finally, an undeniably small number of Germans in Austria frankly desired the destruction of the Habsburg edifice and the unification of all German lands under the Hohenzollerns. Essentially democratic, these radically unpatriotic Austrians were momentarily distressed by Bismarck's disregard for parliamentary forms during his early years as adviser to the Prussian king. Later, like many of the Prussian liberals, they were willing to grant him absolution when he proved emphatically the virtues of the renovated Prussian army.[5]

The battle of Königgrätz left little room for unhurried and pleasantly unclear discussions of the Teutonic future. Bismarck had brutally expelled the Habsburgs from the German heartland, and thereafter Austrian Germans who were convinced of the superiority of their nationality fundamentally had only two choices to make. They could continue their mission of "civilizing" and leading the non-Germans left to them after Hungary achieved her great gains of 1867, or they might, decorously or otherwise, recognize Prussian hegemony and labor for an integral union of all Germans under Hohenzollern auspices.

At first glance it seems that these two tendencies opposed Austrian patriotism to German nationalism. But the patriotism of those who remained loyal to the Habsburg state was always heavily influenced by their consciousness of membership in the German nationality. Even Austrian Germans who embraced Marxian Social Democracy in later decades never totally disencumbered themselves of a degree of national pride, which they unwittingly revealed in their programs to end nationalistic strife.

Outright irredentist, pro-Prussian sentiment did not prosper on a large scale right after 1866, for a goodly number of Austrian Germans who disliked the traditional conservatism and the internationalist tone of the Habsburg court were not yet ready to trust Bismarck, even when he introduced universal manhood suffrage in the North German Confederation. Moreover, while the Austrian defeat of 1866 definitely forwarded freedom of speech and of association in Francis Joseph's western domain, newspapers and political clubs had to be cautious in uttering ideas that bordered on treason.

The *Grazer Telegraf* preached eventual *Anschluss* with the Germany which Bismarck was confidently expected to create, yet the Verein der Deutschnationalen founded in Graz in 1869 merely warned against Austrian moves that might impede German unification. A similar society established in Vienna in 1867, the Deutsche Volksverein, was quite circumspect in asking for no more than a joining of the Austrian lands which were once a part of the German Confederation with the territories following Prussian leadership. Both associations desired special status for Galicia and Dalmatia, since such arrangements would surely enhance German chances to dominate the territories which made up Austria after 1867.[6]

These small-scale gropings for a German Nationalist program aroused some resentment and denunciation from Liberal and Catholic student groups who disliked Bismarck's earlier treatment of the Prussian Diet or who feared his dynasty's Lutheranism. But their disapproval and the Austrian government's attempts to stifle enthusiastic student celebrations of German victories over France in 1870–71 did not inhibit the steady growth of yearning among German Nationalist students for some type of union with the new German Empire—direct, confederative, or through military alliance.

During the development and the resolution of the struggle between Bismarck and Napoleon III, Austrian affairs were in the hands of ministers who were enjoined by Francis Joseph to conciliate the Czechs and the Poles. The failure of their efforts did nothing to reassure the more headstrong of the German Nationalist students, while the return of the German Liberals to power late in 1871 eventually provoked the rise of the very countermovements—the outright Pan-German, the Christian Social, and the Social Democratic—which an unknown Adolf Hitler loved to analyze and evaluate in his Vienna days.

Even in 1871 the imposing Liberal phalanx in parliament included a minority, chiefly younger deputies, who were dubious of German Liberalism's ability to becharm the other nationalities into an acceptance of continuing German predominance in return for material prosperity, full freedom for the individual citizen, and protection against "clericalism." Increasingly worried about Czech insistence upon the unity of Bohemia, Moravia, and Silesia as a first step in the re-creation of a Czech kingdom comparable to Hungary, they espoused the cause of special status for Galicia. By giving the Poles of that crownland a maximum of autonomy, they would eliminate Galician representation from the Reichsrat and thereby render forever improbable parliamentary approval of laws that would endanger Germanism in the lands claimed by the Czechs.

Their version of Galician autonomy, by no means an original concept with them, was rejected by their leaders in favor of a compromise which virtually surrendered Galicia to the dominant Polish aristocrats there without stripping the crownland of its right to send deputies to the Reichsrat. The Czechs meanwhile continued to boycott the Reichsrat, and their absence from Vienna undoubtedly helped to deflect the Liberal Party's

elders from serious concern over the German position in Bohemia
and Moravia.[7]

The financial crash of 1873, with its attendant scandals that
reached high into the upper echelons of the Liberal Party, was
another deterrent to the "constructive action" impatiently demanded by junior party members and by German Nationalist
students. After May 8, 1873, when the Bourse collapsed under
the weight of wild speculation and overextended credit, the
Liberals were constantly under fire, and their endeavors to turn
aside the fury of the unwise and of the defrauded left little energy
for defense of Germanism. The sullen quietness of the Czechs
and the embarrassments of depression do not entirely explain
the leaders' passivity. A week or so after the crash occurred,
Herbst, a shining star of the Liberal galaxy, vigorously turned
on the "youngsters" who would have subordinated libertarian
and material goals to the safeguarding of Germanism in threatened areas. Liberty never could be sacrificed to shallow nationalism, and Germans had only to work to prove their continuing
capacity to lead in Austria.[8]

At a time when the Czechs with their policy of passive resistance were ineffectually striving for the same status the Magyars had obtained, Liberal emphasis on cosmopolitanism was
a gesture which the circumstances briefly permitted. In later
years, when out of power, the Liberals struggled unconvincingly
to prove that they really were aware of German superiority
and eager to maintain it. A new generation of voters either dis-
believed them or, bored by the unending nationalistic bickering, cast ballots for parties which stressed social and economic
betterment.

It was Georg von Schönerer who first arose as the spokesman
of German Austrian disenchantment with Liberalism, and the
painful similarity between his dogmas and Hitler's National
Socialism should not blind the observer to the momentous influence he exerted upon a generation of political leaders whose
ideologies still live in modern Austria. Politically dead by 1914,
regretfully discounted as an effective tribune even by the totally

unimportant young Hitler, Schönerer nevertheless was the symbol not only of an inflated ethnocentrism that would destroy an ancient empire for its own purposes but also of a growing revulsion of the masses against an unrestrained capitalistic system whose impersonality made thousands pine for the order that manor and guild once represented.

Schönerer's background was a cogent exemplification of the changes which were being wrought by the great economic expansion of the nineteenth century. His grandfather, a plain migrant to the city of Vienna, had eked out a living as a caretaker and house painter, but Schönerer's father was measurably higher on the social scale. A self-made man, his engineering skill, evidenced by the Semmering railway line, brought him a good income and entrance into the lesser nobility. Young Georg was born in Vienna in an administrative building of the Südbahn, attended the usual schools in the capital, and then went to cities and towns in the future Hohenzollern Empire for business and agricultural training. A favorite Nazi story of later years placed him on Prince Schwarzenberg's Bohemian estate in the fratricidal year of 1866, where he supposedly was impressed for all time with the disciplined behavior of the Prussian troopers. Three years later he became the squire of his own estate, "Rosenau," in Lower Austria, where he worked hard to indoctrinate the peasants with soil betterment procedures, schemes for athletic clubs, and plans for cooperative fire protection.[9]

His energetic crusading was rewarded in 1873 with his election to the Reichsrat. Conventionally enough he called himself a Liberal, but his first term was more significantly conditioned by the fact that he represented rural communes and by the circumstances arising from the depression which coincided with his appearance in parliament.[10]

Schönerer was soon playing the part of a vigorous reformer, anxious to cleanse the noxious air of the Bourse-dominated capital with fresh breezes from the virtuous countryside. Genuinely shocked by unpleasant disclosures, he opposed measures which would have brought relief to financially embarrassed banks, which he bluntly called "swindle enterprises." He wanted sure checks on usury and on peddling, particularly since the latter was deemed so much of a threat to small businessmen. Overshadowing his sniping at the cabinet's failure to root out all vestiges of ambiguous "influence" and favoritism, however, was his continual insistence on order in the state's financial system.

Schönerer's earliest theorizing undoubtedly centered about his concern over the deficit and over the obviously unsatisfactory tax system. First of all he would have reduced the tie with Hungary to a mere personal union. In this way Austria would have lost her great-power status, which, to his mind, her citizens could no longer afford. An end to the *Ausgleich* with Hungary would mean sensible reductions in defense expenditures, and a close alliance with Germany would give Austria protection without degrading her to the position of a helpless satellite.

Certainly at this point Schönerer had no idea of *Anschluss* with the German Empire. Like most Liberals, he wanted insurance underwritten by the best army in Europe. Unlike many of the Liberal leaders in Austria who were still wary of Bismarck's espousal of universal manhood suffrage, he wanted the alliance to be cordial and intimate, implying a degree of coordination of economic and social policies transcending mere military collaboration. In his first term he went no further, though twice in important parliamentary debates he uttered sentiments which thrilled the more ardent German Nationalist student organizations and aroused the indignation of all who had little liking for comparisons that reflected on Habsburg glory.

At the height of the Kulturkampf in Germany, Schönerer lost patience with the Austrian cabinet's far milder campaign against the Roman Catholic Church. "The glances of the Germans in Austria in the direction of kindred Germany will not be lessened by such proceedings," he warned in 1876, the year he disassociated himself from the dominant Liberals.[11] If such a comment might have been expected from almost any German Austrian parliamentarian who had reason to taunt the government, Schönerer's remarks in the hot budget debate of December, 1878, made him a marked man. Austria-Hungary had just occupied Bosnia-Herzegovina, and a new defense bill was anticipated. Ever motivated in these early years by a sincere desire for a balanced budget, Schönerer fully expected the new turn in foreign policy to lead straight to bankruptcy. "More and more we hear in these [German] lands the cry: If only already we might belong to the German Empire, to be liberated at last from Bosnia and its complications. . . . In the state of Austria now almost everything is rotten." [12]

Impatient anger rather than dark thoughts of secession or treason had mastered Schönerer in this speech, though immediately he became the darling of the most determined German Nationalists in the capital, the students at the University. Their adulation probably meant little at first. As time passed, Schönerer drew closer to many of their extreme views. He had already practically given up hope of recalling the Liberals to their duty to the "people," and he had daringly defined patriotism as "doing what the Crown wants." The Liberal cabinet had sponsored the formation in parliament of a "sort of political demimonde, whose members change their opinions in accordance with the price that comes their way." Elsewhere one might discern "political eunuchs" who always voted as the regime desired. The voters had an apt description of parliament, he added—it was only a machine to grind out per diem allowances.[13]

Much of Schönerer's time before 1879 was taken up with attempts to improve the lot of the farming population. He constantly fought for tax relief and tariff protection, urged more rural schools, demanded conservation of forests and streams, and in general pictured a sterling but depressed peasantry which had to be rescued from the grip of cold-blooded usurers and unresponsive theoreticians of laisser faire. On several occasions he complained vociferously of violations of the freedom of the press and of the rights of meeting and association. The German Students' Reading Club in Vienna was dissolved by the government late in 1878, and Schönerer almost achieved a light touch when he recited the number of parliamentary deputies and professors who were members of this "subversive association." Here, however, he was hardly more than an erstwhile Liberal who saw no harm in a bit of national fervor.

Noticeably absent from Schönerer's early political activities was that accent on antisemitism which he helped bequeath to Hitler. Lagging behind much of the prejudice which had seized the lower middle class and students of Vienna, he merely complained in the Lower House in 1878 of "a tone that might be customary formerly in non-Christian cafés" and of the "continual yapping of the Viennese Jewish and governmental press." [14] Unresponsive Liberalism was still the chief enemy, and only gradually did he equate its deficiencies with the "defects of Jewish blood."

During the next ten years, however, Schönerer emphatically moved closer to the antisemitic feelings of the unruly students and of the artisans and shop-owners of Vienna. He added as well to the German Nationalist movement an undisguised adulation of Bismarck and the Hohenzollerns, possibly the only true contribution he made to that constantly bickering, increasingly fearful segment of Germandom in Austria which stressed its loyalty above all else to German *Kultur*. His changes in emphasis came gradually, and on occasion he did not bother to tie together logically important points in his "program."

In the electoral campaign for the Reichsrat in 1879 no one was unaware of the new trend in government which Francis Joseph had decided upon. The Liberals having split violently over the occupation of Bosnia-Herzegovina, many of their leaders in the cabinet had refused to carry on the direction of Austrian affairs. Fed up with Liberal opposition and weakness, the Emperor had picked an interim cabinet whose chief figure, Count Eduard von Taaffe, so managed electoral affairs that the Czechs were persuaded to return to parliamentary life. Every German politician knew that Taaffe would rely upon Slavic and Clerical elements for support, even though the new "Emperor's man" hoped for a true coalition in which Liberals would participate. In 1879 as well, Andrássy, the Austro-Hungarian Foreign Minister, and Bismarck signed the famous Alliance which most German Austrians had wanted since 1871. The probability that non-Germans would have increasing power in Austria, plus the new situation created by the alliance with the German Empire, considerably speeded up Schönerer's turn toward ever more radical demands.

His own electoral platform of 1879 was consistent with earlier pronouncements. Germanism in Austria should be protected; elections to the Reichsrat should be on the broadest possible basis; the deficit should be checked by reduction of peacetime military service, by a progressive income tax, and by economies in administration; Bosnia should be evacuated and given self-government, if possible under an Austrian archduke; agreements on trade, tariffs, and currency should be concluded with Germany; above all, the special favor which had been lavished upon mobile capital and upon the "Semitic control of money and of opinion" should now go to landowners and to genuine workers and producers.[15] The last plank has undoubtedly been over-emphasized by later Nazi apologists, for Schönerer was still irritated primarily by doctrinaire Liberalism and only desultorily by Jewish businessmen and journalists who identified themselves with its tenets.

In fact, the squire from Rosenau did his best to reenter the Liberal fold in 1879, at least in the sense of urging the party to accept his propositions. His elders could not swallow universal, equal, and direct voting, nor did they honestly see much sense in fighting longer over the Bosnian occupation, which had severely divided their ranks. At a final conference on October 6, 1879, Schönerer dropped the idea of a mere personal union with Hungary and kept quiet on the Bosnian issue. As well, he seemed willing to acquiesce in an alliance with Germany which had no parliamentary ratification and which implied no change in Dualism. But, as expected, the Liberals had no taste for his democratic franchise or for his avowed contempt for their love of untrammeled individualism. He reentered the Lower House as a maverick.[16] Only one deputy, Heinrich Fürnkranz, joined with him to create the "Two-Man Party." [17]

In parliament Schönerer found no contradiction in fighting against a renewal of the Defense Law of 1868, upon which Bismarck undoubtedly relied in drawing up the alliance of 1879, and his own hearty support of the alliance. Nor did he seem to worry over the full implications of an electoral reform which he and three other deputies tried to introduce in 1880. Their bill provided for universal and direct manhood suffrage, with electoral districts to be as nationally homogeneous as possible. In justifying this proposal he argued that the class system in vogue was no protection for Germanism, and, somewhat vaguely, he declared that direct elections were as indispensable for German interests as the creation of special status for Galicia. Decades later Schönerer would be adamantly opposed to a democratic system that endangered Germandom's special position in Austria. In 1880 the vision of millions of disfranchised peasants and artisans temporarily blinded him to the higher call of *Kultur*. To be sure, he did not long cling to the ideals incorporated in this bill, which the Lower House would not even refer to a committee, for in 1882 he mentioned the possibility that vocational representation would be a better expression of the people's will. And in the same year he left no doubt that reform was predicated upon the elimination of the rights of Galicia, Dalmatia, and the Bukovina to send deputies to Vienna.

Heinrich Friedjung, a Jew closely associated with Schönerer, meanwhile had failed to convert the Liberals at the Party Day of 1880 to the idea of a "popular" party which would tie Austria more closely to the German Empire. The Taaffe regime continued to pay the price of the return of the Czechs, giving the Czech language parity in the internal services of the bureaucracy in Bohemia and Moravia and elaborating a division of the University of Prague into German and Czech sections. In 1881 all of the cabinet members who had been distinctly identified with the Liberals quit their posts, though this gesture, even when added to forthright Liberal denunciations of Taaffe, brought no revival of popularity for the party among the increasingly excited students.

Friedjung, Schönerer, Victor Adler, Engelbert Pernerstorfer, Otto Steinwender, and others began to work out a program which would save Germandom in Austria, they hoped, from the neglect of the Liberals and from the headstrong aspirations of the non-Germans. The result of their work was the epochal

Linz Program of 1882, whose clauses inspired a variety of political tendencies among German Austrians down to the final
collapse of the empire.[18] As the best known of the anti-Liberals,
Schönerer had not yet embraced the Jew-baiting of the streets,
and it is noteworthy that Friedjung and Adler, both of Jewish
ancestry, were most welcome collaborators. Schönerer consequently was regarded with distrust by some German Nationalist
students, who were of the opinion that baptism itself could not
wash away "Jewish stains."

To protect and unify those lands of the monarchy which
once had belonged to the Germanic Confederation, the devisers
of the manifesto had little to offer that was new. Personal union
should be the only link with Hungary; Dalmatia, Bosnia, and Herzegovina should be incorporated into Hungary; Galicia and the
Bukovina should either be united with Hungary or be given
special status similar to that accorded Croatia within the Hungarian state. Obviously the realization of these recommendations
would have freed the Germans of Austria from the threat of being
engulfed by a democratic franchise, to say nothing of relieving
them of territories noted for their demands upon the Austrian
treasury.

To guarantee further the German position, German was to
be legally recognized as the official speech of the empire—for
army, legislative bodies, bureaucracy (including its internal
services), and for public records. In all mixed districts there was
to be at least one primary school using German as the medium
of instruction, and in all secondary schools German would be
a compulsory subject. Every examination for state or provincial
office had to be taken in German.

In matters democratic the Program was less doctrinaire than
Schönerer had been in 1880. The franchise was to be progres-
sively extended, with direct and secret voting mandatory. Persons whose freedom to express themselves on all occasions in
parliament was limited by their profession were to be denied the
right to sit there—priests, imperial bureaucrats, important officials of enterprises which dealt with the state, which were in
competition with the state, or which were in the process of

liquidation. The rights of association and meetings were to be honestly upheld, while the press was to be freed from state interference and state influence. The school system was to offer a "good and enlightened" education.

The central government should effect economies in administration, especially by reducing military service for literates to two years. The budget and the imperial debt were to be brought into proper focus, as long as the defense of the empire and the programs to nationalize railways and to continue social insurance were not harmed thereby. To remedy tax inequalities a progressive income tax should replace the existing direct taxes, while luxury taxes and a tax on Bourse transactions should place burdens where they belonged. Likewise, revision of the indirect taxes and of the tariff should be undertaken to cut the cost of the necessities of the poor.

To further economic development, a customs union with Germany was to be created, with provision for adhesion thereto by Hungary and the Balkan states. Artisans and workers were to be compelled to form vocational associations, while corporative bodies representing trade, industry, agriculture, forestry, and the working class should be formed as ultimate advisers on all bills and ordinances advanced by the government. Railroads were to be nationalized, and their rates fixed to stimulate agricultural and industrial production. Canal and river traffic was to be regulated. Insurance should be nationalized at the same time that old age and accident insurance was introduced. Transactions on the stock exchange were to be stripped of "moral and economic dangers."

The general economic code was to forbid adulteration of goods, restrict peddling and the sale of prison-made goods, and require a certificate of qualification from craftsmen. Factory laws were to be reformed, with limitation of child and woman labor, establishment of a normal workday, and penalization of employers for accidents suffered by their employees. In legal affairs justice was to be quick and reasonable—fixed fees for lawyers and penal colonies for criminals.

To arrest the decline of the peasantry, tax relief, credit institutions, state help against indebtedness, and revision of legacy and homestead regulations were demanded.

Last of all, the alliance with Germany was to be consecrated by a formal state treaty, while Austria's interests in the Near East and the Mediterranean were to be strongly upheld. Surely this final point indicated, as did the tenor of all of the Program's provisions, that the framers were intent upon reforming, not abolishing, the Austrian state-complex. The economic and social content of the Program was symptomatic of a general dissatisfaction with Liberalism, rather than with the continued life of the monarchy. It was this positive accent which indubitably drew a variety of followers to Schönerer at first, since he was the most influential of the Program's publicists. But it was not long before other tribunes levied with equal profit upon the democratic and reformist premises found in the manifesto. Karl Lueger skillfully united Clerical-Conservative distrust of laisser faire with more than a touch of economic antisemitism to assume leadership of the eventually potent Christian Social movement, while Adler and Pernerstorfer rather quickly turned to a Marxist orientation. During the vital 1880s, however, it was Schönerer above all others who won the attention of those who wanted a greater share of the empire's wealth and who were intensely perturbed over the future of Germanism in the empire.

The original phrasing of the Linz Program was totally devoid of antisemitism, but Schönerer's first positive adhesion to such a tendency actually preceded the publication of the Program. Alexander III's inhuman harrying of the Jews in Russia led to a large-scale migration of the persecuted to neighboring countries and created much sympathy for these unfortunates in Liberal circles in Austria. While important Liberal politicians importuned Taaffe to protest to St. Petersburg and the Vienna Municipal Council voted funds for the relief of those who had escaped, Schönerer tried to have the Lower House add to its protocols protests signed by various citizens against the immigration of Jewish refugees. One Viennese petition he unsuccessfully sponsored baldly asserted that the Russians had good cause to take steps against the Jews. Did not the tsarist government repeatedly

declare that "the unproductive and generally pernicious conduct of many Russian Jews had called forth the universal aversion against them?" [19] This protest warned that labor was already too plentiful in Austria and that the Christian character of
the state would be imperiled if these Jews were not kept out.

Schönerer did not actually propose a bill in 1882 which would
have prohibited or limited the entry of Russian Jews. Sincerely
concerned over the depressed condition of artisans and small
businessmen, he would have opposed the immigration of any
sizeable body of potential competitors. Nonetheless, a positive
antisemitic gesture had been made, and the first issue of what was
to be Schönerer's chief journal for two decades, the *Unverfälschte
Deutsche Worte*, on July 1, 1883, unhesitatingly stated that no
Jew, even though he might speak German and be a German
Nationalist, ever could be accepted as a German.[20] Such an
assertion was "racial" in its thought-pattern, though Schönerer's
next move toward well-defined antisemitism was still inspired
by economics rather than by dubious anthropology.

The Linz Program had called for the nationalization of all
railroads, and in 1884 a first-class controversy arose over the
fate of the privately-owned Nordbahn, whose privilege or franchise was to expire in 1886. This line, identified in the public
mind as a Rothschild enterprise, had made enormous profits after
its early and somewhat troubled years of operation, and the
people of Vienna particularly resented the nexus between its
dividends and the high price they paid for foodstuffs and industrial raw materials. The Taaffe regime had consistently assumed control of railroads, though it was pointed out that these
lines, before nationalization, ordinarily were in financial trouble.

Schönerer and the rising young Lueger quickly assumed
leadership of those who were absolutely opposed to a renewal
of the Nordbahn privilege. Massive petitions offered to parliament and well-attended protest meetings in Vienna were the
means employed to dramatize the case for nationalization.
Schönerer's utterances emphasized the role of the "wealthy Jew,"
of a Rothschild, in the Nordbahn's fight to exist as a private
corporation. He lunged at the "Jewish coal barons" who wanted

to retain their "transport-usury." When he melodramatically intoned a warning against "the vampire in the Mark of Austria," he immediately identified this bloodthirsty being as "Rothschild and Company." It was the power of Rothschild and Company before which the ministers and "possibly even higher factors in the state" bowed.[21]

The Taaffe cabinet discovered fairly quickly that it could not count on enough votes in the Reichsrat for approval of the new privilege it had negotiated with the Nordbahn. Vienna was not the only area which deafened the deputies with cries of dismay, and Schönerer was unquestionably the decisive gadfly. He never failed to compare the Nordbahn's practices with the worst excesses committed during Liberalism's heyday, and his denunciations of Rothschild and Company were pretty well purged of the relative care with which he had heretofore treated the "Jewish question." Goaded to a supreme fury by the realization that a second bargain negotiated between state and Nordbahn might pass, he exceeded his previous comments in a Reichsrat debate of January 27, 1885, where he bluntly spoke of the "system of exploitation pursued by the Jewish nation." [22] It is true that he was doubly stimulated by unpalatable events on this occasion, and no one ever doubted Schönerer's low boiling point. The German Clericals were wavering in their attitude toward the new Nordbahn proposals, while the cabinet rigidly refused to relax the antilabor "emergency conditions" existing in Vienna and Wiener Neustadt. But Schönerer was already convinced that the Jews were the chief enemy, and unilaterally he added to the Linz Program on May 1, 1885, a significant twelfth point: "To carry out the reforms aspired to, the removal of Jewish influence from all spheres of public life is essential." [23]

Antisemitism thereafter was a constant with Schönerer. Student pressures and the acclaim which he heard lavished upon other "democrats" who played the racialist tune undoubtedly prepared the way for his wholehearted conversion. R. A. Kann also has offered the opinion that any crusade against laisser faire had to attack the Jews, who "had joined the liberal fold as an almost compact ethnic religious group." He pointed out that "the assault upon the Jews was further fed by the fact that numerous individual Jews were participants in the speculative enterprises of the 'roaring seventies.' " This authority on the multinational empire concluded, however, that Schönerer and other Austrian antisemites of his period never really desired "the official initiation of discriminatory measures against the Jews." Their goal "was essentially nothing but a fight to influence public opinion." [24]

Once Schönerer was convinced that mass support of an attack on Liberalism was improbable without a simultaneous campaign against the Jews, his was the voice which echoed most effectively the clichés popular in antisemitic circles. Ironically, he softened his blasts at the end of the century only when a new and equally blinding light revealed Roman Catholicism as the archfiend on guard against German purity and unity.

Ritter Georg's adoption of racism should not obscure his more praiseworthy actions of the early 1880s. He continued to defend vigorously the citizen's right to express his opinions freely and to join political societies without hindrance from the police, though of course it cannot be disputed that his entire emphasis was put upon defense of the *German* citizen's rights. Late in 1882 he and Fürnkranz gave substance to the Linz Program by moving the consideration of a bill that would have abolished or minimized child and woman labor and reduced the working day to ten hours. Here transparently he wished to goad the regime into imitating Bismarck's scheme of allaying labor unrest by conciliatory legislation, for no development in Germany was more influential than Bismarck's "social policy" in leading Schönerer to complete adoration of the Hohenzollern Reich.

In fact, his blindness to any imperfection in the German Empire was strikingly illustrated by his vehement protests against Taaffe's proclamation of emergency conditions in Vienna, Korneuburg, and Wiener Neustadt on January 30, 1884. Avowed anarchists plus a comparatively small group of disaffected laborers, reflecting the real miseries of the proletariat, had committed a series of crimes against individuals, either out of desperation or to underline doctrinal convictions. While Bismarck after 1878 had severely limited the Socialists in their rights of assembly, press, and association, relieving the letter of the harsh laws only at election time, the Austrian government suspended jury trials and resorted to arrests and to deportations from the most affected areas. Schönerer never opened his mouth against the celebrated anti-Socialist laws in Germany, which were in force throughout the realm, but he vigorously pressed Taaffe for an explanation of the far more limited ordinances prescribed for the three industrial areas.[25] The episode was most revealing. Civil rights in Germany might be violated if the founder of the new Reich so recommended. In Austria a "Slav-friendly" regime had no right to hinder the justified protests of honest German laborers.

Though the Nordbahn "crisis" made Schönerer very much of a popular idol, he was constantly reminded in the Reichsrat that he was merely the senior partner of a two-man party. The Liberals still dominated the German clubs of the parliament of the 1880s, and they were Taaffe's persistent critics. They led the fight against the Bohemian-Moravian Language Ordinances of 1880, they constructed the formulas which would have given German clear legal status as the official imperial language, and they debated every point of the proposed creation of a Czech faculty at Prague. Schönerer consequently was often relegated to the side lines when the dominant Liberals began at last to try to prove they were German rather than preeminently cosmopolitan. For instance, in the lengthy but futile debate on the bills making German the state language, the puny "Two-Man Party" offered a pat solution to the incredibly tangled issue. Outside of Galicia, Dalmatia, and the Bukovina, German would enjoy precisely the same status in the western half of the monarchy which Magyar enjoyed in the eastern. Two men proposed this bill, and exactly two voted for it.[26]

Schönerer also was out of harmony with the usual Liberal approach to school problems because of his continuing loyalty to the rural areas which sent him to the Reichsrat. The Liberals were intensely proud of the compulsory schooling which they had introduced during their ascendancy, and they had no taste for a reduction in the years of prescribed education, whatever the complaints of labor-hungry farmers might be. When Taaffe was forced by his German Clerical supporters to introduce a bill making a teacher's appointment dependent upon the coincidence of his religious affiliation with that of the majority of his students, the Liberals were vigorously opposed. Schönerer was quite happy about German Clerical attempts to modify the length of compulsory schooling and to establish half-day schools, but he was suspicious of the religious affiliation proviso, "dictated by a power-thirsty antinational hierarchy." Unlike the Liberals, who wanted no discriminatory yardstick applied to persons seeking teaching posts, Schönerer argued that only Christians should be allowed to teach predominantly Christian, and even predominantly Jewish, classes. No Protestant should be barred from instructing a class composed preponderantly of Roman Catholics, however. In his opinion Protestants were as valuable as Roman Catholics in the great task of destroying in public schools that spirit which was bent upon the corruption of "the German race." [27]

The enactment of new electoral qualification laws in 1882, which enfranchised men who paid at least five gulden in direct taxes, failed to benefit distressed artisans and peasants who might have voted for Schönerer's candidates in the elections of 1885. Only two successful campaigners, Karl Türk and Josef Fiegl, joined Schönerer in the Lower House. The "Two-Man Party" became the German National Union, and eventually it numbered six among its members. After Schönerer's expulsion from the Reichsrat in 1888, however, the Union fell to pieces.

An intensification of the war against "Jewish influence" in Austria colored practically all of Schönerer's activities between the elections of 1885 and his temporary exile from public life that came in 1888.[28] When Taaffe delayed a law which would tax Bourse transactions, he demanded that the "immoral and injurious traffic" carried on "mostly by Jewish speculators" be halted. He introduced lengthy bills to prohibit "press lies" and to abolish the publication of material which would arouse impure thoughts, particularly illustrations of naked or lightly clad women or advertisements which would expedite unsanctified sexual intercourse. Though the bills properly avoided naming a particular class or group as chief offender, their author later admitted that he was aiming at the "continuing shameless falsification of public opinion by the corrupt Jewish press." [29] As well, he and his cronies in parliament insisted that increasing irregularities in installment buying and in the use of premiums, lotteries, and other "come-ons" be legally corrected. Again, the Jews were singled out as the principal transgressors.

On April 28, 1887, Schönerer distinctly moved from mere strictures aimed at "Jewish-Liberal" economic sinning to complete racial antisemitism. In his Reichsrat speech of that day he deplored the custom of accepting "aliens" as Germans, whether they were Jewish, Negro, Chinese, or Singhalese, simply because they learned to speak German, accepted Christian baptism, or became religiously neutral. Antisemitism was now to be the main pillar of the national idea, and the German who supported Judaism and its agents was to be treated as a renegade. "Our antisemitism is not directed against the religion of the Jews, but against their racial peculiarities, which have not changed under past oppression or under present freedom." The Jews were the creators of "the social question in its present alarming form," and antiradical measures were useless as long as exceptional laws against the Jews as the originators of anarchism and nihilism were not in force.[30]

A month later Schönerer put teeth into his arguments by recommending the passage of a law prohibiting the migration or settlement of foreign Jews in Austria. Some years earlier he had translated into German the Chinese Exclusion Act of the United States, and with the word "Jew" substituted for "Chinese" this text had been widely circulated and lauded by antisemitic circles in Austria. Attempts to rally all deputies who were alarmed by the sudden incursion of the refugees failed when Schönerer and his more violent colleagues insisted on stating, rather gratuitously, that an exclusion act was made even more imperative by their own sure conviction that in a short time all Austrian Jews would be placed under "special legislation." Only nineteen members of the Lower House voted to send Schönerer's bill to committee. In addition to the co-sponsors two Democrats and eleven Clericals supported the general idea of excluding foreign Jews from Austria. One of the Democrats was Karl Lueger, who had not yet found a completely satisfactory political home.[31]

The proposal of a new school bill in 1888 by the Clerical Prince Alois Liechtenstein inspired Schönerer to make even more evident his antisemitic bent. A meeting of the Verband der Deutschnationalen in Vienna accepted a lengthy memorial he had prepared in which he insisted upon the segregation of Jewish students from Christians and the absolute exclusion of Jews, even if they had become Christian, from teaching posts. To safeguard the Christian nature of the state, Jewish schools should be supervised by a few Christian teachers. To be sure, Schönerer was especially concerned over Liechtenstein's demand that bishops judge the capacities of teachers for religious instruction, and his stiffening attitude toward the Jews was subordinate to his distaste for increased Roman Catholic influence in educational affairs.[32]

In view of Schönerer's catastrophic loss of temper over a real or supposed insult to the Hohenzollerns in 1888, it is rather interesting to note that his growing displeasure with Habsburg Austria was highlighted by this basically negative campaign against the Jews and not by incessant, glowing apostrophes of the Second Reich. He and Türk unsuccessfully moved the creation of a permanent tariff union with Germany, at least in the sense of a common policy on grain, flour, livestock, wine, and timber. With no luck he renewed the attempt to have the alliance of 1879 ratified by the parliaments of both empires, hoping thereby to make it a "fundamental law" as far as Austria was concerned.

Outside of parliament Schönerer had greater opportunity to sway his listeners, and there his actions on occasion revealed more significantly the love he bore Bismarck and Bismarck's master. Among the students of Vienna and Graz he was a true folk-hero, though their fellows in Prague never quite fell under his spell.

Had there been universal suffrage in Austria in the 1880s, there is no doubt that Schönerer would have secured a large following in the Reichsrat. But his first decade of real prominence also revealed those defects in strategy which in the end left him a neglected demagogue rather than a throne-shaking tribune. First, he was not interested in a large party or in the grass-roots activity which would have kept enthusiasm at a constant level. Second, he was so much enraged by the "derelictions" of the press, which jeered at his every move, that he was markedly unsympathetic to the founding of a daily which could have printed his "line" with sufficient repetition to make new converts. Third, in a decade notorious for constant switches of personal allegiance and for splinter groups whose dates of origin and demise are still difficult to ascertain, he disclosed a positive talent for quarreling with the closest of associates. The German National movement might dissolve in a hundred tendencies before Georg von Schönerer would brook opposition or suggestion from his fellow travelers.

In the first shock occasioned by the replacement of the German Liberals by Taaffe, democratically and nationalistically minded Germans embarked upon the formation of societies which aimed at the preservation of Germanism from ambitious Czechs and Slovenes. Typical of such activity was the Deutsche Schulverein, founded in 1880 to protect the German language in "threatened areas" and to encourage the establishment of more German schools everywhere. Schönerer, Pernerstorfer, Victor Adler, and Otto Steinwender were some of the earliest members, and in four years it had enrolled 90,000 adherents. Its funds were expended for Jewish communities as well as for Christian as long as German culture was forwarded. At the height of his popular appeals against the Nordbahn, Schönerer demanded that subventions for Jewish schools be cut off and that the Schulverein support the principle of not hiring Jews as teachers. Moriz Weitlof took the lead in opposing such a move and dissolved a Vienna branch of the society when it sided with Schönerer, who then resigned from the Schulverein in 1886. In a few weeks he and other pronounced antisemites were allowed to organize a Schulverein für Deutsche, which never seriously competed with the prestige and the scope of activities of the older Schulverein. Claiming 20,000 members in 1889, it was extinguished by order of the cabinet a few months after its leading light was jailed for his exuberant loyalty to the deceased William of Hohenzollern.[33]

Less overtly nationalistic in tone was another ephemeral society of the 1880s which Schönerer first flirted with and then deserted, the Österreichische Reformverein. Its founders were well-known antisemites, Josef Buschenhagen, Karl von Zerboni, and the somewhat more moderate Robert Pattai, and the ostensible purpose of the association was protection of the hand-workers. The job of saving native craftsmanship from over-whelming competition was abetted by the printing and circulation of stamps whose crude Jew-baiting messages were glued to letters, postboxes, and kiosks. The Reformverein also sold silver effigies of hanged Jews to be affixed to watch chains and models of "Polish Jewish types" to be utilized as heads of canes. Another specialty—stationery glorifying Schönerer—did not suffice to keep Ritter Georg a happy member. The Reformverein was too "Austria-minded," too accommodating in its attitude toward Taaffe, and, possibly most important, it supported Lueger's candidacy for the Viennese Municipal Council in 1884. Lueger ostensibly was still quite close to Schönerer in the common fight against Liberalism and its cohorts, but their comradeship was strained by the former's continuing friendship with Dr. Mandl, a Jew, and by a natural rivalry in the turbulent politics of the capital. Schönerer, Fürnkranz, and a few others resigned, reserving their time and talents for the more easily controlled Deutschnationale Verein.[34]

This political club, also founded in 1882, was never as vulgarly antisemitic as the Reformverein, though Schönerer in 1885 sharply reminded his relatively few fellow members (773) that he could not compromise with those who merely disliked Jews for economic reasons, who could not see as clearly as he did that a Jew ethnologically could not be a German. The Deutschnationale Verein excluded Jewish members from the beginning, and a year after its establishment Pernerstorfer, the first chairman, quit because he was unsympathetic to unqualified attacks upon all Jews. He carried with him the control of the Verein's journal, *Deutsche Worte*, thereby forcing Schönerer to take the responsibility of creating a "pure" journal, the rather famous fortnightly *Unverfälschte Deutsche Worte*.

In the meetings of this Verein Schönerer beat down opposition with aplomb and rather quickly enlisted as a complement to his tiny parliamentary fraction a core of loyal supporters. There he arrogantly equated Lueger's "democracy" with republicanism and republicanism with eventual domination by the Jews, even though he and Lueger cooperated generally in the Reichsrat at the time. There again, in Olympian mood, he declaimed that, though he and his followers embraced no personality cult, they bowed before Bismarck in true love and reverence.

If the Taaffe regime and a thoroughly outraged Emperor had to swallow the latter utterance in 1884, their true feelings became manifest once Schönerer had been jailed and stripped of his title. On September 16, 1889, the Lower Austrian Governor's Office dissolved Schönerer's most successful Verein, charging it with the spread of unpatriotic sentiments and of antisemitic propaganda which eventually would disrupt public order. In response to Schönerer's emphasis upon a few, totally loyal, supporters, the organization numbered only 1,200 members when the government destroyed it.[35] Its fortnightly *Unverfälschte Deutsche Worte* had a circulation of from 3,000 to 5,000, though only 1,698 paying subscribers were on record in 1885.[36] By assuming the deficits incurred under such circumstances, Schönerer kept a tight control over editorial policies.

Schönerer's happiest associations in the 1880s, transcending the bitterness which often disfigured his relationships with his more intimate colleagues, were with the volatile German Nationalist students of Vienna. It took some time to win their attention, and even his famous speech of 1878, seemingly full of yearning for unity with the German Empire, was taken as nothing more than a sign that they had a friend of oratorical ability in the Reichsrat. At the end of the 1870s he was introduced to the fraternity "Teutonia," but he was more at home with the brothers in

"Libertas." In 1878 the latter had decided to initiate no more Jews as members, but this action preceded their association with Schönerer. Student clubs which, strictly speaking, were not fraternities also began to rally to his banner as the 1880s advanced, and eventually a majority of the German Nationalist fraternities and clubs compelled their members to subscribe to his program. A minority in Vienna never considered him a leader to be absolutely obeyed, and his influence in Graz and Innsbruck always was limited by the facts of geography which kept him in Vienna much of the time. In Prague he had a minimum of appeal at first, because the German students there needed Jewish allies against the ever-rising Czechs. Later, when Schönerer represented a Sudeten district in the Reichsrat and particularly during his intense vendetta against new language ordinances in 1897–98, he did become a force among the younger Germans in Prague.

It is extremely likely that Schönerer's antisemitism was intensified by the rapport he enjoyed with Viennese student organizations and with the "old gentlemen" who were alumni of such groups.[37] In 1883 and 1884 a large segment of the German student body at Vienna formed a union which was outspokenly anti-Jewish, and their stress was on "race," never on religion. They discussed the increasing percentage of Jewish students at the University and bewailed the number of Jewish lawyers, doctors, and professors being produced. When Schönerer actively embraced the idea of abolishing all Jewish influence on Austrian public affairs in 1885, he was merely repeating what a majority of German students at Vienna had been saying for some time.

If it can be rather easily proved that antisemitic tendencies were well developed among the nationalistic German students at Vienna and Graz prior to Schönerer's conversion to such leanings, it is generally admitted that he conclusively increased irredentism among them. The singing of "The Watch on the Rhine" and the ostentatious wearing of cornflowers by undergraduates had been noted before he won commanding influence over them, but his perpetual praise of Bismarck and the German

Empire gave his youthful audiences a definite object for their affections. The Austrian government, armed with a hazy law that forbade political activities by student organizations, repeatedly disbanded the more excitable societies. Since law enforcement in Austria was proverbially genial, if not sloppy, it was easy for dissolved groups to reform under a new name.

A high point of Schönerer's popularity with the young students was the riotous commemoration of the work of the recently deceased Richard Wagner in March, 1883. Years later Hermann Bahr, the critic and author, graphically recalled the scene in his autobiography. Young Bahr belonged to the fraternity which played host to the mourners, and, when enthusiasm for Bismarck's Reich was overflowing, he rose to add what he later called "my cheap symbolism" to the cause. Using what undoubtedly passed as a good Wagnerian figure, he implored Germany to pity and rescue grievously atoning Kundry (German Austria), who yearned for a redeemer from beyond her borders. There was an instantaneous roar of approval, a clanking of rapiers, hand-clapping, and the inevitable rendition of "The Watch on the Rhine." A poor police commissioner declared the meeting dissolved, but only Bahr heard him. Finally, police reserves were summoned and the order given to clear the hall. As the police went about their disagreeable task, Bahr came face to face with Schönerer, who was swinging a rapier and, elemental with rage, ordering total resistance to the police. Forty years later Bahr could not erase from his memory Schönerer's rabid fury.[38]

Closely allied with the beer-drinking, saber-dueling fraternity life of the universities was the continuing enthusiasm for gymnastics. The *Turnen* movement had sacrosanct roots in the War of Liberation against Napoleon, and its revival in Austria in the 1860s was part of a renewed accentuation of nationality and "blood" among the Germans there. But the gymnasts of the *Turnen* were also profoundly affected by the ideals of 1848, which stressed equality for all in a liberal atmosphere, and a large number of Jews were enrolled in the most important Viennese *Turnverein*.

Such a situation had aroused Schönerer's protests by 1885, but it took two years to expel the Jews from this Erster Turnverein. The unpleasant task was actually fulfilled by Franz Kieszling, long active in the Turnverein's affairs, but the victory was short-lived. The expelled Jews founded a new *Verein* and were admitted to the general Austrian gymnasts' association, the Deutsche Turnerschaft. A general feud resulted, with Schönerer's sympathizers eventually forming their own general association of athletic clubs.

Schönerer actually played quite a small role in the *Turnen* movement. He willingly encouraged the "Aryan" wing and applauded their adoption of his motto, "Through purity to unity," but he failed to entrance the gymnasts as effectively as he did the university men.[39]

The Emperor and Taaffe had sincerely hoped for Schönerer's defeat in the election of 1885, but his status as a deputy forced them to endure his provocations.[40] Suddenly, on the night of March 8–9, 1888, his ungovernable temper delivered him into their hands.

In March of 1888 the venerable William I was dying in Berlin. The German Nationalists of Austria were inconsolable in their grief, particularly in view of the well-founded reports that an untried and virtually unknown grandson would soon succeed to the Hohenzollern throne. On March 8, about ten in the evening, the streets of Vienna were all at once filled with newsboys hawking an extra edition of the *Neues Wiener Tagblatt*, announcing the death of the aged Kaiser. Schönerer and some cronies had already gathered in Skoda's beer-hall for their weekly rendezvous, and their usual conviviality gave way to solemn reminiscence and the singing of a memorial ode. About midnight the wake was interrupted by another extra edition declaring that the first report was false—the old soldier still lived on!

The dumbfounded mourners, after a few moments of glad relief, grew wrathful over what seemed to them to be a cheap money-making journalistic trick. Schönerer called for vengeance upon the guilty, and he and a gang of twenty-seven men descended upon the newspaper's editorial room. What happened thereafter was disputed by witnesses. Certainly the staff on duty at the time of the invasion, including a young woman, was genuinely alarmed. The enraged Schönerer, reportedly wearing brass knuckles and brandishing a heavy cane, shouted at the preponderantly gentile employees: "This is the day of vengeance. No mercy for the Jewish devils. On your knees, you Jews, and beg pardon! By spreading lying reports you have tried to make capital out of the death of His Germanic Majesty!"

Printers soon came to the relief of the astounded staff, and in the ensuing brawl considerable property was damaged. The newspaper immediately appealed to the state prosecutor, the Reichsrat duly quashed Schönerer's immunity, and a sensational trial ran its course on May 4–5, 1888. Lueger, still on good terms with the accused, wryly declared that a stupidity rather than a crime had been committed, but the court was duly severe in its verdict. The sentence passed on Schönerer included expulsion from the Reichsrat, permanent loss of title of nobility, a five-year suspension of active and passive political rights, and a four-month prison term. The party circulated numerous petitions and engineered demonstrations aimed at ameliorating the judgment, but to no avail. Most picturesque of the spectacles of loyalty was a parade of 200 carriages to Schönerer's home on the day of the announcement of the verdict. Karl Lueger naturally was on hand to show his sympathy.[41]

Schönerer's conviction and temporary banishment from active political life cut deeply into his following. His earlier growls against the Habsburg monarchy, when adequately mixed with antisemitism and social consciousness, had not been taken too seriously by many who voted for his disciples. But the essentially disgusting scene in the office of the *Neues Wiener Tagblatt* convinced many who had applauded his philippics against Liberalism and who had winked at his antisemitism that such blind devotion to the Hohenzollerns left no room for the survival of Austria as an historic entity. The sudden vision of an extinguished Habsburg fatherland was too great a shock to their habitual modes of thought. Nor were all of his closer comrades eager to bank on their chances of profiting from his "martyrdom." There were other parties and other leaders with whom one could get ahead.

Karl Lueger attracted many of Schönerer's strays, particularly those who saw no moral difficulty in combining Roman Catholic piety with hearty denunciation of the Jews. Other disillusioned followers, as wary of clericalism as they were of laisser faire, joined the German People's Party, founded in 1895. This organization catered primarily to those who had admired Schönerer's stalwart resistance to the aspirations of non-German Austrians but who had been repulsed by his irredentist behavior. Characteristically, the new fraction's initial program demanded special status for Galicia and legal guarantees of German as the state language.[42] Lueger was much more general in his assertions of undying love for historic Germanism, and so it was the religious factor which primarily determined the allegiances of those who had abandoned Schönerer.

The obvious defection of a large part of his popular following did not ruffle Schönerer, for he constantly predicted that the fidelity of a few would suffice to realize the ultimate union of all Germans. Great was his indignation, however, when one of "the few" directly disobeyed his injunctions. The traitor was Ernst Vergani, who had been elected to the Reichsrat in 1887 with Schönerer's direct support. While his leader was locked securely behind bars Vergani enlisted enough moral and financial aid to launch a daily late in 1888, the *Deutsches Volksblatt*. In line with his absolute opposition to a nationalist daily, Schönerer virtually excommunicated Vergani a month after the paper was first published. Quite abjectly Vergani and his embarrassed collaborators signed a protocol explicitly divorcing the new journal from any tie with the party, but Vergani's renewed pledges of eternal fealty to Schönerer did not long survive his urgent need for appreciation and support. By 1890 the two men were totally estranged, and the *Deutsches Volksblatt* soon attached itself to Lueger's growing throng.[43] The switch in allegiance was typical of many who had once revered Schönerer. His obstinate insistence on absolute acceptance of his strategy was bearable as long as no alternative was in sight. Lueger, with his personal charm, his obvious determination to enlist the broadest kind of support, and his undeniable gift for swaying the Viennese mob, was the inevitable gainer when Schönerer's disciples wearied of iron conformity to their leader's will.

The appearance of the *Deutsches Volksblatt* brought to Vienna Karl Hermann Wolf, whose journalistic talent and oratorical skill were for some time at Schönerer's disposal. Wolf was suspect, of course, until he ended his association with Vergani. He then began publication of the *Ostdeutsche Rundschau*, a weekly which for a decade mirrored his determination to create mass support for the German Nationalists. From the beginning Schönerer and Wolf were fated to disagree, and it is rather amazing that Schönerer desisted from the usual ultimatums until 1902, the year following the party's greatest electoral triumph. By temperament Wolf was a shrewd politician, not above election deals and business arrangements which Schönerer, with all of his unpleasant traits, contemptuously spurned. Significantly, Wolf was well acquainted with the prosperous German community in Bohemia, which Schönerer had never effectively wooed, and he knew that their antisemitism was more of a conventionality than a firm principle and that they were not enamored of the idea of competing with their fellow German businessmen in a great unified *Deutschland*.

Wolf's adhesion to Schönerer coincided with the squabbling that attended Schönerer's imprisonment and the first issues of the *Deutsches Volksblatt*. When the government reluctantly permitted a Deutsche Volksverein to be set up in January, 1890, by many of the members of the dissolved Deutschnationale Verein, Schönerer sulkily refused to become its leader. Rejuvenated by his success in driving Vergani from the party and exalted by his opportunity to eulogize Helmut von Moltke on the latter's ninetieth birthday, however, Schönerer grandly announced on October 25, 1890, "The leader is not dead—he lives and is ready to work!" [44]

Work actually meant preparation for the imperial elections of 1891. The old slogans were dutifully repeated, but Schönerer had implacably resolved to defeat former friends who no longer followed his directives. Anyone who ran as his "man" had to sign a declaration of complete obedience to his dictates, and the Czechs and Jews were practically lost sight of in the battle to punish such heretics as Vergani and Fiegl. Such negative tactics, when added to the ground swell of secession that had come after the trial, rewarded the party with but two seats in the Lower House.[45]

What these two German Nationalist deputies did in parliament was overshadowed by the growing conflict between Schönerer and Wolf over the rising might of Christian Socialism. During the Nordbahn crisis Lueger had enjoyed almost equal billing with Schönerer in the eyes of the resentful middle and lower strata of Vienna, and now his superior technique as master of the homely yet witty phrase thoroughly enraptured a majority of the members of the Deutsche Volksverein. When the elections of 1895 pointed to a Christian Social control of the Municipal Council of Vienna, Wolf begged Schönerer to unite with Lueger's following. Schönerer agreed, if Lueger would cast off Vergani and the *Deutsches Volksblatt.* This step "Handsome Karl" was not willing to take, but his astute refusal to accept the mayoralty because he lacked "sufficient" backing in May, 1895, simply augmented his attractiveness to Wolf and an impatient majority in the Deutsche Volksverein. For once Schönerer yielded to the protests of his comrades, if only to the extent of resigning his post as chairman of the Volksverein. He counseled abstention from the new municipal balloting, but the increased number of seats that fell to the Christian Socialists in September, 1895, was proof of his momentary impotence.

Wolf had undoubtedly delivered strategic votes to Lueger, but their partnership scarcely lasted a year. Sure that he had Vienna under control, Lueger disdained Wolf's warnings to avoid ostentatious fraternization with clear-cut Roman Catholic associations, and a meeting to "clarify" their differences ended in a brawling, shouting encounter between their partisans which police had to disperse. The *Ostdeutsche Rundschau* lamely sued for Schönerer's forgiveness, and Wolf penitently admitted his grievous miscalculation. In the Municipal Council eleven members quit Lueger as protest against his "betrayal" of Germandom, but most of the men elected as Nationalists moved smoothly into the ranks of the Christian Socialists. The attempts by Emperor and regime to keep Lueger from wearing the mayor's golden chain brought one last pitiful squeak from Schönerer's camp. After Lueger's fourth election the Emperor himself asked the popular hero to decline the honor. When Lueger acceded, Schönerer's small band castigated him for ignoring the wishes of the people. As was customary, the Christian Socialists replied that their denouncers were but lackeys of Rothschild and Company and worshipers of Wotan.[46]

As the imperial elections of 1897 approached, Schönerer was cajoled by his worried confederates into renouncing his resolve never again to sit in parliament. With Wolf back in the fold, party strategy boldly put Schönerer up for election in the farm areas that surrounded Eger in the heart of the Sudetenland. The "Egerland" had long been a Liberal stronghold, and Schönerer heretofore had not dazzled the Sudeten Germans. With nearly every qualified voter casting a ballot, he thoroughly drubbed his Liberal, Social Democratic, and Christian Social rivals. What had been lost in Vienna was surprisingly retrieved in the marchlands to the northeast, for three of the four party members who also won their seats in the new Lower House had been returned by Sudeten areas. Among them was Wolf, whose oratorical effectiveness was of decisive importance in the terrain he knew best.[47]

Most appropriately, Egerland's election of the most intransigent of Teutonic voices in Austria coincided with the greatest collision between Czechs and Germans the monarchy suffered in its last years. Before Schönerer and his tight little fraction could properly reply to the speech from the throne, Badeni, the Minister-President, issued a new language ordinance for Bohemia, soon followed by a similar decree for Moravia.

Past "aggressions" against Germanism in the Taaffe era had been reluctantly suffered by a majority of German Austrians, but now it seemed to them that a determined stand had to be made. As Schönerer rushed to arms, he did not need to search obscure Viennese alleys and the pleasant countryside for mass support—the Germans of Austria were overwhelmingly behind his standards.[48]

The chief forum for the battle between Badeni and the irate Germans was the floor of the Reichsrat. Schönerer and Wolf were in the forefront of the obstruction and disorder, seizing the president's bell and engaging in fisticuffs with their Czech antagonists. Schönerer seemed to reserve his bitterest feelings for the Polish president of the Lower House, who was blamed for the new restrictions on parliamentary misbehavior. The rabid German had cards prepared on which were printed epithets describing poor Abrahamowicz, the hapless president. Among the phrases employed were "government flunkey," "Badeni's tool," "biggest liar in Austria," "Polish horse-trader," "murderer of Galician peasants," "ravisher of the rights of the people," "seasoned delinquent," "bootblack," "Polack swindler," and "hangman." At the end of this ugly catalogue, Schönerer recommended the lamppost for Abrahamowicz.[49]

The banishment of Badeni from high office logically bestowed upon Schönerer a degree of popularity he never before had tasted, even in the exciting days of the attempt to nationalize the Nordbahn. A new generation of students, bored by old grads' retelling of that epic struggle, abruptly discovered that Schönerer did have unmistakable glamor. As is the way with students, however, they were not minded to accept his leadership without proffering some ideas of their own. And, just as Schönerer had quickened his pace toward full-blown anti-semitism as a result of his sampling of undergraduate opinion in the early 1880s, so did he digest and utilize the strong anti-Catholic tendency that certain student orators manifested late in 1897.

Distrust of the Church of Rome was nothing new among intellectuals and would-be intellectuals in Austria. Joseph II was a great hero among progressives of all varieties, and the remembrance of Bismarck's Kulturkampf lingered long after its chief features had been repealed or ignored. Schönerer himself never deserted the Liberal camp in so far as their legislation of the 1870s curbing the influence of the Roman Catholic Church was concerned, and there can be no doubt that he welcomed the resurgence of anticlericalism among the students as Badeni departed. The Church was assaulted because its German-speaking political champions inevitably were restrained in their national fervor and because Taaffe's regime, cursed as the source of all German woes, had partially depended on the votes of devout Catholic German deputies. Most recently, Badeni, son of ultramontane Poland, reportedly had sanctioned Lueger's inauguration as mayor of Vienna in return for Christian Social promises to help quell the anticipated storm over the new language ordinances. And, despite considerable political and denominational evidence to the contrary, suspicious German students were sure that the Czech renaissance walked hand-in-hand with international Catholicism.

On December 11, 1897, a medical student named Födisch called upon his fellows, who were assembled in the great courtyard of the University of Vienna, to prepare for liberation from the "deadly Roman foe." Once freed, they could obtain a genuine national education within the German Christian Protestant Church. Next day in the Sophiensaal, Theodor Rakus, another medical student, ardently called for a renunciation of loyalty to Roman Catholicism—*Los von Rom!* (Away from Rome!).[50] Neither the term nor the spirit behind it was new. More to the point was the question: Did the enthusiastic response of the students mean that the undeniably disturbed German Catholics would sacrifice their spiritual ties to a newer devotion?

Födisch's implication that Lutheranism alone could offer the "right" kind of training for Germania's sons raised painful questions within Schönerer's coterie. Protestantism's great emphasis on both the Old and the New Testament could mean the implanting of a Jewish ethos in the minds of future generations, worried the *Unverfälschte Deutsche Worte*. Would it not be better to substitute the *Edda* for the Old Testament, since talk of Christian-Aryan culture was mere babble and poor camouflage for the "fact" that what was Jewish could not be Aryan? [51]

Almost a year after the preliminary impulse from the students,

Schönerer in the Reichsrat consecrated *Los von Rom* as the all-important watchword "in this fateful hour." Early in 1899 selected members of the party adopted a neat formula he had devised. When 10,000 Roman Catholics had seceded from their church, then the party leadership would renounce communion with Rome. On schedule, Schönerer was received into "Bismarck's Church" on January 15, 1900, after party records indicated that 10,000 others had taken the momentous step. Efforts by sincere Lutheran pastors to make a good Lutheran of Schönerer were met with his bland confession, "I am and remain a pagan." [52]

In view of the centuries-long connection between the Habsburgs and the Roman confession, *Los von Rom* was but another symptom of Schönerer's conversion to total irredentism. The dynasty was subjected to taunts that went far beyond the unsubtle recommendations that its civil list be cut. When Badeni tried to hang on to office, Schönerer ruthlessly asserted that the Emperor was obviously uninformed of parliamentary opinion and proposed the creation of a special advisory group representing all parties, with an archduke as chairman, which could give the Emperor its joint estimate of all pending laws and ordinances. With heavy sarcasm he advised Francis Joseph not to expect many German Austrians to celebrate the Imperial Jubilee in 1898, since Habsburg gratitude was living up to its proverbial reputation by harassing fine Germans with pro-Czech ordinances. "I say partly with satisfaction, indeed perhaps with pride: We cannot mourn that today, at the end of this century, people speak of a dying state of Austria and of reviving German people in Austria." [53] Somewhat earlier his colleague Türk succinctly predicted that if German Austrians could not secure protection from Austrian laws and constitution, then they would seek it outside of Austria.[54]

Anti-Habsburg and anti-Roman Catholic tendencies were meshed with a new, logical, and yet surprising approach to the alliance with Germany. Late in 1898 Prussian expulsions of Poles and Czechs of Austrian citizenship created protest and unrest among Slavic deputies in the Reichsrat. Count Thun, the Minister-President, was obliged to placate the vote-power-ful clubs of the Slavs, and his remarks in parliament were sufficiently sharp to cause a distinct unpleasantness in Berlin. Infuriated by such an insolent disregard of the Prussian right to conduct Prussian affairs without hindrance from anyone, Schö-nerer's confrere Iro announced that the party would welcome an abrogation of the alliance. Then, said Iro, the German Em-peror could transmute into deed his often expressed promises to protect Germans who lived outside of his empire. Solidly backing Iro, Schönerer disdainfully wrote off Austria's effective-ness as a German ally. The basic elements in the Austrian army were as good and as brave as always, but the "Tower of Babel" within the military administration guaranteed defeat from the beginning of hostilities. Let Germany look elsewhere for a power that could be relied upon; the German Emperor would always protect Austria and its Germans.[55] Here, of course, Schönerer's fraction in a sense solved the problem of remaining true to a Germany which was allied with a regime they considered to be inimical to Germanism. If the alliance lapsed, the death of the polyglot realm would be hastened, and nine million worthy Germans would enter upon a new life under the superb guidance of the Hohenzollerns.

Wolf had some reservations about the stiff line that had de-veloped from the assault upon Badeni, but he soon agreed that *Los von Rom* was first-class strategy and was quite deferential in acquainting Schönerer with his own views on policy. The last years of the decade were almost totally deficient in constructive parliamentary activity, for the Czechs turned all of their talents to obstructive behavior when Badeni's ordinances were sus-pended. Schönerer cared naught that the Reichsrat was dissolv-ing into impotence, but a majority of German deputies still were sufficiently devoted to Austria and to parliamentarianism to reconsider the idea of a partition of Bohemia into German and Czech areas. Wolf anxiously suggested that the party make a public stand before private bargaining became general knowl-edge, and he implied it would be quite difficult to "swim against the stream." Schönerer swept aside the hint, resisting partition absolutely and postulating full recognition of the primacy of the Germans in Austria.[56] Since the Young Czechs were equally determined never to surrender the territorial integrity of Bohemia, Moravia, and Silesia, the battle lines were drawn for the elections necessitated by the dissolution in September, 1900, of the hopelessly divided Reichsrat.

The violence of feeling aroused by the language ordinances was attested by a noteworthy increase in seats for the German Nationalists. Schönerer's unyielding insistence on German supremacy went over well with the voters, who sent twenty-one of his candidates to the new Reichsrat. The party had campaigned openly on a "Pan-German *Grundprogramm*" and its deputies, for the first time in the movement's history, formed a parliamentary club which called itself Pan-German rather than German Nationalist. In short, primary stress was on securing an integral connection with Germany. Austrian problems as such took second place.

The impressive victory was nullified in a year's time by a complete breach between Schönerer and Wolf. The latter had never been fully forgiven for his flirtation with Lueger, and Schönerer constantly was irritated by Wolf's poorly concealed desire for a big party and by his recommendation that *Los von Rom* be soft-pedaled in the elections of 1901. Wolf was not trustworthy in Schönerer's eyes on other issues, for he had been lukewarm in opposing the partition of Bohemia and even thought well of having Pan-Germans appear at the Emperor's reception for members of the Delegations. For a brief moment Schönerer seemed rid of his ambitious lieutenant, who resigned his mandate in November, 1901, because of accusations which he could not entirely refute. It was customary for deputies in such predicaments to resign and then to run for immediate reelection as a means of securing a vote of confidence from their constituents. A majority of the Pan-German deputies forbade Wolf to seek this rehabilitation, but he refused to obey. Winning reelection, he was forced out of Schönerer's group, taking five deputies with him. As a parting thrust he and his schismatics took the name "Free Pan-Germans." [57]

Sheer personal rivalry, despite all of Schönerer's disclaimers, had much to do with the final break. Yet the incident inspired Schönerer to recall to his followers his own basic strategy, which Hitler condemned as faulty when he wrote his critique of both Schönerer and Lueger. If one reads carefully what Schönerer said on February 27, 1902, however, it is apparent that his grand design was not far removed from later National Socialist procedure. Schönerer simply failed to develop the apparatus necessary to keep and increase the following his program had won in 1901.

If there is to be a breakthrough, it will be based on a trustworthy elite. History is always made by a few; [it is made] by the masses only if they have joined themselves to a few persons or groups. . . .

If people sneeringly refer to me as the old enemy of the majority principle, they are partly right, for I have steadily declared myself first and foremost for the principle of authority.[58]

In 1904 eleven of the fourteen deputies still loyal to Schönerer voted to dissolve the Pan-German parliamentary club formed in 1901. Clubs were not necessary to protect Germanism, they had decided, though their action palpably was inspired by Schönerer's ancient grudge against party combinations which lost sight of the chief objective by getting involved in day-to-day issues. A modicum of unity for the disbanded fraction was afforded by their participation in the Alldeutsche Verein für die Ostmark, founded in 1902, and by the line laid down under Schönerer's careful supervision in the *Alldeutsches Tagblatt*. This daily had been established in 1903 as a counterweight to Wolf's *Ostdeutsche Rundschau*, for Schönerer's old animus against a Pan-German daily was overpowered by his fear that Wolf would suborn all of the faithful. To make things financially easier for party and subscriber alike, Schönerer discontinued publication of the *Unverfälschte Deutsche Worte* and strenuously begged all who loved Germanism to buy or to make donations to the new journal.[59]

Schönerer's last term in the Reichsrat, for such it was to be, revealed a certain relaxation on his part in that subordinates often delivered the fiery tirades which had been his specialty. He arose occasionally to blast the British for their treatment of the Boers or to request the regime to buy a hotel in Geneva which was being vulgarly commercialized as a result of Empress Elisabeth's stay there prior to her assassination. (Here he wished to honor the memory of a lady sprung from the ancient German House of Wittelsbach, let it be firmly stated, and not the family into which she was married.) When Bülow, the German Chancellor, refused to investigate alleged mistreatment of Germans in Hungary, Schönerer seemed almost befuddled as to what to say. He finally and lamely concluded that, if the decisive elements in the German Empire would never stick up for Austro-Hungarian Germans, then there was no purpose in maintaining the alliance. But it was rare that he did not emit "Heils" to the German Emperor and his empire, no matter what the subject of debate might be, and he was incredibly proud of the new German navy, whose mission he interpreted to be the propagation of German majesty and power throughout the world.[60]

It was the Pan-German Franz Stein, though, who reminded older deputies of the vituperation of the previous decades. When there was discussion of a possible Italian faculty at the University of Innsbruck, he snarled that it was an historical fact that the Habsburgs had sold, betrayed, and deserted the Tyrolese. Overcome by Francis Joseph's decision to support plans for universal manhood suffrage, Stein poured upon the occupant of the throne unheard-of abuse. To give the Emperor two million additional kronen for the civil list was a "sock in the workers' faces." Had not this same ruler "criminally" carried on state business for years by utilizing Article 14 of the constitution? Now he had become a fanatic devotee of calm, and no one dared disturb him while an entire nation went to its destruction.[61]

The proposed electoral reform did indeed mean that the Germans no longer would be the strongest national group in the Reichsrat. Schönerer and Stein despondently revived earlier Pan-German schemes to elect half of the deputies universally, the other half by vocational organizations. With time running out, they implored the "privileged" parliament to give German legal status as the imperial language before all chances to do so had evaporated. Once again there were motions to give Galicia and the Bukovina special status, to cede Dalmatia to Hungary. Foreseeing the inevitable, Stein in December, 1905, brusquely wished the "dying state" a speedy and painless end, "because this state has absolutely no interest for us." In April, 1906, he repeated his fervent wish, "so that the German folk in Austria in the future, happily outside of this state, can exist under the glorious protection of the Hohenzollerns." [62] In November, 1906, Schönerer jubilantly assumed that the misled and basely abandoned Germans of Austria could thereafter find protection only in the German Empire, and in his very last speech in the Reichsrat on January 26, 1907, he gloated over the "courage" demonstrated by the citizens of Hohenzollerndom in the "Hottentot election." The stiff rebuke administered by the German electorate to Social Democrats and Catholic Centrists who had hoped to slow down colonialism, militarism, and inflated nationalism was intoxicating news for Schönerer. He did not need to bother further with matters Austrian. The right course for Germandom had been set, and inevitably the trumpets of deliverance would sound for the oppressed brothers beyond the Inn. "Heil dem Deutschen Kaiser! Heil dem Deutschen Reiche!" [63]

The Austrian general elections held in the spring of 1907, preceding Hitler's permanent move to Vienna of the same year, almost annihilated Schönerer's extremist faction. The aging leader suffered a most ignominious defeat in the Egerland, collecting only 909 votes while a Social Democrat received 4,830, an Agrarian 1,623, and a Christian Socialist 1,042. The tempestuous Stein, who had taken on the role of heir-apparent in parliamentary affairs, was overwhelmed by a Free Pan-German in Asch. Exactly three Pan-German candidates were victorious in a new house of 516 members, whereas Schönerer had thirteen to depend upon four years earlier in a house of 425. Wolf's hated dissidents increased from eight to fourteen, but the great victories went to the Christian Socialists and Social Democrats. Their popular vote was 720,000 and 514,000, respectively, among German voters, while Schönerer's men picked up a paltry 20,000.[64] The results bore out the gloomy prophecies uttered by Schönerer and Stein, for the German masses indeed had been "deluded" into favoring internationalism, both Roman Catholic and Marxian. How comforting had been the earlier elections in the Hohenzollern Reich! How superior was the political sagacity of its voters!

Schönerer's lonely trio in the Reichsrat submissively repeated his lines, but one of them, Malik, frankly admitted that the Pan-Germans had simply gone on the defensive. An active policy no longer was feasible. Consequently, the annexation of Bosnia was deplored, anti-German demonstrations in Lemberg were protested, and attacks upon the Slavs, the Roman Catholic Church, and the Jews were delivered from time to time.[65] In 1911 one more candidate was selected to join the three chosen in 1907, and the popular vote for Pan-Germans did increase by 6,400. True to Schönerer's consistent distrust of coalitions, the four refused to join the more than one hundred German deputies who created a "National Union" in 1911, arguing that the new organization would be corrupted by traffic with the regime.

Meanwhile Schönerer generally eschewed fickle Vienna for his comfortable estate, receiving adulatory messages from the remaining faithful on his birthdays and leading pilgrimages to Bayreuth and to Bismarck's tomb. A photograph taken in 1912 in Friedrichsruh showed the seventy-year-old veteran enormous in girth but as arrogantly erect as ever. His respectably bald pate was offset by a grandly florid beard, while his heavy-lidded eyes resembled a bulldog's, ready for fight even as age made its mark. In 1913 he was persuaded to return to Vienna to celebrate the centennial of the battle of Leipzig, and in a speech that ran more than an hour he repeated all of the slogans of the past. Claiming that more than 70,000 had answered the call to desert Rome, he counseled these "valiant souls" to listen to what William II had to advise in religious matters, since Protestantism had no pope.

Young Hitler had betaken himself to Munich five months

before his erstwhile idol solemnly celebrated the great blow
against Napoleon. In a sense, however, Schönerer's parting words
were for him:

> Pan-Germanism is and was my dream! And I close with a Heil
> to the Bismarck of the future, the savior of the Germans and the
> moulder of Pan-Germania!
> All hail the second Bismarck, three times hail! [66]

The future leader of the Third German Reich has given
testimony that his personal sympathy for Schönerer, so strong
when he first arrived in Vienna, was gradually transformed into
sympathy for Lueger.[67] By 1913 he probably had already developed in his mind his analysis of Schönerer's basic failure,
which takes up more than twenty pages of *Mein Kampf.*[68]
First, Hitler was convinced that the Pan-German leader lacked
"an actual knowledge of human nature" which led him to neglect
the masses for the sake of the bourgeoisie. Second, the Pan-
German group was trapped into taking part in sterile parliamentary life and consequently "deteriorated to the level of
ordinary political parties of the day and lost the force to oppose
a catastrophic destiny with the defiance of martyrdom." The
beer-hall was exchanged for the floor of the Reichsrat, and so the
movement "ceased to be a people's movement." Third, Schönerer's fight against Roman Catholicism was incorrect in both
its assumption and conclusion. His movement "made itself impossible in numerous small and medium circles through its fight
against the Catholic Church, thus robbing itself of innumerable
of the best elements which the nation can call its own." Hitler
was particularly sharp in criticizing Pan-German leadership for
providing the masses with two enemies, when the full force of
the blows should have been aimed only at one. "As soon as the
wavering masses find themselves confronting too many enemies,
objectivity at once steps in, and the question is raised whether
actually all the others are wrong and their own nation or their
own movement alone is right."

What did Schönerer do that was acceptable in Hitler's sight?
He "correctly" realized the nature of the "race problem," and

he foresaw better than anyone else the end of Austria and all the perils such a downfall would entail for the true Germany. For these virtues Schönerer's career and ideology were subjected to numerous Nazi appraisals, all based upon the massive account first published by Eduard Pichl between 1912 and 1923. To spare devout Nazis whose reading time was limited, shorter résumés were prepared so that the herald of National Socialism in the Eastern Mark would not be forgotten by the faithful.

Hitler's shrewd appraisal of Schönerer's political faults should not obscure the debt which the would-be second Bismarck owed to the old campaigner. The author of *Mein Kampf* bitterly resented the loneliness and coldness of pre-World War I society, and it was Schönerer who first in Austria popularly stigmatized Liberal laisser faire as the source of the rootlessness and materialism that demoralized thousands less sensitive than young Adolf. The vast majority of Europeans who were witness to the exploding industrialism that came after 1860 tried to find psychic refuge from the dislocations such a revolution created, most often turning to nationalism, religion, or to economic radicalism. With Schönerer the prime remedy lay in union with the truly German Hohenzollerns, in a mystic blood-brotherhood whose genius would blot out all social evils. With this Hitler vigorously concurred, and it is obvious that the irredentist and anti-Habsburg propaganda that fills the earlier pages of *Mein Kampf* is but a repetition of what Schönerer and his compatriots had broadcast throughout German Austria.

Schönerer's responsibility for Hitler's antisemitism is less self-evident. The Pan-Germans certainly had preached racial antisemitism during Hitler's youth, though their preoccupation with *Los von Rom* after 1900 considerably reduced their parliamentary and press attacks upon the Jews. Any German Austrian coming of age after 1900 would have been exposed to antisemitic attitudes and propaganda, especially in Vienna, and Hitler most likely combined Schönerer's racialist themes with the "popular" anti-Jewish slogans and stories which the *Deutsches Volksblatt* turned out in profusion. If Schönerer's unoriginal and cloudy theories of "race" had some stimulus upon later

Nazi efforts to demonstrate "scientifically" the superiority of the Nordics, the vulgar Jew-baiting of a Streicher was more akin to the columns of the *Volksblatt*. National Socialism used both approaches, and both were available to the frustrated young Hitler in Vienna.

Anti-Liberalism, adoration of the Second Reich, and racial antisemitism—these were the legacies bequeathed by Schönerer to the creator of the Third Reich. Unluckily the younger man had the demagogic genius the elder lacked, and the credit due Schönerer as a critic of social injustice is forever compromised by the tragic fulfillment of his arrogant national egotism between 1933 and 1945.

The Jews in Austria

ANTISEMITISM has deep and ugly roots in the world which fell heir to the decaying Roman Empire, and the nineteenth century, which brought Jewish emancipation to a point never before reached in Western society, was not able to escape its heritage. Indeed, there is considerable reason to suppose that the emancipated Jew who tremulously reached out his hand for the trappings of gentile culture was more hated than the Jew who kept to his ghetto and his orthodoxy.

The traditional distrust which Christians had for their Jewish neighbors was transmuted into a lively jealousy as a fiercely competitive society developed after the shocks which shook the Austrian Empire in 1848–49. The old bitternesses which centered about the scene of the Crucifixion were often supplemented by economic and even social grudges. For many millions it was easy to lump together religious, economic, and social prejudices in arriving at antisemitism. The Jews were really accepted and sometimes honored only by the sectarian German Liberals, with whom they associated in business, in politics, and in the professions. The conservative peasant and the harassed artisan or shopkeeper were easily convinced by demagogues, particularly after the crash of 1873, that the Jews were godless and heartless exploiters, manipulators of the crushing international competitive systems. Vigorous and deep-seated antisemitism was no novelty in Austria when Hitler was born in 1889, though the decade which preceded his birth had witnessed a notable acceleration of its potency and ubiquitousness.

The wealthier and more socially secure Jews in Austria only rarely sought to counteract many of the abusive insults

and accusations showered upon their coreligionists. Some undoubtedly felt that their own conversion to Christianity and
their acceptance by many social arbiters removed them from
danger. As solid Liberals, as patrons of the arts and of charity,
and as investors in Habsburg bond issues, they even allowed
themselves a judicious appraisal of the "Jewish question."
Possibly they joked about grandfather's life in the ghetto as
a modern American lawyer might smile over his grandfather's
secondhand furniture store. At least one of them, Ludwig,
Freiherr von Oppenheimer, after a rather transparent attempt
to hide his identity under a nom de plume, [1] tackled the issue
in an interesting discussion published in 1882. In view of the
general refusal of the great Viennese dailies to descend to controversy with the voices of antisemitism, Oppenheimer's analysis of the Jews in Austria is particularly valuable.

Admitting that the Jews had made great strides forward in the
immediately preceding years, Oppenheimer openly wondered
if the noteworthy progress since emancipation might be bringing with it most serious dangers for Jews and gentiles alike.
He paid special tribute to those Jews who had helped construct
the railway net in the empire, thereby banishing forever the
threat of famine, even though this creditable work was ever
tainted with the lust for rapid profits. Rather sadly, he warned
such speculators that the masses would probably hate them, for
such was the usual fate of a parvenu whose prominence rested
only on his money. The extravagances of the nobility are smiled
at, whereas those of the "matadors of the Bourse" are reviled.
The contemptuous "Hepp, Hepp" spat at the cajoling Jewish
peddler actually signified less genuine dislike than the smiling
and sycophantic greetings which accompanied the progress of
a lucky Jewish speculator through the stock exchange or
through the salons of his competitors' wives.

Oppenheimer frankly deplored the "decontrol" of the legal
profession, that is, the end of all restrictions upon Jews who
desired to practice law. Popular respect for the judiciary had
not been intensified by the circumstance that all men and every
thing now could find their defenders. The suspicion that

penalties might be avoided or lightened by "friends in the right place" had grown with the increasing penetration of the lawyer class by Jews, asserted Oppenheimer. The "disproportionate" number of Jews going into both law and medicine would have very sad consequences, he felt, though "improvement" might come with time. A return to a *numerus clausus*, or restrictions upon the number of embryo Jewish lawyers and doctors, he implied, was practically unthinkable, however, to say nothing of being unenforceable.

Turning to the question of Jewish influence in the Austrian press, Oppenheimer declared that even the least initiated knew of the many Jews who functioned as editors and editorial assistants on the more influential Viennese papers. In the popular mind the increasing power of the press was equated with the waxing influence of the Jews, and consequently there was no warm sympathy for the press or even a recognition of its vital importance. Oppenheimer, no stranger to parliamentary life, was sure that parliamentarians tended to follow the lead of the press. Only in recent years did he see some of his colleagues struggling against those journalistic pressures which had led the German Liberals into many an error. The more prosperous papers also had adopted attitudes which were easily interpreted as being philosemitic and harmful to non-Jewish interests. Such seeming solidarity was readily misused by the antisemites in their general denunciation of all Jews.

Oppenheimer next considered the constant taunt that the Jews avoided their just share of the task of defending the empire. Granting that the Jewish percentage of active soldiers did not equal their percentage of the total population, at least a lessening of the percentual gap was noticeable over the years. In 1869 Jews made up 3.85 percent of the population but only 1.28 percent of the common active army. By 1880 they amounted to 4.33 percent of the population and accounted for 2.82 percent of the recruits. In time the two percentages would become identical, he felt, for previously the poverty and wretched educational facilities facing Galician Jews automatically disqualified hundreds of their sons for military service.

In summary, Oppenheimer solemnly reminded the German-speaking citizens of Austria that the shutting down of every Jewish school in Bohemia, Galicia, and Hungary meant the extinction of another outpost of German culture and speech. The "Jewish question" had but one solution: complete assimilation. Every other action would be transient and perhaps harmful. What would be the nature of this assimilation? Oppenheimer resolutely rejected a complete mixing of Jew and gentile which would cause the total disappearance of the former. He hoped rather for an intermingling in which religion alone would differentiate. The Jews had to keep their religion, which certainly was no threat to the state nor an honest hindrance to assimilation. Never should they surrender it in favor of apathy, indifferentism, or mere rationalism. Yet he had no flaming zeal for the maintenance of a Jewish "purity" that would guarantee the survival of Judaism. He fully expected that someday "Aryans" and "Semites" would intermarry as all of the European "Aryans" had in previous ages. Until that time, he implied that religion alone should set the Jews apart.[2]

Oppenheimer's position in the Austrian Lower House as a deputy of the great landowners of Bohemia, plus the obvious derivation of his name, made his discussions especially newsworthy. He represented the process of social assimilation already inaugurated by the Viennese branch of the Rothschild family, and he revealed the frank worry which emancipated and prominent Jews experienced when they scanned the ferment of the 1880s. In a sense he was answering the doctrines preached by Vogelsang's antisemitic *Das Vaterland*, which operated in such close connection with ultrarespectable and conservative Catholic circles that its very concern with the "Jewish question" was chilling evidence of growing antagonisms.[3]

As Taaffe's regime became more and more estranged from the German Liberals in the 1880s, *Das Vaterland* tended to play the part of an independent supporter of much that Taaffe proposed. The *Neue Freie Presse* consequently fought many a battle with Vogelsang, thereby enlarging the importance of his pronouncements. Rarely did it attempt to answer his thesis that the Jews were responsible for much of the economic malaise afflicting the peasants and the laborers. When *Das Vaterland* shouted for a cordon, no matter how expensive, to keep Jews who were fleeing Alexander III's pitiless empire out of Austria, the *Neue Freie Presse* merely printed descriptions of the persecutions in Russia, avoiding the issue of whether or not a "Chinese wall" should be erected.[4]

Earlier in the spring of 1882, however, the newspaper most often accused of being the tool of international Jewry had lost its patience and had quietly but effectively turned its guns on the antisemites. Ostensibly it was decrying a meeting of Viennese artisans who met as "Christians" to listen to tirades against the Jews. In actuality it acutely analyzed in a few brief sentences the reasons which had recently made antisemitism fashionable. Bad harvests drove peasants to mortgage their lands; to wipe out their obligations they hopefully assailed the Jews. The merchant who had to accustom himself constantly to new challenges, whose profession was never fully learned or mastered, blamed the Jew for all of his travail. The proud owner of rolling estates, hard pressed by the competition of American cereals, cursed free trade as a "Jewish invention." If all the Jews disappeared from the globe, then the Protestant ethic would come in for denunciation in Austria, opined the *Neue Freie Presse*. The modern state was overcast with storm clouds, and it was easiest to blame the unpredictable weather upon the Jew.[5]

Oppenheimer's cautious optimism and the *Neue Freie Presse's* rare yet telling candor did little to arrest the growth of antisemitism in the 1880s. Vogelsang's "interpretations" soon were so much eclipsed by violent agitators that the accusation of 1880 had practically become the accepted "fact" of 1907. The absence of a fanatically anti-Jewish political party of any strength in the Lower House elected in 1907 should not be construed as a waning of prejudice. For the moment it seemed better to most deputies either to pull hard to keep the empire together or else at least to fight for even greater recognition of one's own particular nationality. Burned into the consciousness of many a "little man," however, was the conviction that the Jews were tricky and sometimes crooked, out to grab all of the lucrative posts in business, the professions, the government, and the arts. When Austria succumbed to National Socialism decades later, it was a simple task to reawaken these convictions.

Between the years of Hitler's poverty in Vienna and his grandeur as its overlord, Dr. Leo Goldhammer published a statistical study of the Jews of Vienna which illuminates the problems which Oppenheimer discussed and which the anti-semites loved to exaggerate.[6] First of all, it seems wise to note the extraordinary increase in the number of Jews in Vienna as that city expanded after 1850. In 1857 a mere 6,217 Jews made up slightly more than 2 percent of the population. By 1910 the Jews numbered 175,318, about 8.6 percent of the population. The incorporation of new suburbs after 1880 reduced the Jewish percentage of the total population, for in 1880, the year which saw the beginning of a decade of virulent agitation, the Jews had made up 10 percent of the total.[7]

In Hitler's days of vagabondage the heaviest concentration of Jews was to be found in the Leopoldstadt, a big district which sprawled between the Danube proper and the Danube Canal. Here a third of the generally poverty-stricken citizens were Jewish; they tended to be the woebegone peddlers and hand-to-mouth tradesmen whom Hitler disdained and hated. The Leopoldstadt was the site of the old ghetto, so that the Jews who made money always felt psychologically impelled to move to the Inner City or to the relatively pleasant Alsergrund district. In these two districts they made up one-fifth of the population. The Leopoldstadt by no means took care of all of the indigent, for over 17 percent of the people living in the raw and desolate Brigittenau were Jewish. In general the Jews tended to congregate in the center of the city or in the livelier districts which touched the Ring. In the newest districts, save for the Brigittenau, they were not often seen.[8]

Oppenheimer's expectation that Jews and Christians would tend to intermarry with the passage of time seemed to be borne out by Goldhammer's research. In the four years prior to the coming of World War I, one out of every six Jews who married picked a "confessionless" consort. Since Christians often married "confessionless" persons who really had been born into Judaism, assimilation clearly was on the march.[9] Whereas there always were more females than males in Vienna from 1880 through 1910, there never were enough Jewish women in Vienna to marry the Jewish men resident there. Though this situation tended to "straighten out" in the thirty-year period mentioned, 1,000 Jewish males still theoretically had to compete for 965 Jewish brides as late as 1910.[10] This ratio undoubtedly helped the process of integration, which many established Austrian Jews looked to as a sovereign "solution."

It would be quite impossible to guess how much ink and time went into the antisemites' discussion of Jewish participation in the Austrian educational system. If Czechs and Germans were ready to battle in the streets over language qualifications for governmental posts, antisemites were more than prepared, particularly in Vienna, to sound the tocsin against Jews who "dared" to avail themselves of the imperial schools. The statistics for Hitler's last few years in Vienna do indicate that the Jews were athirst for knowledge and that they had distinct preferences in the kinds of knowledge they sought. Whatever the sins of the old empire might have been, there was no persecution of Jews who were guilty of the above desires; nor, in view of the unrequited howls of their enemies, was there indication of any limitation placed upon their ambition, save that of competence.

It will be remembered that 8.63 percent of the inhabitants of Vienna in 1910 were Jewish. Down to 1914, their children made up approximately 7 percent of the attendance at primary and intermediate schools. Then the proportion of Jewish students in Mittelschulen, whether Gymnasien, which stressed preparation for the University, or the Realschulen, which emphasized vocational and industrial training, increased almost sensationally. By 1913, 27.6 percent of those enrolled in the Mittelschulen were Jewish. These students definitely preferred the Gymnasien, for their diploma opened up far more avenues than did one from a Realschule. Almost 35 percent of the youngsters in the Viennese Gymnasien were Jewish in 1913; only 18.4 percent of the enrollment of the Realschulen was Jewish. To avoid the confusion which percentages alone occasionally convey, it should be added that in the last year of peace a total of 5,710 Jews were being taught in the Mittelschulen, in comparison with 14,956 non-Jews.[11]

The antisemites who raged over the number of Jewish lawyers and doctors in Vienna and who maintained that Jews were uninterested either in making the earth blossom or in creating new art forms constantly used the registration figures of the University of Vienna as their text. In the five academic sessions of the University prior to Sarajevo, the number of students increased from 9,090 to 11,115; the percentage who were Jewish went from 25.09 percent to 27.54 percent. Medicine seemed to attract most of these young men, for they comprised almost 29 percent of the persons under that faculty in 1913–14. Second in interest were law and politics, of whose neophytes 20.51 percent were Jewish during the same session. The Faculty of Philosophy was least enticing, for here only 16.33 percent of those registered were Jewish. To balance mere percentages, it would be well to say that in 1913–14 1,167 Jews were studying medicine at Vienna, 1,051 law and politics, 568 the liberal arts.[12]

During this same academic session 660 Jewish students went to the Technische Hochschule, making up 20.67 percent of the enrollment. Far different was the story at the Hochschule für Bodenkultur, or Agricultural University; only 2.37 percent of its future experts were Jewish. The presence of a mere 27 men in the midst of 1,114 non-Jews was explained by Goldhammer as being a direct result of the antisemitic attitude of the student body. To Austrian hatemongers who did not live to see the muscular young farmers of modern Israel this ratio was proof either of laziness or agrarian incapacity among the Jews. At the University for Veterinary Medicine the Jews again were not strongly represented; possibly the hostility of the Christian students kept the percentage at a little over 4 percent. The Academy of Fine Arts which rejected Hitler certainly was not as well attended by the Jews as the lectures at the University of Vienna or even the classes in architecture and applied sciences available at the Technische Hochschule. Sixteen Jewish students accounted for a mere 6.42 percent of the budding artists of 1913–14.

Most popular of all of the Viennese institutions of "higher learning" with the Jews was the Export Academy, which trained men for world trade and international finance. If one were to believe even half of the antisemitic utterances of the last years of the empire, one would anticipate that the classes were overwhelmingly Jewish, that Baron Rothschild had thousands of eager imitators. Given the long centuries in which the European Jew had been allowed no livelihood save that of a trader or moneylender, it is surprising that only 30 percent of these incipient tycoons were Jewish on the eve of the war that would destroy much of the Central European trade complex.[13]

Aside from the unending complaints that the Jews would soon dominate all business, all medicine, and all legal affairs, it was almost as fashionable among the antisemites to dilate upon "Jewish criminality."

Goldhammer's statistics are particularly full on this point. Sensibly, he divided offenses against state and society into what might be called "crimes" and "misdemeanors." Among the former were included murder, manslaughter, theft, robbery, embezzlement, fraud, and severe assaults upon other persons. Misdemeanors embraced usury, criminal negligence that led to the death of others, and financial derelictions which eventuated in unjustified bankruptcy. In the years between 1902 and 1913 the percentage of Jews condemned for crimes tended to decline, and this ratio always fell below the Jewish percentage of the total population of Vienna. For the years 1911–13, for instance, only 6.38 percent of convicted criminals were Jews.

Quite different was the percentage of Jews condemned for misdemeanors. In the same period 1911–13, 28.13 percent of the convictions were against Jewish malefactors. As might be anticipated from the preceding paragraph, Jews were primarily guilty of misdemeanors linked with usury and bankruptcy. They made up 40 percent of the persons tied in with illegal bankruptcy procedures and 30 percent of those convicted of exacting excessive interest. And yet no Jew had been found guilty of usurious practices in the 1902–4 period, whereas five non-Jews were so implicated.

In the field of true crimes the Jews were most often found guilty of fraud. They accounted for 16.57 percent of the convictions in the 1911–13 period, a proportion almost double their share of the total population. With almost all other criminal activities, however, they tended to be well below their percentual strength. Their share of the convictions for theft, forgery, and robbery was rising slightly, so that in the period above mentioned they were responsible for 7.34 percent of the unfavorable verdicts.[14]

The vicious competition which afflicted the business life of the most recent Jewish migrants to Vienna, plus the undoubted shock they suffered in moving from villages and cities they had known for years, might have accounted for many of their transgressions, which seemed to center about monetary matters. They rarely committed brutal or passionate deeds. Their faults rather were those of a group which had to scramble unceasingly for security. To men who worshiped Siegfried while reviling Hagen, however, it was better to be a violent warrior than a sly trickster. Though the Viennese Jews most likely sinned against each other more often than against their Christian neighbors, their disproportionate share of convictions for financial irregularities fed the flames of the resentment that all men nurture against the rich and successful.

Adolf Hitler had convinced himself that the Jews were guilty of yet another affront to humanity, namely, the management of prostitution. He wrote in *Mein Kampf*:

> In no other city of western Europe could the relationship between Jewry and prostitution, and even now the white slave traffic, be studied better than in Vienna, with the possible exception of the seaports of Southern France. . . .

An icy shudder ran down my spine when seeing for the first time the Jew as a cool, shameless, and calculating manager of this shocking vice, the outcome of the scum of the big city.[15]

The most inexperienced amateur in the field of human behavior is aware of the difficulties which beset any investigation of commercialized prostitution in any stage of the world's history. For a hundred lurid and sensational accounts there may be one slight article which pinpoints responsibility; the twentieth-century American jury has found it easier to convict "vice lords" of income tax evasion than of pandering. Bribes and the frank conviction that someone has to furnish prostitutes if decent women are to be unmolested play their part in the conspiracy of silence.

No one seemingly has made even a preliminary study of the directors, if there were any, of the Viennese traffic in prostitutes. The only judicious review of this social problem was H. Montane's, [16] published some years after Hitler dragged Kubizek through the depressing Spittelberggasse, where the girls sat at the windows between customers.[17] If anything, Montane's report indicated almost unlimited autonomy among these unfortunates. The laws encouraged the very type of organization which Hitler was sure existed, but relatively few women *seemed* to be effectively controlled by either state or vice lords. The melancholy rows of houses on the Spittelberggasse, strategically close to infantry and cavalry barracks, did indeed imply some sort of organization. For every admitted "district," however, there seemed to be thousands of free lances who must have been as chary of "ring" control as of state control.

Legalized prostitution in Austria dated from the period of German Liberal ascendancy, when it was decided that the police should control rather than suppress. The statute of February 6, 1873, required that all professionals be registered and undergo a medical examination by a police doctor. Any female over fourteen years of age could practice this profession as long as she could prove mental competence and carried her Health Book. Further medical examinations came at stated intervals, and a diseased woman had to go to the hospital for treatment. The law worked badly from the very beginning, for few prostitutes wanted to lose time in hospitals.

In early 1874 it was estimated that only 10 percent of the presumed 15,000 streetwalkers in Vienna were complying with the law. Even some of these were driven underground by the well-meant missionary efforts of certain bureaucrats who tried to reclaim the ladies for society. Housing problems also arose, for the person who rented all or a part of a dwelling place to a registered harlot ran the risk of prosecution down to 1879, when a high court finally agreed that such a landlord was not *ipso facto* a pimp. A few doctors as well helped to weaken the force of the law by declaring women disease-free when the opposite was the case. Such dangerous deviations forced the government to authorize only municipal doctors to carry out the inspections.[18]

Secret prostitution flourished despite stiffer penalties, surveillance of notorious cafés, and strict prohibition of the wearing of alluring costumes by "waitresses." The professionals detested the idea of periodical examinations and the opprobrium which came from public licensing. In 1900 the government offered a compromise. Dancers, barmaids, and the like who entertained male guests in their own homes for fees might simply register with any police commissioner anywhere in the city. They thereby retained a degree of privacy and were spared the Health Book and its rules. Only 375 women had taken advantage of this relaxation of the rules as of 1910, however.[19]

The regulations of 1900 also raised the age of activity to sixteen, but by 1911 only a girl of eighteen might apply for a license or for simple registration. Brothels were supposedly outlawed by a rule which forbade more than three prostitutes to live and work together, but the police surgeon's report for 1907 calmly mentioned six bordellos alone in the Inner City.[20]

Propositioning was a normal occurrence on the main streets of the capital and in certain favored cafés. The best-dressed and most expensive cocottes wandered through the Volksgarten even when the roses were not in bloom or angled for the handsome and the well-heeled at the expensive restaurant in the Stadtpark. On big nights at the concert halls they contrasted strikingly with the frozen busts of the great composers. Should anyone protest their presence, their voices rose in righteous indignation, for they had their "rights." The older and less inviting specimens competed for soldiers, students, and rough laborers at the cheap dance halls in the Prater or in suburban beer gardens. One locale, a brewery in Ottakring, was so notoriously exploited that it usually was off-limits for the military. In spring and summer, of course, the inns serving new wine doubled as spots for casual assignations.[21]

In 1913, Hitler's last year in Vienna, only 1,879 women were registered with the police as professional prostitutes.[22] Montane was certainly to be trusted when he declared that these were but a small part of the picture. It is possible that every single woman involved in the traffic was dominated by and preyed upon by an all-knowing ring. It certainly cannot be proved otherwise. But a rationalizing group of purveyors of sin would have no reason to operate in defiance of the mild regulations; most prostitutes were carrying on despite the law, it seems quite clear. The *Deutsches Volksblatt* would have delighted in exposing "big shot" Jewish white-slavers had it been able to do so. In the shadowy world of sexual indulgence it was easy to name anyone as the heartless exploiter. Hitler, the pure and blameless prophet of "The Flame of Life," [23] simply foisted all of the responsibility upon the Jews. His conclusion fitted the pattern he had already worked out.

Though Kubizek was convinced that his friend Hitler was antisemitic long before leaving Linz, the future murderer of the Jews went to considerable pains to leave a far different impression in *Mein Kampf*. He would have had his followers believe that he knew of no "organized hostility against the Jews" when he arrived and that he first thought that "the language of the antisemitic Viennese press was unworthy of the cultural traditions of a great race." As time went by, he wrote, the "great" Viennese press, as opposed to the antisemitic, began to repel him with its unending adulation of the Habsburgs, with its attacks on William II, and with its "wretched wooing of France."

Then came, he recounted, the gradual realization that Karl Lueger, Christian Socialism, and antisemitism merited "open admiration." [24] Without a doubt this conversion to hatred of the Jews or, as is more likely, the intensification of a previously developed animus against them was abundantly nourished by the *Deutsches Volksblatt*, a paper which was the acknowledged apologist for Lueger's regime and the one truly vicious calumniator of the people whom Lueger no longer found it profitable to attack.

The editor of this daily was Ernst Vergani, long celebrated as a particularly valuable adjunct to the mayor's party. Born in the stormy month of March, 1848, the son of a governmental supervisor of saltworks in Galicia, he also was trained in the administration of mineral properties. In 1881 he married a wealthy lady in Lower Austria, whose dowry included a metallurgical refinery, became mayor of the town in which they resided in 1884, and was elected to the Austrian Lower House in 1887. Though the representative of well-fixed townsmen, he joined Schönerer's relatively small antisemitic following, soon coming to the conclusion that these German Nationalists needed a newspaper; Schönerer disagreed, but Vergani convinced the rest of the fraction's leaders that the scheme was feasible.

The appearance of the first issue of the *Deutsches Volksblatt* in December, 1888, was the signal for an unending conflict between its founder and the German Nationalist Führer. In four months bankruptcy was avoided only by the use of Vergani's personal funds plus contributions from the only two collaborators who stuck with him until 1890. When Schönerer got out of jail, he obstinately refused to accept the paper as a party organ or to reestablish relations with Vergani. The latter traveled to the home of his unbending ex-friend to beg for help but ended up signing a protocol admitting that the *Volksblatt* was in no way the voice of the German Nationalist group.

This utter capitulation only increased Schönerer's venomous enmity when he spoke to the faithful, while the Taaffe regime also confiscated the more violent issues. It was impossible to sell copies in the state tobacco shops or in railroad stations, at least for quite a few years. With the lifting of this restriction circulation reached a high point of 45,000 to 55,000 in the years 1893–1904. Earlier, 18,000 sales a day had been considered quite good.[25]

The *Deutsches Volksblatt* of 1907 was still edited by Vergani, who had moved ever closer to Karl Lueger from 1890 on. Indeed, one could not find a more devoted chronicle of the glories of Christian Socialist Vienna than this basically vulgar sheet, with its unchanging injunction, "Buy only from Christians!"

To get some notion of the ideas purveyed by this classic example of gutter journalism, let us look at the issues of the last three months of 1907, those months in which Hitler had to reconcile himself to his rejection by the Academy of Fine Arts and in which his frustrations must have increased.

First of all, Vergani's stories and editorials took issue with the dictum attributed to Lueger, "I decide who is a Jew," by refusing to accept the convert to Christianity as anything other than a Jew. Whenever baptized or unbaptized Jews got into political parties or became very influential in particular professions, the effect was always the same. They could not help bringing on decomposition and corruption.[26] Such an assertion seemed to place the *Deutsches Volksblatt* clearly with those who preached the theory of racial "blood" defects among specific groups. Actually Vergani did not get involved in such disquisitions. He was content to memorialize Count Gobineau, whose ideas became sacrosanct to the racialists, as a man whose death twenty-five years before had deprived the world of one of its greatest thinkers.[27]

The *Deutsches Volksblatt*, to speak plainly, stayed closer to the prejudices of its readers, who usually found it convenient to dislike their Jewish neighbors and competitors for economic reasons without delving into mystical analyses of blood. It delighted in reporting cases of Jewish derelictions: the man who belabored his family's Christian maid because she had slapped his seven-year-old son when the latter called her a "dirty sow"; [28] the operator of a brothel who was leading maidens and married women into a life of sin, after being involved earlier in a sex-blackmail scandal in which she had used her own daughter as bait; [29] the old lecher who had been rightfully assailed by a young Christian girl in his employ when he made indecent advances.[30] In short, a nauseous conglomeration of sex and prejudice, fact and invention kept the readers happy.

A petty incident in Galicia illustrated all too clearly the journal's determination to besmirch the Jews. A dispatch from Lemberg on November 12, 1907, recounted rather breathlessly the shocking story of Uhlan Lieutenant *Kohn*, who had attacked a *Generalmajor* with drawn sabre after being stripped of his commission by a court headed by the *Generalmajor*. His assault was foiled by courageous fellow officers, and he had ended up in the hospital badly wounded. "So ends the career of one Jew as an officer," pontificated the *Volksblatt*.[31]

Next day the story was corrected with apologies to no one. There had been no court-martial and no dishonorable dismissal and no attack upon a superior officer. A Lieutenant *Kuhn* had simply been involved in a tavern brawl, which was broken up by the *Generalmajor* and other officers.[32]

Orthodox Austrian antisemitism of the day naturally looked askance at any Jewish influence in the revered army. If a disorderly lieutenant could not be tagged as a Jew, at least it was not hard to find "expert" appraisal of Jews as soldiers. Russia had recently lost a war to Japan, much to the surprise of the rest of the world, and there had been the usual rash of books by generals explaining the debacle. One such worthy, E. J. Martynov, wrote of an "inborn" Jewish cowardliness in the face of the enemy. The *Volksblatt* shuddered over such authoritative comments. The Austro-Hungarian forces had better take steps to counteract such weaknesses, especially in Galicia, where so many reserve officers were Jewish.[33]

Even more illogical were the attempts to link antimilitarism with the Jews of the empire. The German citizenry of Austria was not foolishly pacifistic, according to Vergani's cohorts. It was only the swindling "Jewish press" that shouted for reduction in armaments and men. These infamous press lords wanted to estrange the army and the people so that it would be easy for the Marxian Social Democratic commanders, in the pay of the Stock Exchange, to take over the state.[34] It is dubious that even the readers of the *Volksblatt* could accept such an unlikely picture of the Rothschilds slipping wads of kronen to the bespectacled leaders of the proletariat. Their oracles had somewhat less trouble in using the celebrated legal duel between the journalist Maximilian Harden and certain Prussian officers as an indication of Jewish plots to undermine the armed forces of all states.

Harden's stories had implicated some of the best names in the higher echelons of the Prussian army as participants in sexually perverse practices. The *Volksblatt* was happy to milk the sensational testimony given in the resultant trial for even more than it was worth, but it self-righteously balanced its prurience with crude invective against "Herr Maximilian Harden, alias Isidor Witowski." The commotion he had stirred up in the Viennese "Jewish" press was compared to scenes in a pigsty when the swill was dumped into the trough. Harden was the pigherd "from whose mouth flowed a broad stream of those spicy details which his racial associates greet as the finest of tidbits." But the *Neue Freie Presse* had given away the game by asserting that no one now in Prussia could have any objection to a Jew's receiving a commission in the army there. To block this supposed Jewish plan to infiltrate into the Prussian officer corps, the *Volksblatt* screeched that "Jewish" papers in Berlin had declared that homosexuality was a sickness to be pardoned when Jews were accused of it.[35] In addition to likening Harden to a pigherd, Lueger's organ had more compliments to add when its target was found not guilty of libel: "a journalistic freebooter and brigand whom men hire to render their enemies impotent," "a onetime buffoon from Posen" who made a business of degrading every authority and who spat upon highly placed personages.[36]

While the Harden trial gave ample opportunity to exploit

scandal while stimulating prejudice, a native controversy coming soon thereafter gave the *Volksblatt* the more difficult
duty of covering up for its idol, Lueger. The issue was old,
for it concerned the degree of Jewish influence in Austrian
universities. The antisemites continuously bewailed the percentage of Jews among the professors and students of the
universities, for, as Vergani's journal put it, the Jews never
denied their allegiance to that speculative trend of mind which
was a menace to true knowledge (!).[37] Their increasing control
of the medical faculty of the University of Vienna was extremely dangerous, for they would graduate other Jews who
would do anything to make money and who would misuse indigent patients without conscience.[38]

The radical wing of the enlarged Christian Social party, like
the *Volksblatt*, was determined to play up the university question. An interpellation put to the Minister of Education protested the appointment of Jews to the faculties of Prague and
Vienna, alleging that such men would stoop to corruption and
would favor and pamper their brothers.[39] Most significantly of
all, Karl Lueger announced to the sixth Austrian Catholic Day
on November 16, 1907: "We have still another great task to
perform. It concerns the conquest of the universities. The
universities cannot any longer be a soil for subversive ideas,
for revolutions, for lack of patriotism and agnosticism. . . ."[40]

The mayor's prestige, the constant rumors that he would be
Francis Ferdinand's first minister-president, and the importance
attached to academic freedom by all liberals combined to stir
up waves of controversy. Professors and students held protest
meetings, unless they happened to be clerical-minded, while
the Lower House listened to Thomas Masaryk's acid comments
on the "philosophy of the all-highest wine shops" and on the
"theology of the City Hall's beer cellar." [41]

The *Volksblatt* preferred to protect its incautious hero by
hammering at the old theme of "too many Jews in the universities." Even where the Christians were in the majority, as with
the Law Faculty in Vienna, enough of them were sufficiently
philosemitic to guarantee the triumph of Judaism. Every year

fewer Christians were able to attend secondary schools thanks to their increasing poverty, and the richer Jews were crowding them out.[42] Masaryk's strictures were answered with reams of statistics on the religious preferences of students and professors in the imperial universities. The newspaper assured its readers that even these figures did not reveal the true virulence of the "infection," for it was impossible to discover how many of the Christians had come over from Judaism.[43]

In short, the tremendously vital question of academic freedom was ignored or, at best, obscured by a tedious repetition of the "Jews in the universities" scare. They were the medical charlatans, the greedy lawyers, the venal professors, the freethinking secondary school teachers. The enormity of Lueger's blunder was illuminated by the *Volksblatt*'s devious defense; better to batter the Jews than to explain away Lueger's premature call to arms.

The attitude taken by Vergani's journal toward Jews in the arts is of considerable interest, for the first inkling most Americans had in 1933 of the real nature of National Socialism came with the beating of Jewish musicians, the departure from Germany of many of its literary lights, and the gradual prohibition of "Jewish" music, art, and literature. *Mein Kampf* contains an explicit denunciation of the part Jews have played in creating and re-creating some of the treasures of Western culture, but the *Volksblatt* curiously did not berate all Jewish artists and their productions.

When a comedy entitled *Gretchen* by Gustav Davis and Leopold Lipschütz was produced, its low tone was deplored but no attempt was made to identify the religion or background of its authors.[44] The Pan-German paper, on the other hand, refused to give their names or the name of the play because they were but Jews pandering to the worst public tastes.[45] The *Volksblatt* also announced that a young virtuoso named Mischa Elman would give a concert and that Bruno Walter would lead the Vienna Philharmonic and soloists in a performance commemorating the twenty-fifth anniversary of Wagner's death. Nothing was said of their Jewish antecedents, though Vienna was a city which always took pains to ascertain such matters.[46]

If some Jews were spared and if the *Volksblatt* did not automatically equate mediocrity with Jewish artistry, it could nevertheless put on some rabble-rousing exhibitions when it so desired. Great were the lamentations when the Raimund Theater was leased to a firm which included the names of Franz Lehár and Herr Karczag, the well-known impresario.[47] These gentlemen, to be sure, had gladdened Vienna with their merry widows, but should their spirit also dominate at the venerable Raimund, with its "truly German" atmosphere and tradition? They and their brothers of the "Jewish operetta gild" never made room for anyone else once they got control of a theater. The Raimund would become nothing more than another venture in the Semitic theater industry.[48] In fact, the theater as a whole was in decline, overwhelmed by "Jewish parasites." At least a provincial prize should be offered for the best drama written by a native "Aryan." [49]

It should be remembered that the Jew who became Christian earned no credit with the *Volksblatt*. "Once a Jew, always a Jew" was the unchanging credo, and the great Gustav Mahler was no exception. His departure brought not a tear from the artists of the Imperial Opera, said the *Volksblatt*. He dared not make a round of formal farewells lest he suffer a complete rebuff from everyone. To soften the sting, his friends arranged a concert at which he directed his latest symphony—before an empty hall! As a final act of desperation his most intimate companions planned a demonstration of homage at the station from which he was to depart. Again, a fiasco without limit, for outside of the planning committee, only a few Jewish students appeared. Exactly one member of the Imperial Opera bothered to come! Never had an artist, composer, and opera director left Vienna under more ignominious circumstances. The *Volksblatt* ended its crowing by making fun of the Beethoven letter which Mahler's friends gave the departing musician as a gift. The most revered of German composers were dragged into the antisemitic mud when necessary.[50]

To summarize, the *Deutsches Volksblatt* was stridently antisemitic, clerical in a rather restrained way, and definitely committed to the furtherance of Lueger's fame. It carried plenty of advertisements to make up for its less than impressive circulation figures, and it offered a better than average coverage of foreign news. It was eager to splash its pages with sex scandal at the same time that it accused Jews of printing magazines brimming with exposés of prostitutes and pederasts.[51] In short, it was a worthy predecessor of later Nazi excrescences, if one excepts its refusal to swallow the most fantastic ritual-murder tales[52] and its occasional failure to tag particular notables as Jews. Hitler doubtless added much to his stock of poisonous prejudice by reading Vergani's *Volksblatt,* which was admittedly the worst of the "racialist" publications.

In the autumn of 1907 Lueger's Christian Socialists merged with what was left of the Conservative Catholic fraction, thereby creating the largest single party in the first Lower House to be elected by universal manhood suffrage. The mayor's new disciples were not wholeheartedly welcomed by the more rabid antisemites in the old party, and the *Deutsches Volksblatt* was quick to voice its suspicion that the converts were too clement in their attitudes.

Just as Lueger was subjected to the first blasts of his critics over the university question in November, 1907, the *Volksblatt* jumped on his most recent allies for their failure to comprehend the need for antisemitism. Catholic Conservatives often had looked askance at the Christian Social emphasis upon the Jewish "menace." The *Volksblatt* asserted that Cardinal Schönborn himself consorted with the *Neue Freie Presse* to challenge Lueger's zealots. Another newspaper, *Das Vaterland,* which represented the Catholic Conservative point of view even after amalgamation, had deviated far from the ideal course since the death of its great editor, Vogelsang, complained the *Volksblatt.* If all of the journals in Austria had failed to fight the Jews, if all had deserted the battle for German interests in Austria, then political developments would have taken a much more frightening turn.[53]

The *Volksblatt* at least was correct in accusing *Das Vaterland* of modifying its antisemitic tone drastically between 1890, when Vogelsang died, and 1907, when Hitler was getting thoroughly initiated into anti-Jewish press techniques. A sampling of the stories and features which filled the Catholic Conservative paper during Vogelsang's editorship leaves no doubt of his suspicion and contempt for the Jews. Ten years before Hitler was born, a political survey brutally stated in *Das Vaterland:*

It is not our fault if again and again we have to refer to the specifically Jewish character of the press which calls itself Liberal. In business life there is a rather commonly recognized rule that the modern Jew cannot leave any goods in their genuine and unadulterated form. He waters the best wine and clips the ducats. Just so do our press Jews conduct their affairs.[54]

When Germans and Czechs clashed over the latter's nationalistic demands, Vogelsang's journal blamed the Jews for the trouble:

Judaism with its naturally cosmopolitan interests is the natural foe of national autonomy and with its profit-seeking tendencies the enemy of inner peace in our Christian empire. Judaism is the third party which rejoices over the strife of Germans and Slavs.[55]

Germans who had proclaimed war on the Roman Catholic Church as a postulate of the Germanic spirit had ended up noticing with chagrin that thereby they had only paved the way for a Jewish conquest; the more cunning race had duped them.[56] Jews were at the bottom of attacks upon authority and discipline, upon anciently grounded statute and hallowed order. Their clamor was part of the Paris Commune and it was they who unceasingly propagated communism, nihilism, in short, radicalism in all of its colors.[57] The only colors they conscientiously avoided were the imperial colors, for they were not distinguished by a marked spirit of patriotism. *Das Vaterland* sneered that half of the contingent the Jews should have supplied in Galicia had to be filled with Christian lads.[58]

Nor can the modern investigator be entirely sure that Vogelsang's reporters were immune to the temptations of mixing sensationalism with their war on the Jews. A correspondent in

Berlin wrote of a shocking desecration of Good Friday per-
petrated at a bock beer establishment near Spandau. There
congregated young Jewish merchants and stockbrokers by the
hundreds with their non-Jewish mistresses. The latter were
forced to see how their swains respected a day so sacred to
sorrowing Christians.[59]

Vogelsang personally was careful to avoid some of the excessive statements he allowed others when he composed his
editorials. Repeatedly he insisted that the Jews had not forced
themselves into a position of dominance, but that the Christians
had spinelessly surrendered to them the control of state, society,
and economy. Therefore Christians could not seriously plan to
drive the Jews from the empire in order to recapture lost power
and prosperity. They had no right to complain or even to
wish that the Jews would depart. The Jews, despite their
recognized ethnic and religious peculiarities, had been accepted
by the Habsburg monarchy. To want to deprive them now of
their individuality and their religion would be a legal and moral
impossibility. A demand that Christians be granted the holiest
right of religion had as its counterpart a respect for the Jewish
faith.

Austria was a Catholic Christian land in which the Jews had
a special place. They were not to push for complete equality,
for they were but guests of the house of Austria. They had to
respect the empire's order, but they were never to be disturbed
in their religion or in their nationality.

That they cannot force upon us, the children of the house, their
exotic peculiarities, that they cannot strip us of our religious and
ethnic character, that they consequently cannot rule, direct, lead,
teach, or command us in any way is obvious; to stop them from
doing so, we need only to be resolute Christians and Aryans and to
express our character in custom and law, in trade and in traffic.[60]

Vogelsang's *Vaterland*, despite the distinctions he was wont
to insist upon, was a powerful antisemitic voice before Vergani
ever launched his venture. Apologists for Vogelsang can insist
correctly that their social reformer was primarily aroused by

Jews as powers in the economic realm. It is equally correct to infer that the tone of his newspaper encouraged every type of antisemitism, whatever his ultimate purposes might have been.

The *Vaterland* of 1907 was a greatly changed organ. Occasionally it alluded to stories of Protestant intolerance and persecution of Roman Catholics, though it sturdily ignored Schönerer's *Los von Rom* campaign. Attacks on Jews were kept to a minimum, and its approach to the problem of nationalism was quite colorless. It carried few advertisements, and there is no reason to question the supposition that the Catholic Conservatives completely dictated its opinions.

When one Hitzky implicated himself in a ritual murder, *Das Vaterland* loftily dismissed the fellow as one who was known from previous litigation as "very excessive." The paper identified him as a Jew, but no further comments were made.[61] Whereas the *Volksblatt* was sure that dirty literature was a Jewish specialty, *Das Vaterland* restricted its columns to nothing more than a generalized attack upon pornography, with no specific offenders named.[62]

The old flicker of vicious antisemitism came only at rare intervals. When news from Paris announced changes in some newspaper editorships there, the name of Édouard Drumont appeared. Drumont was widely famed for his assaults upon French Jews during the Panama scandal and the Dreyfus affair, and the subdued *Vaterland* at least paid him the compliments a retired general might send to a still active colonel. Drumont's fame abroad, said the Catholic Conservative daily, was based upon the manly stance he took in face of the Jewish danger. Only a man who had close knowledge of the "republic of Rothschild, Herz, Dreyfus . . ." would really understand what that meant, concluded the Viennese paper.[63]

Ordinarily the *Vaterland* of Hitler's first regular stay in Vienna did not try to revive Vogelsang's earlier diatribes against the Jews. When Lueger spoke of the battle for the universities, the rather aristocratic *Vaterland* implied that anticlericalism in general was the foe. It published interpellations which bemoaned the appointment of Jewish scholars to university posts,

but without comment.⁶⁴ When a Jew was elected mayor of
Rome, his republicanism distressed the paper as much as did his
religion.⁶⁵ No attempt was made to hide *Das Vaterland*'s deep
conviction that Austria should live in a manner befitting the
sentiments of her large Catholic majority, but the tone was
moderate and the phrasing polite. The devout antisemite of
1907 had far better chance of limiting his horizons further by
reading the *Deutsches Volksblatt*.

The financially troubled Pan-German newspaper of 1907, the
Alldeutsches Tagblatt, was too much interested in besmirching
and berating Catholicism to offer as steady a diet of antisemitism
as that supplied by Vergani. It also busied itself with those non-
clerical Austrian Germans who had either failed to recognize
Schönerer's overpowering genius or had deserted him. Judaism
consequently had to face only infrequent blisterings and its
followers were spared the almost unspeakable filth dumped upon
the Catholic clergy by the Pan-German paper.

Just before Christmas, 1907, Schönerer's mouthpiece went to
extremes rare even in the overheated press circles of Vienna. It
alleged that an earlier issue of the *Correspondence Journal for
the Catholic Clergy of Austria* had carried a suspicious warning
from one priest to his fellow priests. The father in question advised his brothers never to hire a housekeeper unless a reliable
physician would vouch for her good health. To the *Alldeutsches
Tagblatt* it was at once assumed that the clergyman had con-
tracted syphilis. If the church would not admit the need to
reform the laws on marriage, at least it might modify the
privilege of keeping concubines if only to stave off syphilitic
infections.⁶⁶

It is rather difficult to understand why such surmises were
not silenced by confiscation on the part of the authorities, for
seemingly less poorly founded stories and accusations were being
so handled in 1907. When the anti-Catholic journal was able to
point its finger at a properly tried and convicted clergyman,
then it devoted columns to the full description of his misdeeds.
Such was the case of a forty-eight-year-old priest in the
Marburg region who was sentenced to fifteen months' imprison-

ment for seducing two girls aged fourteen and fifteen. The priest's role as teacher of religion in the schools was strongly underlined by the reporter.[67]

The paper did not always wait for trials or even indictments to cudgel its Catholic foes. When two thirteen-year-old girls swore that an elderly priest had improperly caressed them during his teaching of the art of playing the melancholy zither, the story was written up as proof that all parents should quit the church to save their daughters from celibate lusts.[68] When the state failed to prosecute, the *Tagblatt* printed more tales against the priest and further complained that a stepfather of one of the girls was afraid to appear in public. The peasants of the parish, it seemed, had fully supported their spiritual leader.[69]

When there was a lack of contemporary cases of clerical misbehavior, or accusations of same, the indefatigable staff went back to the Middle Ages for combustible material. An eminently logical choice for clergy-baiting was the infamous practice of *jus primae noctis*, the right of a feudal lord to spend the first night of a peasant's marriage with the peasant's bride. The *Tagblatt* disingenuously declared it did not know what the Church, as guardian of the sacrament of marriage, had done to arrest this barbarism during the days of knights and serfs. It did not doubt, however, that some of the clergy had exercised this right when they were lords of domains, paying gladly whatever fines were imposed by their confessors for their transgressions. To "enlighten" the shocked reader further, the article went on to declare that the papal budgets of the fifteenth and sixteenth centuries contained large incomes from taxes on public prostitutes and that bishops were empowered to collect fees from clergymen who kept concubines.[70]

Collecting evidence against Catholic nuns, who rarely were spared by European anticlericals of any age, was obviously a more difficult task. When two nuns of an orphanage in Graz were fined for overstepping their disciplinary rights in punishing a girl in their charge, the *Tagblatt* jubilantly seized upon the case. Had they not kept the girl in a strait jacket for an entire night? Had they not confessed using a wire whip? Dismissing them with paltry fines of twenty and ten kronen was a disgrace that could be wiped out only with the complete repudiation of the Church by all Catholics, argued Schönerer's columnists.[71]

If it was almost impossible to calumniate Catholic nuns, it was easier to get at Catholic ladies who were noted for their devotion to Lueger and the Christian Socialists. The secretary of the Ottakring branch of the Christian Women's Union was singled out for mention because some property she owned was being used as a brothel. What sort of behavior was this from a member of Lueger's "League of Amazons?" The fact that the prostitutes paid a higher rent was explanation enough, opined the Pan-German report.[72]

Kubizek remembered that Hitler was apathetic rather than actively hostile in his attitudes toward Roman Catholicism during their winter together in Vienna.[73] When *Mein Kampf* was written, its author was most critical of Schönerer's fight against the Church, since it alienated "innumerable of the best elements which the nation can call its own." [74] No doubt the youthful Hitler was much more interested in the *Deutsches Volksblatt*, with its steady flow of racialist rot; on occasion, the Pan-German organ as well reverted to antisemitism.

For instance, it was so enraged by the production of *Gretchen* that it refused to give the title of the comedy or the names of its authors in the "review." Why should it identify two Viennese Jews who had turned out another smutty piece for the "Judapest Orpheum Company" and for an audience that reveled in the wisecracks of the half-world? [75] The production of three one-act plays by Hans Müller caused a similar reaction. This dramatist was "revealed" as a much applauded member of the "Viennese literary ghetto" whose works were better appreciated by Jews even when cleaned up a bit.[76] Yet the announcement of Gustav Mahler's last concert before he departed for America was carried in an irreproachably correct manner, in marked contrast to the vicious feelings manifested by the *Volksblatt* with regard to Mahler.

The *Tagblatt* at times seemed to be more interested in proving that Lueger and Vergani were not sincerely antisemitic than

in demonstrating its own undying antagonism to the Jewish
population. Vergani was accused simultaneously of being a
millionaire and of allowing a Jewish enterprise to advertise in
his journal—during the Christmas holidays at that! [77] Lueger
and his party colleagues might blame anticlerical agitation upon
the Jews, but in actuality they were accustomed to make use
of the "Jewish press" for their pronouncements and treated the
Jews as their brothers, said the Pan-German paper.[78]

While Lueger indeed had become far less frenzied as success
and illness alike softened his earlier prejudices, he was not yet
beloved by the *Neue Freie Presse* nor fraternally embraced by
the Jewish community. But truth was an endlessly expendable
commodity with Schönerer's dwindling disciples, who were
willing to proffer the wildest of tales to hold their ever-waning
public.

On the first page of the issue of November 27, 1907, appeared
an article by one M. Joksch which was not rivaled in sheer
fantasy by any other article in any other journal of the period.
The now-forgotten author of this atrocity against sanity was
sure that he had the true explanation of the current financial
depression affecting the world, and he was going to expose what
the rest of the press was keeping secret. Thanks to a letter from
a friend who knew the situation well, the readers of the *Alldeutsches Tagblatt* would be informed of the dark forces at work.

The crisis centering in New York was the result of a dia-
bolically calculated plot which aimed at the conquest of the
world. Two great forces were struggling with each other:
Jesuitism, represented by Morgan, Rockefeller, and the like,
versus a coalition of organized Jewry and Freemasonry represented by "Roosevelt-Roswelski" and the courts and official-
dom of the United States. The bearer of these tidings was
convinced that the world would suffer however the struggle
went. Already the Jews and Freemasons, who scoffed at all law
and at all morality, had extorted an enormous fine from Rockefeller through the courts they controlled. He and his fellow
Jesuits then utilized the yellow press to throw the masses into
a panic which eventuated in tremendous withdrawals of funds

from savings banks. In the resulting chaos Morgan and Rockefeller bought out shaken businesses for trifling sums. Europeans
were being subjected to the reverberations of these intrigues,
paying more for capital they required and even running the risk
of having one of the new gangs of brigands dictate the type
of government and religion to be adopted. The stability of
states and the freedom of the church were definitely endangered.

Schönerer's fading journal was rarely so ridiculous. It was
more caustic and more dirty-minded in its attacks upon Roman
Catholics than upon Jews, but basically it was only a feeble
voice preaching a fanatic loyalty to the Hohenzollerns. Its
advertisements, moderate in number, constantly offered busts
of Bismarck and Schönerer and a great array of pamphlets
which preached the Pan-German gospel. It stressed stories deal-
ing with the defense of Germanism in Bohemia or in the Tyrol,
and it grandiloquently used "Deutschland" as the locale for all
Austrian news, "Deutsches Reich" for all German news. The
economic coverage was primitive and the fine arts were usually
ignored unless an "evangelical" group or author were offering
their talents to the public.

In summary, the young Hitler of 1907, who already was
beginning to hate the Jews, should have enjoyed most Vergani's
Deutsches Volksblatt. Das Vaterland would have been too
Olympian, too detached, while the *Alldeutsches Tagblatt* was
too much deflected by the "Catholic issue" to concentrate satis-
factorily enough for him upon antisemitism. Yet these con-
trasts are extremely relative, for the most urbane antisemitic
asides from *Das Vaterland* found some response in Vienna.
That three newspapers, however varying the emphasis, could
face the public as representatives of avowed prejudice, if not
hatred, was but another symptom of a sick society.

As Hitler sank further into poverty and bitterness during his
second winter in Vienna, he personally began to experience
other evidences of the ugly side of Viennese life, for a sick
society has many faces. Just as important for his future career
as the antisemitic pap which nourished his resentment was his
constant struggle to avoid proletarianization. He won in that he

never joined a labor union. He became a bum instead. And in the long hours of idleness with which he indulged himself there was plenty of time to analyze the shortcomings of the polyglot empire which the Habsburgs had accumulated.

"This Babylonian Realm"

ADOLF HITLER likened the Austria of his youth to "an old mosaic; the cement which held the single little stones together had become old and brittle; as long as the masterpiece is untouched, it can still pretend to be existent, but as soon as it is given a blow, it breaks into a thousand fragments." [1]

He recounted in *Mein Kampf* his yearning for the coming of "the hour of doom of this Babylonian realm," since it "promoted everything non-German." [2] The individual nationalities were shredding the old loyalty to dynasty to bits, and even Vienna was less and less a German city.

While fanatical young men like Hitler were anxiously awaiting the empire's demise, more than a few self-appointed "experts" were advancing plans to arrest nationalistic inflammation. In the years of Hitler's stay in cosmopolitan Vienna, what instances of national collisions might gladden his German sympathies and simultaneously reduce schemes of federalism and equalization to academic games?

Soon after Hitler's permanent move to the capital there was a clamorous demonstration at the University involving German and Italian students. The question of granting educational facilities to the non-German nationalities of Austria had embittered the lives of thousands and had sometimes threatened the collapse of representative government. Improved educational opportunities meant better chances for bureaucratic and professional careers, which in turn meant less likelihood of a near monopoly of prized positions by the Germans. In November, 1907, the Italian students of the University of Vienna asked the rector to allow them to use a lecture room so they might discuss their lack of an Italian law faculty at the University. Since this demand was standard with irredentists who naturally cared nothing about remaining under Habsburg rule, the rector refused. About 200 Italian students then assembled to denounce the rector. As one of them tried to deliver a speech, a large number of German students interrupted with a provocative bawling of "The Watch on the Rhine." The Italian spokesman angrily shouted, "We want the same rights you have," and a pitched battle followed. The Germans prevailed with their canes and umbrellas and celebrated with another rendition of "The Watch on the Rhine."

Next day the classrooms of the University were closed by order of the rector, but the encounters continued. The Italians stoutly sang the Garibaldi Hymn as the Germans fell back on their staple anthem. Jeers and insults were exchanged, and here the Italians were well supplied with ammunition that must have hurt the Germans sorely. Several weeks before, the daring German journalist, Maximilian Harden, had been sued by Count Kuno Moltke in Berlin as a result of Harden's extraordinary revelations about Moltke, Prince Eulenburg, and their "circle." [3] The Italians as a matter of course taunted the Germans with allusions to the effeminacy and perversion implied by Harden's articles. The catcalls ended only when the deputies of the nearby Reichsrat insisted that the commotion cease. Similar disturbances took place at the University of Graz. [4] Did Hitler pay any attention to the incidents? He tells us:

> In Vienna I saw the passionate contempt and the bottomless hatred flare up more than once with which the Italian was "devoted" to the Austrian State. The damage that the House of Habsburg had done to Italian liberty and independence for centuries was too great to have been forgotten, even if the will to do so had been present. [5]

Five months after Italian students protested their lot in Vienna and Graz, a solitary Ruthene student in Lemberg murdered the governor of Galicia to bring attention to Ruthene grievances. The victim, Count Andreas Potocki, had the customary Polish disdain for "helots" of Ruthene ancestry, and he amiably allowed

Polish electoral commissioners to manipulate election results a bit even in 1907, the year of the introduction of universal secret manhood suffrage. Since the Ruthenes already were being cheated of half the Reichsrat representation due them on the basis of population, their hatred for Potocki was not inconsiderable. The murderer, a third-year philosophy major at the University of Lemberg named Miroslav Siczynski, was additionally excited by knowledge of the death of a Ruthene peasant at the hands of Polish police.

Potocki usually held many audiences on Sunday, and the twenty-four-year-old Siczynski was allowed to come in after lunch. Whipping out a revolver, he fired a volley of five quick shots, hitting the governor on the forehead, the chest, the right foot, and on the hand without causing immediate death. Several doctors who were summoned could give no hope, and the dying Potocki asked that the Emperor be told "that I have always been his true servant." As the assassin was led from the governor's residence, he shouted to Ruthene peasants outside, "This is the payment for national injustice!" In prison he declared that his deed was strictly his own method of avenging injuries done Ruthenes in elections. The police ascertained that he had been imprisoned several years earlier for taking part in a demonstration against a minister-president visiting Lemberg. Siczynski luckily escaped the death penalty, possibly because his deceased father had been a clergyman and a deputy in the Galician Diet. Indeed, he even escaped the imprisonment to which he was condemned by fleeing Austria and making his way to the United States.[6]

Of all the Slavic groups within Austria, the Slovenes had been the most tractable down to 1908. The Poles, it is true, were ordinarily the most cooperative, but their amenability to imperial desires was costly. The Slovenes had recently worked quite sincerely for the electoral reform, and the outbreak of violence in Laibach on September 18, 1908, was something of a surprise. Laibach was the principal city of Carniola, where in 1910 there were 491,000 Slovenes to 28,000 Germans. Had trouble been reported from Styria, where 983,000 Germans faced 410,000 Slovenes, no one would have been taken aback. Six thousand Slovenes in Laibach, nevertheless, after a fiery anti-German meeting, attacked a German-owned casino, smashing its windows and furniture. This mob then turned on the homes and places of business of German merchants, the German Gymnasium, and even the German kindergarten. The police were too few to restrain the marauders, so several infantry battalions were called in. They took over the patrolling of the streets just before midnight, bayonets fixed, and gradually restored calm by morning. Only thirteen demonstrators had to be arrested. After a lull on September 19, the riots were renewed on September 20 with such severity that the soldiers were forced to fire, killing two and wounding several. The Germans of Styria, alarmed for their brothers of Carniola, staged protest marches in Marburg and Cilli, two towns famed for German-Slovene bitterness. In the end, of course, the violent agitation died down, though it indicated all too plainly how brittle was the cement holding together the mosaic.[7]

A few days prior to the Slovene outbursts in Laibach, important Austro-Russian discussions were held at Buchlau in Moravia between the foreign ministers of the two empires, Aehrenthal and Izvolsky. In return for the Austrian privilege of annexing Bosnia and Herzegovina, the Russians were to have the right to send their naval forces through the Straits. When would the bargain be consummated? To this day, it is impossible to say that a precise timetable was agreed upon or even discussed by the two diplomats. A fortnight after the meeting, however, the rumormongers were getting close to guessing one of the top-secret decisions, namely, the annexation of what Austria-Hungary had occupied and administered since 1878.

The *Neue Freie Presse* in its morning edition of October 2 discreetly prepared the public for coming events. A dispatch from Budapest told of widespread rumors and discussion in regard to possible annexation of the two territories (still legally Turkish). There was as well an interview with the leader of the Croatian Party in the occupied lands, who pleaded for incorporation with Croatia under definite constitutional guarantees. The evening edition of the great newspaper quoted a "spokesman" of the Independence Party in Budapest to the effect that annexation was logical and necessary, as long as Magyar historic rights were protected.

On October 4 the *Neue Freie Presse* vigorously supported the project of annexation in a leading editorial, holding that there was little difference between occupation and annexation after all. It also significantly published a report from Paris which told of a special letter from Francis Joseph to the French President, which had been delivered on the previous afternoon. This was the famous notice which Aehrenthal had the Emperor send to all of the great powers. The Austrian Ambassador to the Third Republic had, for practical reasons, "jumped the gun" on his fellow ambassadors in Berlin, London, and Rome. Next day the news of the delivery of the rest of the imperial letters was made known, along with the announcement that Bulgaria had proclaimed her complete independence of the Turks. On October 6 there was a formal rescript from the Emperor definitely confirming the talk of annexation.

At first there was general approval of Aehrenthal's forceful move. Two leading politicians of the South Slav Club declared that they were filled with joy over the news. One regretted that the inhabitants of Bosnia and Herzegovina would not have immediate representation in the Delegations then meeting, while the other issued the usual warning about Magyar intentions to profit from the situation.[8] Albert Gessmann, cabinet minister and leading Christian Socialist, was moved to call Francis Joseph a true "prince of peace" in a ponderous speech that stressed the necessity of bringing lasting order to the empire's Balkan limits.[9] In the Delegations' meetings there was not a single statement of disapproval; for once the estranged Germans and Slovenes, even the permanently embittered Czechs and Germans, were united in astounding agreement. Actually, Kramář, the Young Czech leader, and Šusteršič, a renowned South Slav figure, did reveal to the press some reservations and a general lack of overwhelming enthusiasm, but only after several days of reflecting upon reports from Belgrade and St. Petersburg.[10]

The October sessions of the Bohemian Diet contrasted ominously with the apparent unanimity of the Delegations' meetings. A week after Francis Joseph officially announced the annexation of Bosnia and Herzegovina, Czech and German members of the Diet meeting in Prague staged a fracas of scandalous dimensions even by Austrian standards. The trouble began with provocations from a Czech deputy, who insolently waved a lump of sugar in the face of the famous Pan-German, Karl Hermann Wolf. Herr Wolf had been accused in the past of less than ethical connections with the "Sugar Trust," and he reacted as expected, leaping from his desk to knock the lump from his tormentor's hand. He then tried to attack the Czech but was restrained by some fellow deputies.

The encounter lured a goodly number of Czechs over to the German benches. Jibes led to outright insults, and in a few moments a wild brawl was in progress. Violence seemed to be limited to cuffing and boxing of ears until a German representing the supersensitive German town of Eger decided to overawe the Czechs with his own famous physical prowess. He jumped upon a desk to obtain a preliminary advantage, only to be jabbed by one Czech who then spat upon him while another grabbed him by the hair. The German's predicament seemed to inspire his conationals to resort to an old parliamentary prank. The air was soon filled with flying ink bottles. One Czech deputy had his face soaked with ink, but German deputies, including Wolf, bore traces of Czech reprisals. As the deputies began to run out of ink bottles, a hefty Czech dashed to the desks ordinarily occupied by stenographers, seized a large table there, raised it high over his own head, and then sent it crashing to the floor. The newspaper account insisted that the legs of the table snapped like blades of straw.

The chaos lasted for minutes, enlivened by the introduction of all sorts of improvised missiles. The gallery, filled to overflowing, somehow retained its collective composure. After ten minutes of patient waiting for the rioting to subside, the presiding officer prorogued the session. His action brought the wild scene to a close. Everywhere one could see ripped collars and cuffs, hair that had been pulled out, shattered ink bottles, and smashed eyeglasses. Deputies bespattered with ink uselessly dabbed at their faces with handkerchiefs while others searched foolishly for missing buttons.[11]

Three days later the streets of Prague were the backdrop for further Czech-German encounters. The German students of the University had planned an inaugural promenade through the streets, and their clubs assembled at eleven o'clock with the traditional banners and caps. A crowd of more than a thousand hostile Czechs surrounded them and shouted, "Kill the Germans! Down with the Germans! Knock out their teeth!"

A police cordon safeguarded the students for a short while. About 200 Czechs eventually broke the cordon, grabbed as many caps as they could, and inflicted some bodily punishment on the Germans. The latter reassembled at the Deutsches Haus, sang the perennial "The Watch on the Rhine," and repulsed another Czech attack as doctors took care of their wounded. About noon the police were able to report a return to general order.

This report was oversanguine, for a reading and speaking hall belonging to the German students was attacked an hour later. The quick action of the watchmen in telephoning for the police saved the building from real damage, for after smashing some windows the crowd quickly dispersed when the police arrived. The New German Theater also was the scene of anti-German manifestations. While Artur Bodanzky, later to be famed as director of the German repertory at New York's Metropolitan Opera House, was holding a rehearsal of Wagner's *Die Walküre* within the building, a mob hurled rocks at the façade, breaking 100 window panes and nicking the mortar of the façade a bit. The street-lamps outside were demolished, and a vigilant employee of the theater was almost lynched when he tried to detain one of the stone-throwing urchins who had joined the adult demonstrators. The management of the theater courageously went ahead with a children's performance in the afternoon, which was poorly attended. The night's performance of Offenbach's *The Tales of Hoffmann* was made possible only by a considerable concentration of gendarmes and infantry. Czechs who watched the coming of the guarantors of order sarcastically jeered, "Here come the Prussians!" [12]

By December the antagonism in Prague had led to the Diet's adjournment and to the consequent resignation of the Czech members of the Austrian cabinet. Baron von Beck, who had ably directed the struggle for universal manhood suffrage, resigned his post as Austrian Minister-President, to be succeeded by a far less thoughtful and purposeful man. Prague itself was subjected to stringent martial law for twelve days in December. Hitler's dislike for the Czechs, as revealed in the earlier chapters of *Mein Kampf*, undoubtedly went back to the superheated tensions of 1908, if not earlier. Kramář's sponsorship of Neo-Slavism from 1908 on [13] must have been another symptom to young Hitler of the approaching and welcome doom of the Habsburgs.

Mein Kampf also reveals something of Hitler's attitude, possibly retrospective, toward another large segment of Austrian citizenry which was becoming increasingly restless. The Southern Slavs of Austria after 1908 were regarded with less and less confidence by many German Austrians, particularly in view of Serbia's obvious hatred for the Habsburg Empire; Hitler in 1924 spoke of Serbia as "an inexorable and mortal enemy who challenged the monarchy at shorter and shorter intervals, and who would not have given in till finally the favorable moment for the destruction of the realm had actually come." [14]

Because of increasing cooperation between Serbs and Croats within Croatia, the Magyars were most fearful that their hold over that area would slip. To break the back of mounting Slavic discontent, the arbitrary viceroy of Croatia arrested fifty-three Croats and Serbs early in 1909, charging that they were planning a union of Habsburg South Slavs with Serbia. Despite most inadequate and silly evidence, a majority of the accused were convicted at Agram. Slavic opinion was outraged by the ridiculous verdicts, and the cases were appealed. A higher court dismissed the proceedings against all of those convicted, but only after Habsburg Slavs were once again forced to feel that they were inferior citizens.

At the height of the indignation aroused among Slavs by the Agram trials, one of Austria's most respected historians, Heinrich Friedjung, lent his prestige to a most dubious maneuver. The *Neue Freie Presse* of March 25, 1909, included a sensational article by Friedjung which alleged that the most influential leaders of the Serbo-Croat Union were being financed in subversion by the authorities in Belgrade. The historian claimed that his statement was based on genuine evidence, but fifty-two members of the Serbo-Croat Union sued him for libel.

The relatively short trial was most embarrassing for Friedjung. His "evidence" was so badly discredited that he was compelled to admit that the accused were innocent. The well-informed at home and abroad were convinced that Aehrenthal, Minister of Foreign Affairs, or at least some of his subordinates, had turned over the tainted material to poor Friedjung. Aehrenthal later did tell another Austrian intellectual, Joseph Redlich, that he had asked Friedjung to help him whip up a press campaign to supplement war preparations against Serbia. Unfortunately, Friedjung had worked with a high bureaucrat in the Foreign Office named Jettel, whose unreliability Aehrenthal deplored.[15] In sum, a previously fine historian was deluded into playing the fool, the entire Foreign Office was compromised, and prominent Southern Slavs had greater reason to yearn for drastic changes.[16]

Who could achieve such drastic changes? Serbia might well be the Piedmont of the early twentieth century and unite the Southern Slavs. But little Serbia, like little Piedmont, would need the assistance of a greater power, if Slavdom was to have a chance. The increasingly frustrated Slavs under the Habsburg scepter were never completely persuaded that the Romanovs of Russia might be the long-awaited saviors, but Russian influence was undoubtedly waxing in Slavic circles after 1908. The existence of the Duma in Russia, however circumscribed its real powers, wiped out much of the fear of Russian despotism among many Slavic leaders who in honest moments had to admit their satisfaction with the fundamental freedoms allowed in Austria. The Russian failure to aid Serbia in 1909, moreover, by no means destroyed the Austrian Slavs' admiration for limited tsardom, if one can judge by the great popularity of Kramář's Neo-Slavism during and after the annexation crisis.

If the Russian government, then, could count on the friendship of millions of Slavs under Habsburg tutelage, could it also count on their dissatisfaction as a sure sign of potential treason in case of war? Austrian Poles definitely detested Russia and would undoubtedly support the Habsburgs in case of conflict. The Ruthenes of Austria did show signs of succumbing to secret agents sent in from Russia, but the Ruthenes, after all, were devoid of any strong political integration that might help tsardom. No outstanding Czech had gone beyond cultural flirtation with the Russians, and it is dubious that a majority of the Slovenes, Croats, and Serbs of Austria was intent upon a Yugoslav state apart from the Habsburg holdings. It is reasonable to assume, then, that Russia had no more than a few thousand potential fifth columnists in Austria. Given such conditions, the Russian government was compelled to go beyond her easily recognized friends in the empire to secure vital military information needed for future emergencies.

Just as Hitler was leaving Austria for Germany in May, 1913, the Austrian public was given a fleeting yet scandalously piquant look at such Russian machinations. On May 29, 1913, the *Militärische Rundschau* announced that during the night of May 24–25 Colonel Alfred Redl had committed suicide. His motive was extremely lurid for that day, as it tends to be forty years later. Because of homosexual proclivities, he had found himself in impossible financial difficulties and consequently sold military information to an agent of a "foreign power." [17]

Here was a disgraceful affair made to the newspaperman's order. The *Neue Freie Presse* devoted an editorial to the late Redl, blasting his infamy and demanding to know why he had been spared the obloquy of a public trial. Its reporters had been able to ascertain that the traitor had been summoned to Vienna and received by three officers in a hotel. After a "trial" at their hands, he was left with the customary pistol.[18] When the evening edition of the famed newspaper appeared on May 30, a good deal more information had been collected by industrious reporters. First, a new editorial clearly implied that the great power involved was the one which had been most hostile during the Balkan squabbles of the previous winter. Second, there had been worried protests from parliamentarians asking why suicide had been permitted. Was there not the possibility of a nest of spies whose work would hardly be tracked down now that Redl was gone? If Redl, according to rumor, had been noted for his expensive living habits, why had there been no previous investigation?

Further news stories revealed that the treason probably had been going on anywhere from two to ten years. The deceased officer had been given a very responsible part in preparing for the annexation of Bosnia, had been honored with the task of completing a special mission to the German General Staff, and as a result wore high Austrian and German awards. His linguistic talents were marked, especially in the Slavic "idioms." He had studied abroad, where, according to the somewhat self-righteous *Neue Freie Presse*, foreign officers had probably initiated him into the rites of sexual perversion. His most recent duties had been important; after an autumn tour at the vital fortress of Przemysl, he had commanded the 99th Infantry Regiment of the 8th Corps in Prague. Officers who knew him in Prague denied any knowledge of his secret vice. To them, he was simply a tireless worker who rarely dawdled more than an hour in a café, where he concentrated on reading the world press. In fact, he led such an extremely restricted life that his associates knew him but slightly. It was always rumored that his family sent him money to keep up his 36-horsepower Austro-Daimler, which was worth 16,000 kronen.

In the Reichsrat the deputies were asking pointed questions. Was there any outright connivance between the military and the First Public Prosecutor in allowing Redl the easy way out? asked an independent Socialist from Lemberg. German deputies asked the government to explain fully what had happened, to

estimate how much damage had been done, and to say whether
or not other officers were involved. A Ruthene deputy of undoubted loyalty to the empire expressed his extreme criticism
of "officer honor" which conceivably might have allowed Redl
to escape beyond the frontiers.[19] The government did not choose
to answer the interpellations posed by the deputies until June
5. Redl's career meanwhile was thoroughly ventilated in the
press.

Prague sources declared he had made recent automobile trips
to Warsaw and Dresden and continued to insist that he had
enjoyed costly affairs with demimondaines. Vienna recalled that
traitor Redl had taken a large part in the investigation and
prosecution of earlier spies, especially in 1902–3.[20] Berlin was
informed that the mysterious colonel probably had revealed the
invaluable German plans for mobilization and invasion of potential enemy territory, in so far as such plans were linked with
Austro-Hungarian preparations.[21]

The reports which seemed to indicate that German security
had been fatally compromised elicited real moans from the *Neue
Freie Presse* and from the German National Alliance (parliamentary deputies pledged to protect Germanism in Austria).
The newspaper offered a plaintive editorial on the misuse of
Austrian hospitality by foreign military attachés. Such officers
and gentlemen should not use their privileged positions to spin
espionage webs.[22] The German deputies furiously demanded
some sort of explanation from the Minister of Defense and
intemperately shouted for safeguards against subversion in the
future. Their tempers cooled appreciably a few days later when
the Prussian General Staff in Berlin stiffly denied that Redl had
been acquainted with any German secrets. He most certainly
had nothing to do with confidential German data when he was
entrusted by his own government with great responsibilities in
1908–9 during the Bosnian crises. The German spokesman dismissed the case by asserting that there was no reason to suppose
that the German Empire was compromised in any way.

The German statement paved the way for an official revela-
tion from the Austrian government. First, there was the pre-

paratory interview with a "high" military authority. Redl, said this authority, had been selling secrets for the past seven years. As to the effects wrought—they were moral rather than material. Austrian counterintelligence had its first indication of his treachery in the last part of April, 1913. A full investigation by the General Staff and other agencies had followed. Redl was summoned to the War Ministry in Vienna and presented with the evidence. He immediately made a full confession, and, as the "high" authority lamely continued, it was possible that a member of the "investigating committee" chivalrously allowed Redl the fatal pistol. Redl had no accomplices of military rank, and naturally no changes in the General Staff were contemplated.[23] A day later, the Russian consul in Prague vigorously denied any acquaintance with Redl and revealed that he had protested already to the governor, Prince Thun, against such rumors.[24]

The Minister of Defense, Freiherr von Georgi, answered the queries of the deputies of the Reichsrat on June 5. It had been promised that no aspect of the sordid business would be withheld from the public any longer, but von Georgi's recital was not completely satisfying. He denied that the "investigating committee" had put pressure upon Redl to commit suicide or had even given him permission to do so. It was obvious, however, that the army or its representatives had done nothing to prevent the suicide, and the cabinet minister never explained why Redl was left alone for four hours between his "trial" and death, thereby cheating the citizens of a public hearing.

Von Georgi puzzled his contemporaries by revealing that information had gone to foreign states, not just to one state, as previously surmised. He also made clearer Redl's desperate search for money by disclosing that the colonel had been erotically involved with a lieutenant, who had posed as a nephew to screen their constant companionship and who had "cost plenty." The lieutenant had of course been imprisoned, but not for espionage. No high officer, no "lady" had been compromised in any way. There was no link between Redl and the Russian consul in Prague.

The secrets sold to potential enemies were mobilization secrets. Luckily Redl had never been given access to the complete and concrete details of full mobilization, such as routes of march. Von Georgi closed with a plea that the house defeat a motion to allow debate on what he had revealed. Despite opposition from Czechs, Ruthenes, and Social Democrats, the Reichsrat buried the Redl case by voting as von Georgi desired.[25]

Fifteen years later, important new aspects of the Redl case were revealed to a public always avid for spy stories.[26] Early in 1900 Redl had been appointed head of the Austrian military secret service, a sensational detail which von Georgi had carefully avoided in his explanation. During this assignment it was Redl's particular duty to guard rigorously the elaborate work on "Plan Three," which was a supposedly foolproof project for the invasion and quick annihilation of the Serbian Army. Because of the high costs of his own peculiar way of life, Redl sold out to a Russian nobleman visiting in Vienna, who actually was a person high in Russian intelligence.

During the period of Redl's infamous treason, the Austro-Hungarian military attaché in Warsaw was able to purchase extremely valuable Russian information from a Russian colonel who also suffered from financial woes. The information was turned over to Redl, who realized its vital importance and consequently told the attaché that it had been cleverly fabricated by the traitorous Russian. He secretly returned it, of course, to the Russians, who then graciously allowed their renegade colonel to blow his brains out. Unfortunately for Redl, his brilliant repute as a defender of state secrets earned him a promotion, and by 1913 he was chief of staff of the 8th Army Corps in Prague.

His successor, in the course of ordinary counterintelligence work, began to suspect that foreign agents were doing extremely well in ferreting out Austro-Hungarian secrets. A strangely addressed letter turned up at a post office in Vienna, containing a sizable sum of Austrian kronen, and so special watchers were placed on duty near the general delivery window. Their quarry escaped them when they relaxed a moment after days of waiting, but through a gray suede pocketknife sheath left in a taxicab they eventually caught up with Redl. His handwriting at intelligence headquarters matched the script which was on the receipt for the letter picked up at general delivery.

Conrad von Hötzendorf, the Serb-hating director of Habsburg military might, ordered that Redl be liquidated immediately and in complete secrecy, if at all possible. The visit of the officers to the colonel's room had followed and "officer honor" had supplied the necessary pistol. Redl never had a chance to escape from the hotel, for a vigil was kept across the street from the hotel until his body was discovered. In 1914, when the first Austrian attempt to seize Belgrade fizzled out miserably, there was reason to recall the colonel who was not quite a gentleman.

To Adolf Hitler, abandoning Austria in 1913, the Redl case must have been another sign of the corruption and approaching doom of the despised Habsburg edifice. If Germans in this empire were subjected to "undignified submission and fulfillment of all and every extortion," [27] why be surprised that a high-ranking officer of German stock should sell his honor to a potential enemy?

The damage had begun long before, in the struggles of 1848. "The German, forgetting or not acknowledging his origin, sealed his own doom by entering into the service of the revolutionary movement. He helped in awakening the spirit of Western Democracy which after a short time deprived him of the foundation of his own existence." [28]

"The Grinning, Ugly Face
of Marxism"

THE UPROOTED of modern industrial society turn to various panaceas in their search for a new integration of their lives. Nationalism has been most comforting to millions, but millions of others have become devoted followers of Marxian Socialism. In the great European zone of intense industrialization in the period ending with World War I, it was a rare worker or wanderer who did not meet up with Marxist propaganda at one time or another. In Hitler's Austria, in the very year that he moved to Vienna, the Marxist Social Democrats had just won the largest number of mandates secured by any party taking part in the Reichsrat elections. One should immediately add that their 87 deputies by no means controlled the total Lower House membership of 516. But the victory was impressive, and even Hitler admitted that he "rather liked the activity of Social Democracy" [1] in his first months in the capital city.

His reasons for liking what he later called "a pestilential whore covered with the mask of social virtue and brotherly love"? [2] The party's successful struggle for universal suffrage, he reasoned, would be rewarded in time with the collapse of the state he so bitterly hated. Secondly, Social Democrats were endeavoring to improve the conditions of the workers. His first reactions were changed, he testified, when he went to work as a building worker. How much manual labor was performed by young Adolf in Vienna is still a matter of debate. There is no particular reason to disbelieve the story of his first encounter with unionized labor. How often he accepted other construction jobs does not much matter.

On this first job the young provincial was outraged by the workers' rejection of "everything." Most annoying to him was their contention that the nation was an invention of the capitalistic classes. At first he tried to maintain silence, he said. Inevitably he was forced to contradict and to scan Social Democratic literature to strengthen his own points. He left his job when threatened by "the leaders of the other side" with being thrown from the scaffold.[3]

Thereafter his opposition quickly congealed into hatred, if not fear. The sight of a mass demonstration of workers left him depressed and anxious. His reading of Social Democratic newspapers convinced him that they "operated with the most brutal forces of calumny and a virtuosity for lying that was outrageous!" [4] The population obviously was being subjected to an infamous mental terror of terrible effectiveness. To be sure, the bourgeoisie, by past refusals of just concessions to labor, had forced "even the most decent worker . . . from trade unionism into political activity." [5] Out of this regrettable breach between German employer and employee had developed and prospered Social Democracy. Now, what was the real key to "the comprehension of the inner, the real, intention" of this movement? "Understanding Jewry," opined Hitler in retrospect.[6]

Once the future Führer linked Social Democracy and "Jewry" in his reminiscences of the Vienna days, he lapsed into a savage tirade against the Jews and said very little more about actual Social Democratic notions. He swore that the majority of the Marxist leaders in Austria were Jewish and consequently "the seducers of our people." [7] Now, what truth is there in these observations on Austrian Social Democracy? Was it an avowed enemy of the German people? Did it, under a mask, represent the interest of the Jews? One should begin to answer Hitler's accusations with a survey of the conditions which encouraged a Marxian Socialist party in Austria in the first place.

Though Karl Marx had visited Vienna in the late summer of 1848, his lecture there on the recently suppressed workers' revolution in Paris and on English Chartism aroused no real interest.[8] Bohemia and German Austria had already witnessed the organization of benevolent societies among textile and porcelain workers and among printers, as well as the usual violence that accompanied the introduction of machinery, but these weak and confused beginnings had little chance to progress further in the reaction which followed Windischgrätz's capture of Vienna.

A law of 1852 explicitly declared strikes to be illegal, though benevolent societies were barely tolerated. In the early 1860s, while Schulze-Delitzsch and Ferdinand Lassalle were organizing their quite different workers' associations in other German states, the authorities in Vienna sternly rejected a plea for a laborers' union. The same reverses which established dualism in 1867 initiated the true labor movement in Austria, for the constitutional laws which regulated the non-Hungarian portions of the monarchy from 1867 to the collapse of 1918 guaranteed rights of association and meeting.

In the sudden thaw, the followers of Lassalle's "state help" clashed with those who plumped for Schulze-Delitzsch's "self-help." The latter philosophy, with its emphasis on frugality and on apolitical cooperation in matters of consumption and production, soon faded before the superior attractiveness of the Lassallean approach. The heretofore restrained laborers wanted full state aid in return for their peaceful collaboration with society. The price, specifically laid down in a workers' program adopted on August 30, 1868, was high in terms of labor's previous lack of bargaining power: unrestricted rights of association, meeting, and press; universal direct suffrage for all representative bodies; complete religious freedom; abolition of all standing armies and introduction of a "people's army." [9] In Vienna a dozen labor unions were formed during 1868, and, despite the antistrike law of 1852, a series of work-stoppages ensued. In Brünn it was the weavers, in Trieste the metal-workers, in Mährisch-Ostrau the miners, in Prague the tailors, and in Vienna the shoemakers, printers, and railway construction workers.

The climax to the agitation came on December 13, 1869, when about 40,000 Viennese workers peacefully assembled to present anew their basic demands of the previous year. Should universal direct suffrage, absolute freedom of association, and the other requests not be met in the Reichsrat session just getting under way, it might be possible that "the people would again appear in greater strength to make known their will." [10] Next day the ministry introduced a bill allowing labor to organize, though there still were to be penalties upon the use of intimidation and force during strikes, and this bill became law on April 7, 1870.[11]

The cabinet's honest sentiments were better expressed by an order of December 23, 1869, to arrest all of the leaders of the workers' demonstration. The presence of two of these leaders some months earlier at the launching of the German Social Democratic Party in Eisenach had already disturbed the Liberal ministers in Vienna, and an impressive treason trial was held in July, 1870. The sentences varied from six years to a few months. The sensational nature of the accusations made "Social Democrat" a well-known word in Austria, and it is not surprising to read in the memoirs of the period that two young students named Victor Adler and Engelbert Pernerstorfer contributed financially to the imprisoned.[12]

A slight change in the government's attitude came in 1871, when the Liberals gave way briefly to a conservative, "federalistic" ministry. The Social Democrats who were imprisoned received amnesty, and for almost a decade it was internecine bickering rather than governmental arbitrariness and persecution which impeded the development of a "labor" party. The grisly suppression of the Parisian Communards in 1871 had of course forced upon all would-be leaders of the proletariat a searching reappraisal of tactics at the same time that it alerted the property-owners and upper classes to the amount of stubbornness and idealism which even the petty bourgeoisie might evince when aroused. While a Three Emperors' League genially collaborated in an ostracization of republican France, even after Thiers and MacMahon had chastened Paris with fire and powder, Austrian labor was buffeted by the catastrophic economic crash of 1873 and by the confusion and rivalry within the ranks of its putative leaders.

The great contestants of the 1870s were Andreas Scheu and Heinrich Oberwinder, both of whom had been chief defendants in the "treason trial." The latter wanted labor to cooperate with the bourgeoisie, particularly with the dominant Liberals in the ministry, in a common front against "feudalism" and particularism. In 1872 he aroused Scheu's express anger by informing the Ministry of the Interior that labor would accept labor chambers (with parliamentary representation) in place of universal, equal, and direct suffrage. Soon rival organizations and publications attested to the increasingly bitter feud, while Scheu's scandalous imputations against Oberwinder's personal honesty ended in a libel suit in which Scheu was acquitted.[13] Efforts to heal the rift were fruitless, and the numbing effects of the business depression naturally added to the laborers' apathy—indeed, fear of reprisals —as unemployment steadily mounted.

By 1879 a very small proportion of the 4,000,000 industrial laborers took part in any sort of cooperative association or union. All extant varieties of labor associations in 1879 numbered only 206, concentrated in Vienna and Bohemia. At the beginning of 1878, the once promising Arbeiterbildungsverein in Vienna had a few more than 170 members. Of the dozen or so prolabor or "socialist" journals published, some were merely "house organs" of a particular vocational group.[14] Bismarck's final success in securing tough anti-Socialist legislation in the German Empire in 1878 paradoxically helped to reanimate radicalism in Austria. As both moderate and advanced Social Democrats fled Germany for London and Zurich, they carried with them well-developed propagandist talents. The journals they prepared for under-ground passage into the Second Reich were just as easily slipped into Austria, and, emboldened by reviving economic prosperity, Austrian laborers were soon taking to heart some of the really "hard" doctrine emanating principally from Johann Most's *Freiheit*, published in London.

With Most's influence came a renewed struggle between

moderatism and intransigence in labor's ranks. Originally a book-binder, Most had consorted with Scheu and Oberwinder in the first days of freedom that followed the constitutional edicts of 1867, and he was well acquainted with Austrian industrialism and handwork. Five years' imprisonment had been his punishment at the conclusion of the great trial of 1870, and he saluted the regime's grant of amnesty by embarking upon a most provocative "agitation tour" of the more sensitive provinces and cities. Not unexpectedly, he was invited by the police to leave Austria "forever." Elected to the German Reichstag in 1874, his basic distrust of any tactical or "historically induced" compromise with the bourgeoisie hardened into outright anarchism when Bismarck's measures drove him into exile. In a Europe which still conjured up nightmares of another Commune as it avidly read of nihilist outrages in Alexander II's Russia, Most was quickly and rightfully associated with those radicals who eschewed words for deeds.[15]

Scheu had been closest of all the early leaders to Marxist ideology, but now he contributed to *Freiheit*. Karl Marx himself at the end of 1880 glowingly praised Most while denigrating the exiled "party organ" in Zurich.[16]

The London-oriented group sent a persuasive envoy to the increasingly excited laborers of Austria in 1881 in the person of the lanky and slightly sinister Josef Peukert. By 1882 the radicals in the Austrian movement had forced the moderates to found a new journal, the clearest possible sign of political schism, and by the end of the year Peukert had control of what had been the publication for all Austrian Socialism, *Die Zukunft*. More and more the labor movement went underground, since the Taaffe regime's police consistently forbade "Social Democratic" associations. The apostles of direct action were triumphing over those who ever more impotently pleaded for social reforms as preparation for the eventual liberation of the proletariat.[17]

Though Crown Prince Rudolph reportedly sent a lackey weekly to pick up copies of *Die Zukunft* and *Freiheit*, less well-placed colporteurs found guilty of transporting Most's paper received four-year and twelve-year prison sentences. Peukert confided to his closest friends schemes to ignite or blow up the Hofburg, when suddenly two carpenter's helpers rashly threatened the entire future of both moderate and radical socialism in Austria.[18]

On July 4, 1882, these admitted adherents of Peukert's radical majority chloroformed to death a less than beloved shoe manufacturer named Merstallinger, robbing the deceased of several hundred gulden which they planned to use for the good of the "party." When the police tracked the culprits down, the moderates stiffly reprimanded "anarchists" who would mislead the disinherited. *Die Zukunft* rather anxiously argued that every party and every sect had its criminal fringe, though its explanation could not conceal the fact that one of its most recent editors had not long before defected to the anarchist organization in Switzerland.[19] Sure of the chances of a real purge of all troublesome "Social Democrats," the police rounded up dozens of the more prominent directors of radicalism. The jury trial of March, 1883, resulted merely in the conviction of the admitted murderers and of a third carpenter who had known of their plot. The party leaders, including two women, were acquitted of charges of high treason, murder, and robbery, or incitation thereto. Steady bourgeois jurors resisted the state's obvious hope for a "witch-hunt," and several months later Peukert was attentively listened to as he, an invited witness, offered a parliamentary investigating committee his frank opinion of "palliative" social legislation and of the government's persecution of socialists. With intense scorn he accused the regime of staging the *enquête* either to extract information from laborers or to win their votes. The Liberal *Neue Freie Presse* was particularly happy to print his excoriation of Clerical proposals to change the school laws.[20]

Autumn brought further proof to anguished citizens that, to some radicals, Social Democracy meant license to murder and to rob for the sake of revolutionary justice. Two fanatical German exponents of direct action, after taking turns in assassinating a Viennese policeman and a Viennese detective, most cruelly hacked to death a money-changer named Eisert, robbed his office of 8,000 gulden, and then struck down his young children who had witnessed the atrocity.[21] Though the criminals' connection with Austrian Socialism was not proved, their sickening behavior resulted in the cabinet's declaring emergency conditions in Vienna, Floridsdorf, Wiener Neustadt, and Korneuburg. Trial by jury was suspended, socialistic journals were forced to cease publication, several hundred persons of socialist sympathies were expelled from Vienna and Floridsdorf, and Peukert fled to Switzerland. Under the influence of honest fear many workers' associations dissolved themselves, and the cabinet, pleased but hardly satiated, proposed a stringent anti-Socialist law after the parliamentary elections of 1885.

Though the Reichsrat was impressively devoid of proletarian deputies and though its more vocal Liberal defenders of the rights of man were in a decline, it did not blindly accept the formula suggested by the cabinet. After strenuous debate a mere "antianarchist" bill became law in June, 1886, to be valid for two years. It was renewed in 1888 only by the cabinet's use of its right to ordain decrees while the Reichsrat was not in session. When the deputies did reassemble, they grudgingly approved the prolongation. In June, 1891, the Lower House pointedly requested the end of any and all "exceptional conditions" in the cities and towns of Lower Austria, and the cabinet honored the request. The "antianarchist" regulation lapsed at the same time.[22]

Marxists are tenacious exponents of the theory that circumstances shape men, and that conditions which demand specific leadership are rewarded with the appropriate leaders. The conditions of the year 1886 in Austria undoubtedly might be used to buttress this theory, for the man needed to bring coherence and sanity to Austrian labor first began to exert some guidance at the very end of 1886. He was not a complete unknown, for his name was already identified with the elaboration of the Linz Program of 1882. This hero sent by dialectical necessity, since Heaven's interposition was ruled out, was the slight and stuttering physician, Dr. Victor Adler.

Adler had been born in Prague in 1852 to Salomon Markus Adler and his wife. The family was typical of many Prague

Jewish families in that it was fanatically devoted to German culture and downright fearful of rising Czech nationalism. When Victor came into the world, the family was already well-to-do, and a move to Vienna when the future Socialist leader was three led to actual opulence. Salomon Markus moved expertly from loans to land speculation, making enough to build a magnificent home in Oberdöbling.[23] He sent his son when the time was ripe to the "Eton of Austria," the Schotten Gymnasium, which helped form so many outstanding men of the last years of the empire. The young man went on to the University, where he met agreeable colleagues who were invited home to carry on spirited arguments on politics, literature, and art. The atmosphere of Vienna is said to be especially conducive to unsubstantial dilettantism, but Adler did not allow these exhilarating conversations at home and outside of the classroom to devitalize his yearning to be of use to his fellow man. He decided to become a doctor, and he particularly excelled in the psychiatric training then offered. Thanks to his father's ample resources it was easy to attend those who most desperately sought attention, the poor of Vienna.

Unquestionably Adler's first years of practice changed the entire course of his life. His constant vigil with victims of malnutrition and noisome slum conditions explains his hearty cooperation at Linz in 1882 in formulating demands for the quick relief of depressed laborers and their families. He was still a great German patriot in 1882, it should be remembered, close to Schönerer, the incipient Jew-baiter, and to Friedjung, who much later would riddle his own reputation as an historian in a vain effort to confound the "enemies" of Germanism. Yet it would seem that the welfare of labor already was contending victoriously with the dreams of Germania in Adler's mind, for in 1883 he undertook a trip to Germany, France, England, and Switzerland to survey the operation of their respective labor laws. His report to the Minister of Commerce stressed the need for efficient inspectors of factories, but more important than the report itself were the conferences he had had on his trip with such high priests of Marxism as Friedrich Engels and August Bebel.[24]

As the months slipped by it became increasingly clear to Adler that the radical labor leaders were being jailed, exiled, or forced underground while the moderates, contemptuously ignored by the police, were losing all vestiges of self-respect. Under the spell of Engels and undisguisedly appalled by the sufferings of the needy, Adler became a Marxist. The precise time of his conversion is not definitely ascertainable, for he was never noted for a superb command of the accepted dialectic and theory. As a distressed humanitarian, luckily endowed with an inheritance from his recently deceased father, he simply willed the revival of a labor party. In quiet conferences in the back-rooms of coffee houses, at a lively workers' meeting in Schwenders Kolosseum, and in trenchant political broadsides Adler began to put his personality and his ideals before the laboring public. On December 11, 1886, he published *Gleichheit*, openly entitled "Social-Democratic weekly," and for a while the failure of the police to confiscate issues damned Adler in the eyes of the more suspicious workers.[25]

Slowly the misapprehensions aroused by his bourgeois origins lessened, the more so when the guardians of order did find cause to swoop down upon *Gleichheit*. In 1887 delegates of both moderate and radical tendencies were persuaded to agree upon a statement which, after a good Marxist introduction, settled down to the rather traditional pleas for an end to exceptional conditions in industrial areas, for the complete freedom of press, association, and meeting, for universal suffrage, and for punishment of bureaucrats who violated rights of individuals and of associations.[26] In a meeting at the end of the year Czech workers buried their own quarrels and even provided for the entry of German Bohemian laborers into their new association. Adler could well salute the New Year by writing: "The past year has brought us as the most important and worthiest success the rewinning of the solidarity of the entire Social Democratic Party of Austria." [27]

Though Catholic, Democratic, and German Nationalist groups continued to woo with some profit the workers of increasingly industrialized Austria, Adler and his disciples eventually persuaded 110 delegates from the labor associations to meet and found a Social Democratic Workers' Party at Hainfeld at the very end of the year 1888. This village was not subject to the limitations of "exceptional conditions," and its administrator was no overheated foe of labor. The moderates and radicals finally composed their differences under Adler's determined prodding and produced a statement of principles that disclosed a preponderant moderatism. Its prologue maintained, as one might expect, that labor had been enslaved by the owners of the means of production, that increasing poverty and wretchedness would be the lot of more and more men and women, and that the new party would emancipate the Austrian proletariat from its unworthy situation. The word "revolution" was cautiously avoided, and the actual tactical principles laid down smacked prophetically of the revisionist policies denounced though practiced by most of the branches of international Socialism between 1889 and 1914.

First of all, the infant party proudly vaunted its internationalism. No person should lord it over another because of his nationality, his "high" birth, or his ownership of vast properties. Naturally no nationality had any right to believe in its superiority over any other nationality. Second, the party vowed to spread its gospel by all media of communication and to battle for the unchecked use of such media. Third, while refusing to be "deluded" as to the true worth of parliamentary government, "a form of modern class supremacy," Austrian Social Democrats were to struggle for universal, equal, and direct suffrage in elections to all representative bodies and for a decent pay for persons elected to such bodies. Fourth, the fundamental rights of labor in regard to hours, wages, etc., were to be guaranteed by laws which labor would jointly administer. As a corollary, there was to be no hindrance whatsoever to the organization of labor into unions. Fifth, the party demanded an obligatory, free, and nonsectarian educational system, the formal declaration by the state that religion was a private affair, and the total separation of church and state. The sixth and indubitably the most utopian of the specific planks would have substituted "universal arming of the people" for the imperial standing army.[28]

A test of Adler's abilities as a director of proletarian protest came a few months later. The wretched tramway employees in Vienna concluded that their many burdens could be eased only by a strike in the spring of 1889, and Adler immediately supported them in every way possible. Why not defend the victimized employees of a privately controlled public utility that worked men sixteen to twenty-one hours, its horses only four hours every day? Why not fight for conductors and drivers who were compelled to labor most of the "free" day every week to pay for their failure to keep up with complicated and rigorous timetables? Why not arouse support for workers who were heavily fined whenever their trams suffered damage, no matter who was really responsible?

After two weeks of refusing to harness their horses to the trams, the drivers were still far from obtaining all of their demands. Adler jubilantly claimed that the sympathies of most of the Viennese were with the strikers, despite the ugly evidence that state authority—police, army, bureaucracy—was clearly on the side of the company's stockholders. Good! Let the previously naive drivers realize that the masses of the oppressed and suffering had to preserve their own solidarity! When the inhabitants of the factory districts of Favoriten and Hernals showed a bit of true solidarity by interfering with the strike-breaking substitute drivers, however, they were discouraged by dragoons and hussars. Thereafter the trams were escorted by police or military, with four special guards for every "scab." Just as Adler was editorially admitting the gravity of the situation for the strikers, the government stepped in and ordered the company to honor some of the strikers' demands. The hours of work were to be shortened, enforced "layoffs" were to cease, and reforms in the administration of insurance funds were mandatory. If the company had failed to comply, its holdings would have been subjected to sequestration. Though Adler was forced to confess that some of the worst abuses remained, he congratulated the men on their victory and the lightening of their "chains." [29]

In July, 1889, Adler and other Austrian Social Democrats made their way to Paris to take part in the launching of the Second International. They had just founded a new journal, the *Arbeiter-Zeitung*, to replace the suppressed *Gleichheit*, for the "antianarchist" law was still being enforced. The Paris congress decided to sponsor great demonstrations of workers on May 1, 1890, with the eight-hour day as the special objective of the manifestations. Twenty years later Adler humorously acknowledged that he and his fellow delegates wondered how such mass demonstrations could possibly eventuate in Austria, where any bureaucrat's ukase could intervene. On November 29, 1889, the *Arbeiter-Zeitung* nevertheless announced that May Day would be celebrated by peaceful meetings of labor groups in the morning and by simple recreation in the afternoon. There would be no toil, obviously, on this "holy day."

When the great day dawned, Adler was in Cell 32 of the Landesgericht in Vienna. He and a comrade earlier had fallen afoul of "exceptional conditions," and he was forced to begin his four-month sentence at the end of February, 1890. Thanks to the political nature of his offense and the plenitude of his pocketbook, he suffered little material privation, but he recalled in later years that his mental anguish and fits of depression were considerable. Ever since the announcement of November 29, there had been feverish speculation as to the real purpose of the May Day celebration among those who feared and distrusted the workers. The Social Democrats had repeatedly promised that their fete would be peaceful, thoroughly legal, and utterly harmless, but they persuaded few of their pacific intentions. A most intellectual club in Vienna canceled its annual spring excursion so that the wives and children of the members would not be left alone on May 1. It was rumored that reservists would be recalled, and there was absolutely no doubt that all active military men would be on duty on the fateful day. The evening

edition of the *Neue Freie Presse* on April 30 tickled the spines
of its readers with the following:

The soldiers are in readiness, the gates of the houses are being locked,
victuals are being prepared in the houses just as before a siege, businesses are deserted, women and children do not venture upon the
streets, on all minds weighs the impression of a heavy anxiety.

But the editor of Liberalism's most influential journal soon
changed to a more valiant strain:

This fear is disgraceful, and it would never have arisen if the middle
class had not sunk [so] low. . . . Only upon the ruins of the crum-
bled middle class can Socialism move ahead, and if this social order
no longer is protected by the inflexible resolution and by the courage
of the nationalities, but only by the police and the military, then it
is not worthy of surviving. . . . The anguish over May 1 is a
startling phenomenon that vehemently arraigns internal policy, the
leaders of society, and those responsible for parliamentary power.[30]

In jail Adler kept up his writing of editorials for the *Arbeiter-
Zeitung*, and he underlined more than anything else a slogan
which he hoped labor and its enemies would keep in mind.
It was very simple: "We won't be intimidated or provoked."
That was a vast promise to make for all of the less than satisfied laborers of the empire, and Adler was understandably ap-
prehensive when the "glorious day" came. Two party function-
aries came early to report that the rank and file should be
easily kept in line by a thousand "directors," but they also
had to reveal that the wire surrounding the grassy plots in the
Prater had been removed. That meant that cavalry charges were
on the government's agenda in case of trouble, for the wire, if
not removed, would easily trip horses. The tramp of soldiers
penetrated Adler's cell, but no other menacing sounds reached
his ears. At noon one of his earlier visitors dropped by for a
minute to disclose exultantly that no troubles had developed.
After a long, long afternoon and evening Adler heard the
soldiers returning to barracks, a good indication of the success
and orderliness of the demonstrations.[31]

Obviously the laborers who took the holiday and joined the

demonstrations were not preponderantly Social Democratic. Many probably knew little or nothing of Marx or Engels. For a day they presumably did experience some feeling of solidarity, and their cooperation with the party was a reasonably good omen of party successes of a huge order still to come. The observer of the hard-bitten followers of the Communist Party line today is inevitably impressed with the moderate and almost apologetic stand displayed by Social Democrats like Adler. They assured the representatives of the classes they were "fated" to expropriate that they intended no destruction of life and property, and Adler worried incessantly that some hotheads would ruin the party's promises. Was this hypocrisy? Was this merely a tactical delay until the proletariat was more aware of its manifest destiny? An interchange between Adler and Friedrich Engels, the acknowledged interpreter and collaborator of the deceased Marx, during this period is of some help in showing that Adler was already short on revolutionary phrases and long on evolutionary ideas. The latter had written:

The critics of tactics always believe that it is and can be a straight line, while it must be an undulating line, just like world history.

Engels pleasantly answered:

What you say about tactics is only too true. But there are too many who, because of indolence or a desire to avoid troubling their own brains, wish to employ tactics suitable for the moment for all time. Tactics we do not make from nothing, but from changing conditions.[32]

At the Paris meetings of 1889 Adler had offered an analysis of the Austrian situation which proves even today his shrewd understanding of what tactics had to be adopted to forward Social Democracy in the empire. Propaganda and political activity in Austria theoretically were less restricted by law than in any country save France and England, he admitted, but practically the police constantly violated freedom of press, meeting, and association. But, he added, with a phrase that became immortal, "we have despotism tempered by slovenliness. The young movement exploits the latter to catch its breath once again and to strengthen its ranks more effectively." Another great obstacle, which a preceding Czech delegate had passionately stressed, was the jangle of tongues, with its inevitable slowdown of propaganda efforts. The illiteracy of the masses further compounded the problems of publicity, and here Adler put the blame on the Roman Catholic Church. At the same time he conceded that the feudal aristocracy of Austria, with its close affiliation with the Church, was competing for labor's support by sponsoring social legislation. Though such legislation existed mostly on paper, some improvement of the workers' lot was evident. Again, opined Adler, the bourgeoisie itself, when it proffered the ideals of political liberalism, was not unattractive to some proletarians.

Factory inspection was not all it could be, but his Austrian Socialists were determined always to fight for laws that would raise the physical, intellectual, and moral conditions of the proletariat. When capitalism collapsed of its own contradictions, the proletariat's destiny would be determined by the level of spiritual development it had reached. "We have little influence on the coming of this moment, as we ourselves customarily admit—far less than our foes suspect."

Characteristically, Adler joined other speakers in proclaiming that effective aid for the proletariat would come by social revolution and not by social legislation enacted by parliaments. Just as characteristically, he then enthusiastically supported a resolution demanding an eight-hour day, no labor for children under fourteen, general prohibition of night labor and of female employment in enterprises which were peculiarly dangerous for women, at least thirty-six hours of continuous rest every week, and careful inspection of industries. All of these improvements were to be secured by laws and international treaties.

In later years Adler good-humoredly accepted the title "Hofrat of the Revolution." His socialist colleagues from other monarchies in 1889 might well have done likewise. Not only would they agree to distinctly bourgeois methods of reform; the same founding fathers of the Second International decisively rejected the idea of a "world strike" that might have paralyzed European capitalism.[33]

If the Second International's tactical decisions sound fairly tame to later generations, its Austrian cohorts nevertheless had to employ guile and shrewdness as long as "exceptional conditions" obtained in Vienna. While *Gleichheit* still lived, its editor, Ludwig Bretschneider, had to be extremely careful that he did not sell forbidden issues to snooping detectives and that informal conferences of the comrades in his tiny office were sufficiently casual to escape police investigation. Two of Adler's more colorful henchmen during the last months of strict police surveillance were Franz Schuhmeier and Leopold Winarsky. The first, a witty and miserably poor paper-worker, loved to instruct other workers in history, particularly in religious history. His interpretations were gloriously tendentious, as befitted the party's quick realization of the Christian Social hold upon the lower classes. The second, a Hamlet-like youngster who indulged in black or red cravats as well as socialism in his revulsion against his fate as a paper-hanger's assistant, was the party's "glue expert." When placards which the police manifestly would not approve had to be broadcast throughout the working-class districts, Winarsky and some well-chosen adepts were assigned the glue-pots and brushes. And, since Vienna was still much given to the relaxation of the *Fasching* season, even the more serious-minded party directors helped arrange a most successful Workers' Ball.[34]

The virtual end in 1891 of the exceptional decrees discriminating against labor organizations and activity deprived the party of the necessity of resorting to colorful evasion and harassment of the government. As Social Democratic membership rose from 15,498 in 1888 to 47,166 in 1891, Adler stubbornly argued the case for one big issue which would further advance the party and prepare the proletariat for the eventual "liberation from capitalism."[35] Partially to end the slight but annoying sniping from the remnants of radicalism and anarchism, he insisted that this unifying platform should be the battle for universal, equal, secret, and direct suffrage. The proletariat had to be readied physically and spiritually, and the right to vote plus adequate social legislation would win over and revolutionize the poor, destined to be the heirs and executors of the era of the bourgeoisie. So he argued at the meeting of the International in Brussels in 1891, at the Third Austrian Party Day in 1892, and in a pamphlet which the police confiscated in 1893.[36]

The Social Democrats had won no seats in the general elections of 1891, but they were not alone in agitating for electoral reform. The Young Czechs on May 1, 1893, brought in a bill to which Adler at once pledged his party's support, and the summer was filled with mass meetings sponsored by the Social Democrats. Most curiously Taaffe himself, desperate for new sources of parliamentary support, momentarily persuaded the Emperor to chance a proposal that would have bestowed the franchise upon literate males or those who could prove some distinction in military service. His chief parliamentary supporters quickly signified their total displeasure, and Taaffe's long term as Minister-President came to a close.

The rebuff administered by the parliamentarians led to stormy debate at the party's Fourth Party Day sessions of March 25–31, 1894. Adler was blasted for incapacity and weakness when Taaffe's proposal was withdrawn. Should not the proletariat call a general strike to secure the ballot, indeed, to secure the eight-hour day? Adler replied that the fight for the vote would be long and would require many tactical shifts. More, he and the other leaders could not have called a general strike without the discussion that only a party day could provide. Anton Hueber, already a great power in the trade-union movement in Austria, spoke darkly of treason, and his blunt comments forced Adler and the party directorate to propose seemingly stiff procedures for future eventualities. Anything short of real universal suffrage was to be countered with every possible proletarian weapon, even the mass strike, should the bourgeoisie force the workers to this "last step." The campaign for the eight-hour day should be pushed separately, but here, too, all possible stratagems could be employed. Hueber alone demurred, but his resistance ended in good party fashion with his full acceptance of the majority's will. Indeed, it was he who soon was known as the party's chief whip in trade-union affairs. Until nationalism ripped apart their solidarity, the unions, under his influence, tended to follow the party's decisions with docility.[37]

In 1896 the Social Democratic clamor for universal suffrage received rather curious satisfaction at the hands of Minister-President Badeni and a large parliamentary majority. It was decided that seventy-two new seats would be added to the Reichsrat's total and that deputies filling these seats would be elected by all male citizens at least twenty-four years of age. Here, surely, there was a chance for Adler to prove to his comrades abroad that the masses of Austria were becoming increasingly conscious of their vital interests. Fourteen Social Democrats were elected, but none, not even Adler, won a seat from the Viennese common man. All five of the mandates which all men could vote for in the capital went to Lueger and, to use Adler's acerbic phrase, "his jumping Jacks." Why was it easy to fill the streets with men seemingly sympathetic to Socialist ideas, only to have them seduced by Lueger's enchantments? Adler bluntly maintained that his party, despite manly endeavors, was trounced by the important fact that Lueger was lord of Vienna and consequently lord of all Viennese polling booths. He who had all of the apparatus of administration in his hands had only to ape Galician elections to win with little difficulty.

Was Lueger's overpowering personality the only important reason for the slaughter of the Social Democrats? Was it wise to insist solely on voting irregularities and pressures? No, declared Adler, the party should hate as its worst foe the real enemy which produced the debacle in Vienna—the masses' lack of understanding and judgment. Once the masses were made aware of their plight and of their "real" friends, the party would have no worries about sure victory in the future.[38]

If Vienna proved to be an elusive prize during the 1890s, other areas were much more receptive to Social Democratic propaganda. Most of the Social Democrats elected in 1897 represented the coal, iron, glass, or textile centers of Bohemia, where they had won the approval of either German or Czech workers.[39] When Badeni's language regulations produced furious outbursts from most Germans a month later, the party preserved strict neutrality by the usual insistence that national pride was a cloak for class selfishness. It deserted its neutral position, however, when Badeni resorted to a reactionary revision of parliamentary procedure. For the first time in years German Nationalists and Social Democrats were united in action, the former, of course, for the sake of Germanism, the latter for unfettered freedom of speech in the Reichsrat. The target of their invective and near violence was the Polish president of the Lower House, Abrahamowicz, whom Mark Twain described as "a gray-haired, long, slender man with a colorless long face, which in repose suggests a death mask . . . sunk back in the depths of his armchair . . . his chin down." [40] Before Badeni quit in despair, several Social Democrats had been forcibly ejected from the sessions, along with their odd allies, the German Nationalists.

The German-Czech imbroglio posed inescapable problems for the party's leaders. It was theoretically easy to insist that the worker had no country and that all nationalities were equal in the sight of dialectical materialism. The five Czech Social Democrats who entered the Reichsrat in 1897 caused a sensation, nevertheless, when they refused to join in the traditional claims for a Czech Bohemia, Moravia, and Silesia. The Party Day of 1897, acutely conscious of the need to hold Czech and other non-German proletarian support, decided to reorganize the party so that its national components would have complete autonomy in local administrative and press affairs. [41]

An increasingly large number of Czech laborers showed dissatisfaction with such minimal gestures, and their discontent was given due attention at the important Party Day held at Brünn in September, 1899. To ameliorate national turmoil, the historic crownlands were to be replaced by nationally demarcated self-governing bodies, whose legislation and administration were to be controlled by national chambers. Such chambers would be elected by universal, equal, and direct suffrage. All self-governing areas of the same nationality were to form a nationally unified association, though the party recognized the fact that some regions were so hopelessly mixed in national sentiment that there could be no clear-cut drawing of boundaries. A special act of the Reichsrat was to safeguard the rights of the minorities in such conglomerate regions. The executive committee of the party recommended to all of the assembled delegates that German be utilized as an expedient "language of intercourse" in the revamped empire, but its recommendation was not accepted. Instead, a vague formula was adopted leaving to the imperial parliament the decision as to whether or not to adopt a *lingua franca*.[42]

It has been pointed out that such ideas were not too far removed from the remedies previously recommended by the discredited German Liberals of Austria.[43] The Brünn Program inexorably destroyed all hope for the emergence of a Czech "kingdom" of Bohemia, Moravia, and Silesia and indubitably strengthened the Czech National Socialist Party among Czech workers at the expense of the Social Democrats. The elections of 1901 were emphatically indicative of the hatreds roused by Badeni's controversial moves. Adler's most potent vote-getters had little luck selling to their possible constituents the idea of an Austria renovated along federalistic lines. The Social Democratic representation in the Lower House dropped from fourteen to ten, with Adler still unsuccessful in his attempt to secure a mandate. Of the fifteen seats allotted to Czech voters in the fifth or "universal" curia, five went to the Czech National Socialists, who ferociously attacked the implications of the Brünn Program. From 1901 on the Social Democrats found it more profitable to shout for universal manhood suffrage than to strain at further explanations of their cures for nationalistic aberrations.

Young Hitler approved of this Social Democratic concentration upon complete electoral reform, it will be recalled, because it was clear to him that this campaign would hasten the collapse of the polyglot realm. It is highly unlikely that Adler or any of his associates hoped to strangle the empire as fervently as Hitler eventually did. It is more plausible to argue that they wished to preserve the empire, with suitable improvements, until the proletariat was readied to take over. For instance, the decisions of the Party Day of 1901, which followed the disastrous elections, admittedly moved to the right. Revolutionary phrases were soft-pedaled, and there were exceedingly precise demands for full educational opportunities for the workers, progressive income and estate taxes, civil marriage, the yet unattained eight-hour day, proportional representation, and universal suffrage.[44] In short, nothing which would have explicitly distinguished Adler's followers from Bernstein's revisionists or the British Fabians.

Adler finally was elected to the Lower House, thanks to a by-election in 1905, just as his party was becoming extremely excited and gratified by news from tsarist Russia. The ramparts of reaction were falling in the one great country which had most obdurately proscribed Marxist activities, and no one doubted that the decline of tsardom would inevitably induce a liberalization of political life along the Danube. In Hungary Francis Joseph was talking ominously of introducing universal manhood suffrage, though primarily as a punishment for ultra-nationalistic Magyars who were threatening the integrity and unity of the joint armed forces.

When parliament reopened in September, 1905, the Social Democrats and an influential number of Slavic deputies petitioned the Austrian cabinet to prepare at once a law providing for universal, equal, direct, and secret suffrage. Gautsch, the Austrian Minister-President, declined to follow the suggestion, and the proponents of reform were unable to muster the votes necessary to force him to act. Outside of parliament the Social Democrats planned to make electoral reform the chief theme of their Party Day, which was inaugurated in Vienna on October 30. During the first session a paper on "The Austrian Crisis and the Franchise" was cut off by the announcement that Nicholas II had issued a manifesto promising the vote to all Russians in future elections. The overjoyed Social Democrats summoned Austrian labor to demonstrate for its full political rights, and a series of mass meetings and "promenades" followed. On November 2, police and workers collided along Vienna's Ringstrasse, and the next day Gautsch received orders from Francis Joseph to announce that Austrians would be granted what the street agitators wanted.

Though several parties and millions of individuals pined for electoral reform, the Social Democrats unquestionably should be given credit for forcing Francis Joseph to yield in 1905. Just in case Gautsch and his "like" should be thinking that the Emperor had lost his nerve too soon, the Social Democratic organization sponsored new and generally joyful demonstrations of laborers in every important industrial town and city of the empire from Trieste to Lemberg. On November 28, the Lower House was to reassemble after a short recess, and its members were treated to a spectacle which must have been uncomfortable to many of them. For hours workers marched past the Parliament Building, possibly a quarter of a million in all, wearing red arm-bands insisting on an honest version of universal equal suffrage. Simultaneously there were similar processions in at least twenty industrial centers. At Austerlitz blood was shed, almost exactly one hundred years after the small town first became notable for effusion of blood.[45]

In the tiresome debates over the actual machinery of future electoral procedures Adler consistently battled for equity for all. He saw no reason to favor the Germans because of their "cultural importance," he derided suggestions of plural suffrage for the property-owning family man, and, most significantly, he described his party as a state party vitally interested in the cultural development of the empire and in the progress of the empire toward substantial political peace.[46] A close study of the crises and conflicts that accompanied the tedious working out of the new electoral regulations substantiates Adler's surprising description of his party. Again and again he labored to hasten the dawn of the democratic franchise, and it cannot be denied that he acted most suspiciously like a man who wanted the empire to last a good long while.

The undoubted prestige which accrued to the Marxists as a result of their powerful influence in bringing universal manhood suffrage to Austria was matched by increasing tensions within the party itself. G. D. H. Cole has offered the opinion that up to 1907 "the continual struggle for equal and universal voting rights did a great deal to hold the party together in common opposition to the governing classes, which were also banded together, despite their national differences, to resist its advance." [47]

Actually the party had been the object of Czech nationalist infiltration as early as its second Party Day of 1891, but sincere Czech Marxists then had effectively blocked such moves.[48] In general the history of the fateful separatism which overtook the party originates in the trade-union movement and then spills over into the annals of the Social Democratic political organization. In 1896 representatives of some Czech unions asked that there be a division of the Secretariat of the Imperial Commission of Austrian Trade-Unions along ethnic lines, and, when refused, they formed in 1897 a purely Czech Trade-Union Commission in Prague. These secessionists went no further until 1905, when they petitioned the International Secretariat, meeting in Amsterdam, to allow their Commission to function independently as the second trade-union center in Austria. The Vienna Secretariat, represented by Anton Hueber, was resolutely opposed, and the Czech request was denied.

The elections of 1907 added to the growing schism between German and Czech Social Democrats, though the party had reason to feel most gratified with its overall successes. Of the 4,676,636 votes cast, Social Democratic candidates received 1,040,100. German Social Democrats captured about 516,000 votes, while their increasingly distant Czech brethren rolled up 390,000.[49] In German areas, particularly at the supplementary elections, the Social Democrats preached war to the death on clericalism and actually won more than one-third of the votes cast in Lueger's own stronghold of Vienna. The Czech branch of international Socialism was so pleasantly overcome by its capture of seventeen seats on the first ballot that it went all out to grab some more at the by-elections. It pledged allegiance to the accepted thesis of autonomous development for all national groups, but it also favored a second Czech university in Moravia and a goodly increase in Czech schools of all kinds. Seven more

Czech Social Democrats were subsequently elected. German Social Democrats also did well among the Germans of Bohemia, who sent twelve of them to the new parliament. If 41 percent of all of the voters in Bohemia, whether Czech or German, opted for Social Democracy,[50] was this not a bright sign for the future?

The opening of the Fifth Trade-Union Congress in Vienna in October, 1907, destroyed most of the optimism. The possible secession of Czech trade-unions was openly discussed and denounced as potentially catastrophic to the best interests of the proletariat. In Prague the simultaneous meeting of the Czech unions ignored the moans and pleas from Vienna, and the delegates proudly voted to accept as binding only those decisions their own Central Committee might make in the future.[51]

Three years later an altercation between the editors of a separatist daily in Brünn and hard-core centralists ended in schism between the Czech branch of the party and the party directors in Vienna. The Second International's Congress in Stuttgart in 1907 had stressed the need for cooperation rather than amalgamation of party and unions, and the Czech party leaders who finally decreed in March, 1910, that Czech unionists should be served only by the Commission in Prague were denounced by the Imperial Commission in Vienna for violating the directives adopted at Stuttgart.

The embroiled factions took their respective cases to the International's Congress in Copenhagen, where the separatists were verbally spanked while simultaneously assured that unions had to "take into consideration the linguistic-cultural needs of all their members" in multinational states. The Czech delegates resolutely insisted that their actions had been inspired by purely practical motives, such as the need to supervise their own funds. Back home, they ignored the Congress's pleas for reconciliation, and the estrangement became permanent.[52]

The tough-minded young Otto Bauer wrote that the Czech branch of the party obviously was in the grip of an internal struggle between petty bourgeois and honestly proletarian factions. Stung by such an unflattering accusation, the Czech separatists intemperately lumped their German Socialist brethren together with the entire bureaucratic, military, and dynastic apparatus of the Habsburg state. There was no difference any longer in the danger either element posed for the Czech people. The separatists had a commanding lead in the trade-union movement, but they could not secure total control. In May, 1911, Czech supporters of the Commission in Vienna formed a "Czech Social-Democratic Workers' Party in Austria" and pledged support of the old centralist approach.

The German branch of the party recognized the new Czech centralist fraction at the Party Day of 1911, but it avoided a decision as to whether or not to attempt the expulsion of the separatists from the International proper. At most, a condemnation of the Czech separatists was secured from the Polish segment of the party late in 1911, a move which added to the secessionists' conviction that Vienna and the Germans had a stranglehold over Social Democratic affairs.[53]

The elections of June, 1911, were devastating proof of the nationalistic virus at work among Marxist voters of Czech background. The separatists collected 357,623 ballots, the centralists only 19,367. The party directorate in Vienna was both appalled and self-justified by the fact that both segments together rolled up 23,000 fewer votes than had the united party among Czech voters in 1907. Actually the Czech Social Democrats of both persuasions now had two more deputies than in 1907, and this relative improvement was made possible, according to the disillusioned tribunes in Vienna, by a deal engineered by the separatists with bourgeois Czechs.[54]

At Christmas time the separatists gathered in Prague to celebrate their successful emancipation. Unanimously they agreed that German and Polish Social Democrats were trying to wreck their efforts. They reaffirmed their loyalty to the principles of international solidarity but most strongly asserted their conviction "that international solidarity does not stand in the way of the struggles for the nation's independence."[55]

Struggles for the nation's independence? What responsible Czech leader of a "bourgeois" or aristocratic party would use such words even as late as 1911? If Hitler really had liked the

Marxists initially for their espousal of suffrage reform, then his equivocal affection apparently had been justified. A party which was pledged to effect a federal and democratic salvation of the empire had only succeeded in nourishing the ambitions of admitted rebels.

The nationalistic discords which destroyed Adler's hopes for proletarian solidarity within Austria were small-scale manifestations of corrosive national egotism to be found almost everywhere in continental Europe. The Second International harped on the necessity of "exposing" national loyalties as concepts used by the bourgeoisie to mislead the workers, while individual leaders of the various branches of international Socialism were usually to be discovered earnestly engaged in attempts to calm patriotic passions aroused by the unending "crises" in diplomacy after 1900. Indeed, it was one of the genuine honors of pre-1914 Austrian Socialism that constructive theories on conciliation of national strife were developed and discussed by two of its first-rate party theoreticians.

Karl Renner, whose career began with an impoverished rural boyhood in Moravia, read his first socialist tracts and first met up with the complexities of the "Austrian state problem" while fulfilling his army duty. As a young family man he served as a tutor in well-to-do families, studied law, and fortunately secured a post as librarian in the Reichsrat's library. Beginning in 1899 with his *Zur österreichischen Nationalitätenfrage*, he became chiefly noted for his belief that the most advanced cultural freedom for every nationality could be reconciled with a continuing residuum of power at the center, where emperor, chancellor, cabinet, and legislature would provide administrative stability. Possibly because he was a German from Moravia, he emphasized the cultural autonomy of the individual even when the latter was surrounded by members of another nationality. As a former Lassallean he was often subjected to analysis and criticism which picked at his reverence for the state as state. All too optimistically he supposed that problems of a *lingua franca* and of division of jobs within the inevitable bureaucracy would be self-liquidating in the general rejoicing that would follow the grant of full cultural autonomy to every individual citizen. It would be unfair to Renner to imply that his proposals were so vague. If anything, he was elaborately precise in working out his system of checks and balances. Certainly what he proposed was immensely superior to the ambiguities of the Brünn Program. The latter, however, had been the honest result of Czech and German clashes over a state language and over the definition of what truly were "national affairs," that is, matters over which each nationality should have complete self-administration. Renner, the quiet scholar, was unfortunate in being too late. His balancing of cultural autonomy with intrinsically strong state power was the natural brainchild of a thoughtful Socialist who saw every reason to begin the march toward international brotherhood with a preliminary operation within and upon Austria. He happened to be a contemporary, however, of an explosion of Czech national fervor which alone would have rendered quite illusory his reforms. That separatism which found gravely dangerous a direction of trade-union affairs from Vienna was equally suspicious of Renner's proposed demarcation of the cultural from the political and economic. In an era of "realism" such a program was considered to be nothing more than a blind for unceasing German hegemony at the center.

Otto Bauer was the younger of Austria's Marxian theoreticians in the field of ethnocentrism. In his *Die Nationalitätenfrage und die Sozialdemokratie*, published in 1907, he tended to work more closely within the framework of Marxian exegesis than had Renner. Workers of every nationality had been excluded from the possession and enjoyment of their nationality's cultural heritage by the propertied class, he alleged. Through class struggle, however, the workers would seize control of their cultural heritage, indeed, would bring it to full development by their very recourse to class struggle.

Bauer was reasonably close to Renner in his precise delineation of the "democratic state of nationalities," with his nationally demarcated, self-governing bodies within the state and with his especial insistence upon granting a minority living within an area predominantly inhabited by another nationality clear-cut rights to its own school system. He is far more interesting in retrospect as the Social Democrat who in 1907 at any rate seemed to be the chief spokesman for the idea that the empire probably would last and that this survival would be useful for the further emancipation of the proletariat. He saw good reason why greedy industrialist and blindly loyal peasant and small businessman found it profitable and emotionally satisfying to fight for the empire's life. Also, why would a nationality lacking conationals elsewhere strive to kill off the monarchy? Why would a nationality likely to be overawed in another state-complex work for such a dubious change in allegiance? Would the Roman Catholic Church allow its last faithful son to be destroyed? If Austria-Hungary fell, it would be the work of an outside power, the result of the deadly imperialistic rivalries of the day. The strife of the resident nationalities could not encompass its end, and he predicted that most of these same quarrelsome groups would rally to the colors if war should come.

Bauer, of course, was no apologist ever for the Habsburgs. Like Renner, he was hypnotized by the marvelous scope the empire offered for experimentation in brotherly love and in reforming production, distribution, and consumption of the world's goods. World War I stripped him of such optimism, and the shocks of the 1930s drove him to Brünn, where Social Democracy had first grappled with nationalism, and then to Paris, the Second International's birthplace. It is almost superfluous to add that quite a new Danubia was being created as he died an exile in France in 1938, nor is it totally surprising to read that his last important political act was to approve *Anschluss*. If one believes in the inexorable triumph of the working class, it matters little through which larger state-complex the millennium is hastened.[56]

Bauer expressed a commonly-held party fear when he pointed in 1907 to Europe's rivalries as the more likely source of Austria's dissolution. The appointment of Aehrenthal to the Foreign Office in 1906 was a signal for much greater adventurousness, and the crisis over Bosnia in 1908 impelled Adler and other Social Democrats in the Reichsrat to press for a detailed report on the increasing strain in the international situation. Austria-Hungary was to announce to the world, according to the Social Democrats' proposal, that her intentions were completely peaceful and that the natives of Bosnia and Herzegovina would receive full democracy. The Reichsrat did not agree to such propositions, and the Bosnian crisis continued threateningly into 1909.[57] When it reached its final climax in the last days of March, 1909, Adler rose in the Lower House to move once again in the name of Social Democracy that everything be done to spare Europe the tragedy of war. He described the masses as united in desiring peace, not war, whether that war was large, small, on three fronts, localized, or global.[58]

The outbreak of the First Balkan War in October, 1912, inspired Adler to renewed efforts to keep his countrymen from war. He monotonously stressed nonintervention, complete neutrality, and isolation from all Balkan quarrels. He assured his comrades abroad that even the war hawks among the military in Vienna would not move unless Russia committed a direct provocation. His speech was curiously pontifical, for he said, "I believe that the unity of the proletariat cannot remain without influence upon the government." [59]

In November, 1912, Austrian Social Democracy followed up its hopeful pressure upon the home government by direct appeals abroad. Wilhelm Ellenbogen carried the word to Budapest, Renner to Berlin, and Pernerstorfer to Paris. The great climax of the Second International's drive against a possible "bourgeois imperialist" war came in Basel on November 24–25, 1912. The usual manifesto was issued amid sincere demonstrations of fraternal solidarity, and some months later the Social Democrats of the Russian Duma reiterated their hope in a message to the Austrian German Social Democrats that peace and freedom would triumph over hate and war.[60]

A year earlier the Social Democrats had again attempted to interfere directly in Austrian internal affairs, but with less success than in 1905. The summer of 1911 was marked by a drastic rise in the cost of living, which the Social Democrats blamed on the agrarian sympathies of the government. Workers broke out in spontaneous demonstrations, which the Minister-President, Baron Gautsch, accused the party directorate of "arranging." Should there be any more pressure from the streets, threatened the Emperor's representative, force would be resorted to. Earlier in the summer a national election had shown a slight diminution of "red" strength in the Reichsrat, for the membership of the Social Democrats dropped from eighty-seven to eighty-two. Their compensating success in whipping the Christian Social machine in Vienna by electing a majority of the deputies representing the capital in parliament did not seem to impress Gautsch, however. He had promised stern measures in case of further disturbances, and he kept his word.

In September, 1911, Viennese workers assembled before the Rathaus to protest anew the burden of high prices. Police were ordered to break up the concentration, without too much success. Infantry and cavalry were dispatched to the scene, with the result that several persons were killed, quite a few wounded, and many thrown into jail. In the following weeks eighty-two persons were given stiff prison sentences, while hundreds of others underwent confinement of shorter duration. Here was a situation tailor-made for righteous declamations against the cruel tyrannies of a "class" regime.

Just before the Reichsrat assembled, Adler told a sympathetic crowd in the Favoriten district that while it was an error to expect a capitalistic state to give food to every family, there was no reason for the same state to deprive its citizens of available meat just to please agrarian lobbies. The street events had been the logical explosions which followed months of hunger, particularly among men on fixed wages. Thousands had come to think, desperately, "What is life worth to us? Before we die of hunger we at least want to take revenge upon our enemies!"

Adler quickly disassociated himself from such radical thoughts, but he finished by flatly asserting there could be no justice or equality of treatment in courts until the class struggle was over.[61] The man popularly blamed for the repression of protest was not so much Gautsch as his Minister of Justice, Dr. von Hochenburger. When the Reichsrat discussed the disturbances on October 5, Adler took a leading role in repeating his criticisms of the government's vigorous policy. Suddenly there was a commotion in the galleries as a young man fired five revolver shots at Hochenburger. When the excited deputies calmed down enough to resume their work, Gautsch accused the Social Democrats of inspiring the would-be assassin with their "hate speeches."

The cabinet member's assailant had been identified as one Nikolaus Njegusch, a cabinetmaker's assistant from Sebenico. At his trial some weeks after the attempted crime the frail prisoner declared that he was driven to shoot at Hochenburger when he noticed him laughing and joking during Adler's recital of the woes of the common people. Whether provoked or not, he was sentenced to seven years in jail, where he died before his term was completed.[62]

Njegusch's attack upon a sworn defender of Germanism in Austria, for Hochenburger was a ranking member of the German National Alliance, must have fitted in well with Hitler's later theories on Social Democracy. It will be remembered that the young provincial decided early in his Vienna days that the Marxists were the seducers of his people. By 1911 the Njegusch affair could only have confirmed his verdict. After four years of residence in the capital, moreover, he was probably feeling more and more frustration over the fate of his beloved Germans. Karl Lueger, who knew how to charm the German masses without using them for the glory of the "race," was dead, and his lieutenants had little of his magnetism. Schönerer was practically a political nonentity, while Wolf was important only as one of the organizers of the loose and basically inadequate German National Alliance.

And yet Victor Adler had once been fervently devoted to Germanism, and no later than 1906 was speaking proudly of the material culture of Germanism and the development of the German masses.[63] His party was split within Austria because he and others of German background were increasingly suspect among Czech, Polish, and Ruthene Social Democrats. When Hitler fumed in later years that he would never forget the names Austerlitz, David, Adler, and Ellenbogen as indicative of the Jewish orientation of Austrian Social Democracy before 1914, he conveniently forgot that these were the men who were too "German" for hundreds of thousands of Slavs.

After Hitler had deserted Austria for the German Empire, after the war had come in 1914, Adler, like thousands of alumni of the Second International, seemed to revert to what Hitler might have considered an honorable attitude. The legions of socialist faithful had not met this latest of "capitalist, imperialist" wars with folded arms, as had been often predicted and sometimes promised. In the German Empire, where Marxian Socialism was probably strongest, the decision of most Social Democrats in the Reichstag to vote for war credits was merely the most striking example of the collapse of international solidarity. The Austrian Reichsrat was never consulted on problems of war and peace in the summer of 1914, so Adler and his colleagues were spared some of the soul-searching which had faced German and French socialists.

The party and the trade-unions in Austria nevertheless had to give some guidance in lieu of parliamentary activity. First came a manifesto in the *Arbeiter-Zeitung* of July 25, the day on which the empire severed diplomatic relations with Serbia. Quite significantly the editorial stated its understanding of Austria's right to demand reparation for the crime of Sarajevo and of the monarchy's justification in seeking an end to the underground plotting in Serbia which, in the newspaper's opinion, had been tolerated by the Serb government. In more orthodox fashion the declaration continued with an appeal to the Austrian cabinet not to desert peaceful negotiation with Serbia and warned the cabinet that responsibility for a frightful war would not be assumed by the German workers of Austria. Paragraphs which railed at the Minister-President for failing to call the Reichsrat in such a crisis were scissored out by imperial authorities.

On July 28, the day following the posting of mobilization notices, the *Arbeiter-Zeitung* published another pronouncement. Recognizing the inevitability of war and the insuperability of the forces desiring war, the party chairmen rather sentimentally

wafted their "first kiss" to the workers called to the colors
and then cautioned those comrades who stayed at home that war
would fashion a new Austria. The party's most important duty
was to stay prepared for the postwar period. Its organization had
to be maintained, for otherwise Social Democracy's worst foes
would gain the advantage when war ended. To avoid drastic
restrictions, all governmental orders based on the proclamation
of emergency conditions had to be obeyed. By averting collisions with the bureaucracy, organizational life could continue,
though the directorate freely admitted that the party's press
would be under especial strain.

The Viennese Trade-Union Commission similarly underlined
the need for unusual discretion in all Social Democratic organizations in an announcement of August 8, 1914. While it did not
seem likely that the government would hinder unions system-
atically through its emergency powers, some trouble might arise.
The wartime regulations must therefore be obeyed strictly, and
meetings assuredly were to be public whenever possible and
always in full accord with governmental directives. "We must
risk everything to preserve unimpaired the Austrian trade-union
movement for a better future." [64]

It is clear that Austrian Social Democrats, like the vast majority of their comrades everywhere in the belligerent countries,
were swept into an acquiescence they had always sworn they
would spurn, and their obsessive fear that their hard-won organization would be disrupted unless they implicitly obeyed the
government was particularly manifest. To lessen the bad taste
left by such an unidealistic consideration, German Austrian
Social Democrats summoned up a genuine enthusiasm for the
struggle with Russian tsarism, but it was ominous that even
this sure-fire justification left Victor Adler's son Friedrich un-
moved.

He wrote to his father and to his father's associates in the
party's directorate that they were allowing themselves to be
dragged into the ranks of the *Hurra-Kanaille* instead of recognizing the war for what it was, a murderous attempt upon the
proletarian International. Yet Friedrich, unlike the tiny group of

dissidents in Germany, did not quit the party, and in August, 1914, he subsided into an attitude of watchful waiting. Let the regime take all of the responsibility for the war and let the workers remain quiet and resolute until their hour to be heard returned.[65]

Austrian Marxism indubitably had its share of opportunism and was entrapped, like so many of its brothers in the International, by the very fact that it had successfully organized large numbers of workers. Its greatest rallying cry had been universal suffrage, and once the reform of 1907 was achieved, its magnetism at the polling booths failed to increase noticeably. Despite the finely reasoned schemes advanced by Renner and Bauer, it was unable to remain even a party of nationalities, let alone create the atmosphere for a state of nationalities. If no friend of Habsburg dynasticism, its fascination with the possibilities of economic and cosmopolitan advance in the polyglot area dulled its understanding of the frantic Czech and South Slav demands for bona fide equality. And yet Adam Wandruszka, a most perceptive student of Austria since 1867, has called Adler the most redoubtable of the founding fathers of Austrian democracy. If no match for Schönerer and Lueger in oratorical skill, he surpassed both in leaving a deep personal impress upon the party which he had inspired and disciplined so effectively.[66]

More, Adler was incurably honest. When the war had run its first few dreadful months, he permitted himself a philosophical comment which might have found favor even with Hitler. Speaking of the Social Democratic vote in the German Reichstag on war credits, he said: "I know they have to vote for them; I simply don't know how I might force it through my lips, but it has to be. . . . There is only one thing worse than war, that is defeat." [67]

"Symptoms of Debility"

HITLER recalled in *Mein Kampf* that the only friend in Vienna who never left him, the one comrade who shared everything with him honestly, was hunger. Despite constant sorrow and misery, he claimed that he spent his spare time reading, keeping up his interest in architecture, and making visits to the opera. In a city that symbolized idle pleasure to most persons his purchase of a book or of a ticket to the opera was the signal for another bout with hunger.[1] At the conclusion of his reminiscences of the Vienna period he declared that his observations and study convinced him that Austria "showed all symptoms of debility or at least of its unimportance for the German nation in the domain of purely cultural or artistic affairs." [2] Probably the chief reason for Hitler's contemptuous dismissal of Austrian culture and art was his fanatical hatred of any Jewish participation in art, literature, or theater. No doubt his own personal failure to shine as a gifted architect added to his feeling that his native land was ailing.

Had not Hitler been a devout believer in the "Big Lie," which, when repeated often enough, becomes the truth for the multitude, he might have amended somewhat his arrogant dismissal of Austrian cultural endeavor. In Vienna's musical life the works of Richard Wagner were never more popular than during Hitler's years of residence, and in the later, happier days of 1942 the Führer recalled attending thirty or forty performances of *Tristan and Isolde* alone, plus "some Verdi and other works—leaving out the small fry." [3] Of course, the great German hero-composer was dead, and it is quite possible that Hitler was looking for "good" German accomplishments from his contemporaries. That he tried very little to search for any outstanding new talents, whatever his claims to studiousness in *Mein Kampf*, is the conclusion of practically every careful observer.

Yet there were currents and developments in the artistic life of Vienna which could be twisted later on to give an ostensible veracity to Hitler's condemnations. Without attempting anything like an exhaustive review of those years of Viennese activity and creativity in the arts, it is nevertheless important to sketch those happenings which might have influenced Hitler or which in retrospect seemed to all too many intellectually lazy persons to bear out his analyses.

In the realm of music, which was Vienna's acknowledged glory, the opera house continued to be the center of attraction. Vienna's own version of a lyric theater was a comparatively new structure dating from the 1860s. This Hofoper, or Imperial Opera House, reputedly had brought tragedy to its architects, for it was said that one shot himself because the foundation sank while the other died of mortification over the nasty comments which his work elicited from the press. Though the massive exterior was indeed something less than thrilling to look at, the interior arrangements were second to none in Europe. Unlike most theaters built to show off the elite during this gaudy period of high capitalism, the Imperial Opera in Vienna permitted most of its patrons a decent view of what was happening on the stage. When Hitler indulged himself with a performance, he was no doubt far better off than the indigent patron of the Opéra in Paris or the Metropolitan in New York, who might well be favored with an obstructing pillar or a hopelessly situated side seat.

At the beginning of the twentieth century the stage machinery continued to satisfy the demands of most of the works produced, with the inevitable exception of some of the more grandiloquent stage requirements laid down by Wagner. The house required the attentions of no fewer than 700 employees, from the august director to the shabbiest charwoman. Thanks to the rich resources of the Imperial Arsenal, no "super" or *Heldentenor* had to be outfitted with pasteboard helmets or tin armor. The genuine articles, authenticated by learned curators, added a touch imperturbably accepted by audiences which were subject to the haughtiest dynasty in Europe.[4] It is superfluous to add that the show this side of the footlights often dimmed the brilliant costumes and décor even of a Meyerbeer production. To quote Hitler, reminiscing in 1942: "But before the war it was wonderful; never shall I forget the gracious spectacle of the Vienna Opera, the women sparkling with diadems and fine clothes." [5]

At the time Hitler was first getting settled in Vienna, tickets for evening performances ranged in cost from one krone twenty heller to fifteen kronen. Impecunious youth was allowed to stand right under the Imperial box, a most rewarding location, for two kronen. Here Hitler and Kubizek took their places if they were lucky enough to get tickets.[6] Since the krone (crown) was worth about one-quarter of an American dollar of the period, it will be realized that the poor did have some chance to enjoy the offerings of the extensive repertory.

In 1907 a golden age was coming to a close at the Imperial Opera with the retirement of Gustav Mahler as general director and leading conductor. Mahler was almost as controversial an opera director as he was a composer, and it is noteworthy that his Jewish background inevitably added to the controversies. The greatest conductor at the house when Mahler first appeared there in May, 1897, as interpreter of Wagner's *Lohengrin*, was none other than Hans Richter, who was most intimately identified with the Wagnerian festivals at Bayreuth. Richard Wagner's own brand of antisemitism was hardly a secret among his admirers, and the advent of Mahler as rival of the indubitably Teutonic Richter caused trouble from the beginning. In October, 1898, the fiery younger man was honored with appointment to the general managership, having been baptized quite some time before as a Christian. Baptized or not, Mahler was exposed to antisemitic demonstrations at the opera when Richter announced his retirement from the staff.[7]

Mahler's achievements, at least down to the last year of his directorate, were uncommonly fine. If he had one great characteristic as a re-creator of the works of other musicians, it was his fanatical desire for perfection. He was the inveterate foe of ossified routine on the stage and of bad manners in the audience alike. The claque was abolished, as was the seating of late-comers during overtures, preludes, and first acts. The auditorium was darkened to decrease the diversions afforded by jewels and uniforms in the boxes. To create true musical values Mahler felt he had to widen the repertory, restudy those masterpieces which were being offered in a stodgy or slapdash manner, and restore the cuts most commonly made in the Wagnerian music-dramas. He chose as young lieutenants in his drive to secure musical perfection Franz Schalk and Bruno Walter, who were to attain the highest rank themselves in later years as conductors. Midway in his directorate Mahler engaged Alfred Roller as the designer of marvelous stage settings. The first great fruit of their collaboration was a restudied *Tristan and Isolde* of 1903, for which Roller used orange as the predominant color for the first-act scene aboard ship, purple for the ecstatic second-act garden meeting of the lovers, and gray for the hauntingly tragic last act.[8]

Mahler had already staged a magnificent revival of Wagner's early extravaganza, *Rienzi*, and the popular acclaim for Roller's sets in 1903 led almost automatically to plans for completely restudied editions of the Wagnerian tetralogy, *Der Ring des Nibelungen*. *Das Rheingold* appeared in its new investiture in 1905, and *Die Walküre* in 1907, the year of Mahler's departure. The last two works of the *Ring* were produced under Mahler's immediate successor, Felix Weingartner. Lest the reader assume that Wagner was the chief recipient of Mahler's loving and dictatorial care, it should be emphasized that Mozart's operas were also restored with the grace and intelligence they require. Beethoven's *Fidelio* under Mahler was also most highly regarded, and, as general manager, he regaled the Viennese with such novelties as Richard Strauss's *Feuersnot*, Charpentier's *Louise*, Hugo Wolf's *Der Corregidor*, and Puccini's *La Bohème* and

Madame Butterfly, the last actually given after he had conducted his final operatic performance at the house.[9]

Mahler's decision to abandon the Imperial Opera at Vienna for the Metropolitan Opera in New York has been given many explanations. It was said that the singers were increasingly resentful of the iron discipline and endless rehearsals, that the Emperor himself was upset by the enormous costs of the re-studied productions. There was talk of interference from Kathi Schratt, the Emperor's great friend, in regard to a singer cashiered by Mahler and the inevitable talk of possible intrigues engineered by rival conductors.[10] Mahler's own drive to compose and his feeling of ennui and hopelessness in striving for a perfect opera ensemble were the most probable causes of his resignation. With less responsibility, there was bound to be more time for composition.

Felix Weingartner, the next director, had formerly been on the best of terms with Mahler, but he discerned a coolness when they met to discuss the transfer of authority. Despite some solid achievements as general director, Weingartner never quite won the acclaim which generally had come to Mahler, so that his reminiscences of the period may be somewhat prejudiced. Thirty years later he wrote that his first good look at the personnel did not completely satisfy his own standards. "A few really good singers, others whose voices were failing, the ensemble not as good as it ought to have been. Only the magnificent orchestra was as brilliant as ever." [11]

Weingartner was of the opinion that Mahler's success as a composer drove him to slight the opera house a bit. Like all new directors, Weingartner was not satisfied with the repertory he inherited, claiming that it was insufficient in number of works annually performed. Like many another new director, he ran into difficulties with two of the great singing stars—Selma Kurz and Leo Slezak, who would only accept guest performances. His fine basso, Richard Mayr, loyally remained to face overwork that Weingartner deplored and indirectly blamed upon Mahler. Actually Weingartner inherited a rather decent number of first-rate performers, and they did not merit the unconcern he was sometimes guilty of in the last months of his stay.

The first *cause célèbre* which rocked the musical public was a change ordered in the Mahler version of *Fidelio*. Weingartner maintained that he disliked Mahler's scheme of placing the "great" Leonore Overture between the dungeon scene and the finale, particularly since he suspected that the time needed to erect Roller's complicated settings for the last scene was responsible for the "tradition." The overture went where Weingartner wanted it, Roller's last-scene settings were put in storage, and the city was agog with gossip. The new director heard rumors that he was Mahler's "enemy" and that he was an "anti-Semite." [12]

Then came another sensational change from the policies identified with Mahler. Wagner's *Die Walküre* was "subjected" to cuts once again, as had been the custom prior to Mahler's directorate. The leading organ of Wagnerian enthusiasm in Vienna, the Association for Art and Culture, delivered an ultimatum to Weingartner edited by Hermann Bahr, demanding an end to such sacrilege. Should the new director fail to heed their warning, they threatened legal steps.[13] Weingartner argued in later years that the uncut performances of the *Ring* music-dramas wearied a large part of the listeners and positively fatigued the singers to the point of danger. His defense of cuts meant nothing to the solid cheering section which the Wagnerian cult could call upon, and it was not long before youths, armed with scores, gave signals for hissing and whistling at every excision in the performance. To eliminate this annoyance and also the fury of his critics, Weingartner eventually allowed the restoration of all cuts.[14]

Today Felix Weingartner is recognized as one of the very great interpreters of symphonic music during the first three decades of this century. His tenure at the Imperial Opera was not one of his scintillating successes, but it was no succession of crises and misunderstandings, either. Roller's scenic investiture for the *Ring* was completed with the new productions of

Siegfried in 1909 and of *Götterdämmerung* in 1910. On March 24, 1909, Richard Strauss led a performance of his new *Elektra* that both horrified and mesmerized the audience. Puccini's much tamer *Tosca* was added to the repertory in 1910, and a real service to a neglected gentleman came in 1911 with the careful production of Berlioz's *Benvenuto Cellini.* The last novelty identified with Weingartner's years was Richard Strauss's delectable *Der Rosenkavalier,* given its Viennese première on April 8, 1911, after Weingartner actually had given up his post. Franz Schalk was the conductor, and the notable cast included Gutheil-Schoder, "a realistic talent of the first rank for tragic as well as comic parts," [15] as the dashing young nobleman, Frau Weidt as his aging yet elegant mistress, and the incomparable Richard Mayr as the lecherous baron.[16]

For Hitler and other lovers of the lyric drama the last years before the outbreak of the war were distinctly inferior to the riches offered by both Mahler and Weingartner, who were, after all, sensitive and articulate musicians. Hans Gregor accepted the managerial responsibilities in 1911, to be damned in short order for caring only for box-office receipts. It was maintained that he allowed the ensemble to fall into stale routine, avoiding all worth-while exertions himself and caring naught if his personnel did likewise. The famed music commentator, Paul Stefan, acidly pointed out that in one year Gregor gave 120 ballet performances to one performance of a Weber opera and 40 performances of Massenet's cheap *Juggler of Notre-Dame* to 8 performances of works of Mozart.[17] In Gregor's defense, it should be said that he granted the Viennese a chance to hear Debussy's haunting *Pelléas and Mélisande* and also presided over the Schalk-Roller production of *Parsifal* in 1914.[18]

It is pertinent to note that there was another lyric theater in Vienna where Hitler and other enthusiasts could see good Wagnerian performances with a minimum strain upon slim purses. This house was the Volksoper, which began its activities during Mahler's last years at the Imperial Opera under the artistic direction of Rainer Simons, an impresario with a predilection for the sensational at any price. The house began

modestly with such popular items as *Martha* and *Der Freischütz*
and then graduated under its talented leading conductor, Alexander von Zemlinsky, to Beethoven's *Fidelio*, Wagner's *Tannhäuser* and *Lohengrin*, and even the Mozart operas. Down to
1910 its endeavors were financially rewarded by a large and
devoted public support, but thereafter higher costs of production brought on serious troubles. Simons was particularly well
known for his devilish pertinacity in training young singers
who, in his eyes, had real dramatic ability and for his love of
novelties with "big" effects. He introduced Puccini's *Tosca*
to Vienna three years before it reached the boards of the Imperial Opera, and naturally he exulted in giving a warm welcome to Richard Strauss's *Salome* in 1910, since that notorious
thriller was righteously excluded from the sacrosanct house on
the Ringstrasse. In 1908 Puccini's *Manon Lescaut* and Dukas's
Ariane et Barbe-Bleue were added to the Volksoper's repertory,
with Strauss's *Feuersnot* coming in 1912 and Humperdinck's
Königskinder in 1913. Even *Parsifal* was attempted in 1914, to
give the Imperial Opera's production a reasonably priced rival.[19]

   Hitler always preferred less than first-rate Wagner at the
Volksoper to superb Verdi at the Imperial Opera. In view of
his great yen for *Lohengrin*, it is fair to assume that in 1907
and later he was able to witness the steady progress of a gifted
young singing actress who later became a particular favorite of
American audiences. The potential diva was Maria Jeritza, one
of the greatest personalities on the musical scene before and
after World War I. If one casually consults the brief biographical data available on Jeritza in the usual works of refer-
ence, one discovers that she began her operatic career in 1910.
Now, one of her most sympathetic appraisals is by Wilhelm
Wymetal, who wryly declares that she was never a person to
speak of her age, her training, her actual first appearance on
the stage, etc.[20] As the lady herself put it in 1924, "I have a good
memory for anything I have once written down, except dates,
which are apt to escape me." [21] The Volksoper announcement of
casts for the autumn of 1907, however, lists a Fräulein Jeritza,
who was entrusted with the psychologically and vocally trying

role of Elsa in *Lohengrin*. Max Graf remembered her first performances as those of a glowing blonde with a sensuous and brilliant voice, whose long legs and hands eventually acquired gracefulness with experience and with canny tutoring from Simons.[22]

That such a young artist was trying her vocal cords on such weighty material indicates that Wagner was probably the most popular of composers with the public. Fräulein Jeritza sang no fewer than five performances of the dreamy Senta in *The Flying Dutchman* in October, 1908, another intimation of the strength of the Wagner cult. The Volksoper had to sell its wares to the public and Wagner was a fast-moving item. As we have seen, the Imperial Opera between 1897 and 1914 also gave great attention to Hitler's musical hero.

Vienna actually had been the scene of some very heart-warming moments for the creator of *Lohengrin, The Flying Dutchman*, etc. After the fiasco which attended the Paris performance of *Tannhäuser* in 1861, Wagner's spirits were lifted considerably by the cordial reception he received at the hands of the Vienna Opera. It was here in Vienna that he heard for the first time his own *Lohengrin*, written thirteen years before. This particular performance aroused one ovation after another from the audience, and it was definitely Wagner's greatest triumph up to that time.[23]

Vienna, however, also was the home of Edward Hanslick, a most formidable music critic, who had become vigorously opposed to all of Wagner's work. Probably it was Wagner's contempt for Jews which antagonized Hanslick; at any rate, mutual friends attempted to conciliate the two men. Any chance of a real burial of the enmity ended with Wagner's reading of the libretto for *Die Meistersinger* in Hanslick's presence. Without being too far wrong, the critic assumed that Wagner's most unattractive character in the new libretto, one Beckmesser, was a caricature of himself.[24] Hanslick lived for decades thereafter, but one doubts that his venom, somewhat justified, ever really harmed Wagner's cause. Hanslick, after all, was something of a perennial fad, more of an entertainer than a prophet or missionary. He "said in his criticisms what the most mentally limited of Viennese society thought, but he wrote it down in most ingenious form." [25]

Hanslick, whatever his intrinsic importance, was dead by 1907, when Hitler had his chance to hear Wagner performed by stellar casts. Statistics can be both dull and misleading, but a few illustrative of the Imperial Opera's work between 1907 and 1913 may be of value in further demonstrating Wagner's popularity. During the 1907 season, the truly ardent Wagnerite was given the chance to hear fifteen performances of *Die Walküre*, fourteen of *Lohengrin*, nine of *Tannhäuser* or *The Flying Dutchman*, six of *Tristan and Isolde* or *Die Meistersinger*, five of *Das Rheingold*, *Siegfried*, or *Götterdämmerung*, and two of *Rienzi*. If one totals all of the performances of the above music-dramas for the seven seasons between 1907 and 1913, roughly the period of Hitler's stay in the city, the result is, for the Imperial Opera, 426.[26] During the same period, of course, the Volksoper was busily exhibiting some of the Wagnerian dramas. The poorest of vagrants who yearned for the master could hardly have been left without some satisfaction.

If Wagner and his sea of *Melos* had captured Viennese mass approval by 1907, who stood forth as the generation's chief rebel? In view of Hitler's later seizures over expressionism, cubism, and dadaism, it is amusing to find Arnold Schönberg playing the part of chief disturber of Viennese musical sensibilities while the future Führer devoutly soaked himself in the distraught metaphysics of *Tristan and Isolde*. Richard Strauss was a fairly ubiquitous bad boy in orthodox eyes, too, but he and Mahler were generally conceded to be neo-Romantic and consequently "safe."

Today it would be hard to find music more Romantic than Schönberg's early *Verklärte Nacht* (1899) and *Gurre-Lieder* (practically finished by 1901). Both were brimming with Wagnerian asides, though the *Gurre-Lieder* is perhaps closer to Richard Strauss in prodigal use of voices, orchestral and human. The *Verklärte Nacht* was first performed as a string sextet under the sympathetic direction of Arnold Rosé, the great

Viennese master of chamber music recitals. While Mahler and Bruno Walter applauded vigorously, others hissed and shouted in derision.[27] Thereafter Schönberg was a marked man, denounced for anarchism before he was able to justify the accusation. Early in 1905 he conducted the first performance of his symphonic poem, *Pelleas and Melisande,* which one contemporary critic described as "a fifty-minute-long protracted wrong note."[28] The audience seemed to agree with the critic, for there was another tempest, this time much more understandable. Schönberg in *Pelleas and Melisande* had tentatively embarked upon his flight from "the tyranny of tonality."

During the next eight years he built up a loyal group of students and devotees and continued to experiment with atonality and dissonance. Just as Hitler was planning to leave Vienna for Munich, Schönberg had another chance to test Vienna's reaction to two major works. In February, 1913, the finally completed score of the *Gurre-Lieder* was given its première. The presence of nearly 400 persons on stage plus chimes and gongs did not discourage shouts of dismay and fist fights.[29] If this comparatively moderate work provoked such controversy, it is easy to imagine what happened a month later at a far more abstruse concert. On the last day of March, 1913, the Academic Society for Literature and Music sponsored the first performances of Schönberg's *Kammersymphonie,* along with creations from his students, Anton von Webern and Alban Berg. The result was "the greatest uproar . . . in a Vienna concert hall in the memory of the oldest critic writing." The orchestra and the audience bickered with one another, the president of the sponsoring society boxed the ears of a heckler, and one of the composers was accused of using provocative and insulting language.[30]

Hitler's seeming indifference to or ignorance of Schönberg and his school in Vienna is another puzzling thread in the story of the early days. As a Jew and as a blatant modifier of what had been good enough for Wagner, Schönberg was a natural target for creatures like Hitler in Austria before 1914. The retribution was only delayed. Schönberg and Franz Schreker, who had conducted the première of the *Gurre-Lieder* in 1913, were dismissed from the faculty of the Prussian Academy of Arts on May 30, 1933, by order of the German Ministry of Education. In July of the same year Schönberg returned to the Judaism he had renounced in 1921 in a synagogue ceremony in Paris, and in October he reached the shores of the United States.[31] In 1913 he had contended with some genuine intellectual disagreement and a generous amount of horseplay. In 1933 he fell victim to a fanatical movement brilliantly led by one who said: "To me a single German military march is worth more than all the junk of these new musicians—these people belong in a sanatorium."

There is practically nothing in *Mein Kampf* to indicate that Hitler was more than superficially aware of the important literary trends in Vienna, and Kubizek frankly declared that names like "Rilke, Hofmannsthal, Wildgans . . . never reached us."[32] The Hitler who dictated his wild ideas in 1924 lashed out at the Jews for the part they played in press, art, literature, and theater, alleging that they were responsible for "ninety per cent of all literary and artistic rubbish and of theatrical humbug,"[33] but it has been plausibly argued that here he merely echoed vulgar antisemitic editorials. Nonetheless, there was little in Viennese literary activity just before World War I to gladden the heart of a puritanical and patriotically German young man. If Hitler even carelessly read the book and theater reviews of the period, he must have been convinced more than ever of the "degeneracy" and "weak cosmopolitanism" of the empire.

The most effective publicist for the new literary stars appearing in Vienna after 1890 was Hermann Bahr, the erstwhile German Nationalist of the Wagner memorial of 1882; the established reputations by 1907 were those of Arthur Schnitzler, Hugo von Hofmannsthal, and Richard Beer-Hofmann. Just appearing on the horizon was Rainer Maria Rilke, who had achieved his first real fame with *Das Stundenbuch* in 1905. Acting as secondary figures were such writers as Peter Altenberg and Felix Salten, while in a sense Stefan George and his circle were close to the men of Vienna in a common repudiation of naturalism.[34]

Hermann Bahr's zeal for impressionism in place of naturalism can be easily traced to his Parisian sojourn of 1889–90. Paris inspired him to turn out a novel notable for its hero, " a young painter who, after eating red salmon in green sauce, is pursued by these colours." In addition, there are "symphonies of purple perfumes" and "blue vampires" to exorcise the spell of dull old naturalism. After Paris he preached the new faith for a while in Berlin and then traveled in Russia.[35] His revolt was paralleled by the emergence of Stefan George and his coterie from seclusion in 1892, with the first issue of *Blätter für die Kunst* (Pages on Art). George arrogantly dismissed contemporary writing as vulgar or cheap and called for a return to beautiful form as the basis of ideas and action. In the years to come George would continue to show his basic contempt for the masses' power of understanding by punctuating as he pleased, by some willful changes in grammar, and by an obsession for obscure foreign words.[36]

One of the most striking contributions in this first issue of the new journal was a lyrical drama, *Der Tod des Tizian,* by the eighteen-year-old Hugo von Hofmannsthal, whose father was of Jewish stock and whose mother was of Italian Catholic origin. Titian's last great struggle to finish a picture was treated with beauty and poignancy, but the young author's gentle melancholy and softness were prophetic of the tendencies which would triumph on the Viennese scene. In the following year Hofmannsthal eagerly greeted a sympathetic brother in literature when he apostrophized Arthur Schnitzler's collection of dialogues entitled *Anatol.* Schnitzler's Anatol was the elegant and charming epicurean who devoted most of his time to chasing females and who never believed in drastic solutions for anything. Anatol was simply the Viennese gentleman who frankly realized that one could not combat what was palpably in the air of Vienna. Hofmannsthal's greeting was symbolic of what he and Schnitzler basically were to achieve—"pieces of

our very own, precocious, tender, and melancholy, the comedy
of our own souls, our emotions with their today and yesterday,
ugly things reduced to pretty formulas, polished words, gay-
coloured pictures, pure and reticent emotion, agonies and
episodes. . . ." [37]

By 1897 Bahr had taken up residence in Vienna and was
proclaiming a new artistic epoch whose chief heroes were
Schnitzler and Hofmannsthal. Those who clustered about Bahr
to listen loyally were generically known as "Jung Wien"
("Young Vienna"), a term which was also applied to his literary
idols on occasion. Between productions of popular and problem
plays Bahr led quite a literary pack at the Café Griensteidl,
while another impressionist, Peter Altenberg, wandered from
one café to another collecting memories of the city. With his
large horn-rimmed glasses and drooping mustaches, this half-
buffoon, half-prophet turned up at cabarets, houses of pleasure,
and cheap obscene shows with a motley following of bums and
whores, preaching to everyone that the only perversion that
existed was an individual's weakening or diminishing of his life's
energies. He would turn abruptly to young gentlemen who had
just picked up, for a price yet to be paid, the girls of their
fancy and beg them to spare the poor creatures the full blasts
of their lust. The astonished sensualists thought him crazy, but
at least they changed their coarse tone with their companions.
Altenberg was the aphorist of the Vienna group, and he lives
today chiefly as another symbol of the quiet melancholy and
intermittent enthusiasms of his contemporaries.[38]

The imagination is delighted by the possibility that Hitler
with his youthful severity might once or twice have come upon
Altenberg and his unorthodox crew. Again, only imagination
can be appealed to, but it is more than probable that Altenberg
was well acquainted with types similar to Hitler. The vagrants
of the flophouses were his honored companions; his Jewishness
did not seemingly drive them away.

As stated earlier, there is no compelling reason to believe that
Hitler read anything of importance by Bahr, Schnitzler, Hofmannsthal, Altenberg, or Beer-Hofmann while in Vienna.

Nevertheless, it seems valuable to offer here a brief survey of the works produced by such men between 1907 and 1913, for Hitler at least developed certain fixed ideas about general literary activities during that time. First, he asserted that the Jews had a near monopoly of literary productivity; one agrees that Schnitzler, Altenberg, and Beer-Hofmann actually were of Jewish background, while Hofmannsthal had a Jewish sire. Secondly, the books and plays being written were, in his opinion, "awful," "unclean," "trashy," and "obscene." It would be foolish to argue that Hitler was alone in applying such adjectives to the perceptions and observations of the literary world of Vienna. Sometimes it seemed to many that decay was being worshiped for its own sake. That there was a connection between the Jewishness of some of the authors and the obscenity or poorness of the literary production is quite another issue to the "usual" man of education or good sense. It is the tragedy of the Jews in this century that such "usual" men can be heartbreakingly hard to find even in the most literate of nations.

Hugo von Hofmannsthal secured a world-wide audience with the works he produced between 1907 and 1913, though one wonders if this would have been possible without his profitable association with Richard Strauss, the eminently newsworthy composer. In the year that Hitler settled in Vienna Hofmannsthal published his collected poems (*Gesammelte Gedichte*) to show once again his mastery of poetic craftsmanship and his gifts for evoking tender sorrow and lovely color imagery. Next, in 1908, came a less satisfactory creation, the comedy *Christinas Heimreise*, which had atmosphere but inferior characterization. Though dating back to 1904, Hofmannsthal's *Elektra* received a new lease on life in 1909 in its Straussian musical version. To conventional persons the frenzies and the gyrations of the repressed heroine plus the unconstrained physical readiness of her normal sister were shocking even when Strauss incongruously but effectively used a waltz rhythm for poor Elektra's bloodthirsty triumph. With Hofmannsthal Greece became entangled with Freud, not a rare occurrence in German literature after 1900. In 1911 Hofmannsthal supplied Strauss with *Der Rosenkavalier* and Max Reinhardt with a variously received and appreciated version of the old *Everyman* morality play. *Der Rosenkavalier* aroused a few outraged sniffs because of its first-act bedroom scene and obvious moral neutrality, but discreet stage direction and gradual appreciation of the musical values of Strauss's score guaranteed the work a remarkably popular future. Even the person who knows next to nothing about Hofmannsthal usually remembers that he was responsible for the "libretto" of *Der Rosenkavalier*.[39]

Hermann Bahr was even more busy, if less permanently effective, in producing dramas in the period under scrutiny. He was adept at satirizing the assumed infallibility of theatrical producers (*Die gelbe Nachtigall*, 1907), and he did not even shrink from treating a possibly incestuous theme with the comic relief one could never expect from his more serious colleagues (*Die Kinder*, 1910). In 1910 as well he secured a solid success with the farce *Das Konzert*, a witty description of a virtuoso pestered by overamorous students and beautifully understood by a sophisticated Viennese wife. *Das Prinzip*, in 1912, was a sly dig at doctrinaire reformers who are forced by their convictions to grant their children the necessary conclusions of such convictions. Bahr also produced novels during the period, playing particular havoc with sensibilities in describing in *Die Rahl* (1908) how "a famous actress whose identity was guessed relieves a Jew grammar-school boy in one night of love of his virginity." [40]

Arthur Schnitzler would have been expected to write similar farcical material a decade earlier, though from the beginning his characters' smiles always masked possible bitterness underneath. In the years just prior to the outbreak of war Schnitzler seemed to be striving for greater seriousness. At times he actually deserted his gallant officers and their enchantingly complaisant girls for "problems." In November, 1907, as Hitler came into Vienna, Schnitzler was finally completing a novel whose lineaments had kept him anguished and sweating for a decade, *Der Weg ins Freie*. Mechanically it has never been a satisfactory example of his true talents, for it sprawls awkwardly and tediously. Historically it is of great interest, for Schnitzler here attempted to wrestle, as a sensitive Jew, with antisemitism and Zionism. He had known Herzl and had sympathy for the idea of a homeland for the Jews, but, as Sol Liptzin unerringly points out, Vienna was Schnitzler's beloved home. At the same time Schnitzler made clear his conviction that Jews were second-class citizens everywhere and that they were consequently extremely sensitive to any misbehavior of their coreligionists. Assimilation would come only in the far distant future; meanwhile Schnitzler said through his chief character, "The roads to freedom do not run through the lands out yonder, but rather through our inner selves."

While mulling over the recasting of another work which dealt with Jews and their problems in Austrian society, Schnitzler relaxed a bit with the production of *Der junge Medardus*, an historical spectacle whose melodramatic duels and death pacts were not taken seriously by anyone. A year later the public took passing pleasure in a "society" drama, *Das weite Land*, in which Schnitzler treated of fidelity and infidelity to the marriage vows. In 1912 he again abandoned the light touch for a round with the question of the day with the appearance of *Professor Bernhardi*, one of his truly important achievements. The story was drastically unlike the bittersweet romances of the past. A girl is about to die of blood poisoning brought on by an abortion. The hospital which has taken her in is directed by a Jew, Professor Bernhardi. He notices that she has entered into a psychic state of unbelievable felicity, a not uncommon happening among the moribund. A Catholic nurse, aware of the real situation, has summoned a priest to administer extreme unction, and Bernhardi, after persuasion fails, orders the priest not to enter the patient's room and thereby break the spell of her happiness. A scandal is the inevitable consequence, a scandal that reaches right into parliament. Bernhardi resigns his post and is sentenced to two months in jail, refusing all efforts made in his behalf by professional liberals or by politicians who wish to capitalize on a shift in public opinion.

Professor Bernhardi in Schnitzler's hands is as much the honest

physician as he is the misunderstood Jew. The drama does not
stress so much the unhappy position of the Jews as it does the
chances they run of creating seemingly unimportant incidents
which Christians will pounce upon. The author seemed to tell
his Jewish compatriots that they cannot expect full comprehension and tolerance, but, as always, they must be true to their
inner selves. A young Viennese who undoubtedly scorned the
very idea of seeing *Professor Bernhardi* would teach the Jews
two decades later that they could expect no comprehension and
no tolerance. Without Hitler, Herzl's Zionism probably would
have been a passing phenomenon, to which a "Schnitzler special-
ist" might devote a few paragraphs.[41]

Were Hitler's adjectives condemning Viennese literary activity just and perceptive? Bahr was probably "trashy" on occasion, and Schnitzler would be "awful" in attempting to fuse
several plots in one composition. What is "unclean" and "obscene" in literature puzzles the best of pundits and judges,
though there can be no doubt that many of Hitler's fellows in
Vienna were outraged by what they read, saw, or *heard about*
in theatrical and literary affairs. Incest was not a joke to all
Viennese, marital infidelity was not always an occasion for a
shrug of the shoulders, and seduction of the innocent was no
longer considered the prerogative of the renowned. Today one
pays little attention to the "obscenity" of the men who were
writing in young Hitler's Vienna. Their work may be called
precious, inflated, overrefined, brittle, or superficial. Their
themes have long been surpassed in salaciousness by our contemporaries. Hitler, nevertheless, chose to believe in their absolute decadence and blamed that decadence on Jewishness; this
is the political importance of the Viennese literary scene before
1914.

Critics who pounced upon the sexual innuendo of any of the
Viennese literary productions were likely to be the same persons
who viewed with alarm the gradual recognition of Sigmund
Freud as a stimulating commentator upon humanity's behavior.
Freud's great biographer, Ernest Jones, delimits the years 1906–9
as the beginning of Freud's international fame, and he skillfully

describes the great doctor's reactions to the Vienna which held him at arm's length for so long a time. As a Jew who personally abstained from religious observances, the most famous practitioner of psychoanalysis was particularly embittered by the antisemitism of the day and made no bones of his hatred for the city of Vienna. He voted Liberal rather than Christian Socialist or Social Democrat, and some of his happier moments were identified with meetings of B'nai B'rith. In time he concluded that castration fears were the deepest roots of antisemitism, thanks to the Jewish tradition of circumcision.[42]

Hitler's account of his years in Vienna, if it tells practically nothing of his reaction to individual literary pieces and ignores the very existence of Freud, is a bit more illuminating in describing his "passion for architecture." He states that in 1909–10 his escape from unskilled tasks enabled him to work as a "modest draftsman"; he worked far into the night on his drawings, convinced that some day he would be a famous architect.[43] But his contempt for the Habsburg state grew, as did his belief that its culture was debilitated and unimportant for Germandom. "This was true most of all in the field of architecture. The new architecture could not be successful in Austria for the reason that since the completion of the Ringstrasse the commissions were unimportant, at least as far as Vienna was concerned, as compared with the increasing plans of Germany." [44]

The completion of the Ringstrasse was indeed a labor of such proportions that it would not have been unintelligent to anticipate a subsequent period of inactivity or dull repetition. To an unfortunate degree it was difficult for the new generation of architects to secure the commissions they needed after 1900, but only a person of Hitler's limited artistic imagination would find it possible to discern debility and unimportance in the vision of those young men who did so much to modernize architectural ideals in Vienna at the turn of the century. Did Hitler, the frustrated architect, follow with any sympathy the struggles of these iconoclasts of his youthful days? In a conversation of January, 1942, Hitler spoke feelingly of the hypersensitivity and talent of Hansen and Hasenauer, two men identified with the Ringstrasse edifices.[45] Who can doubt that their patent borrowings from the past pleased both the young and the mature Hitler far more than the experimentations of his contemporaries?

Yet it is not fair to imply that the concept of a Ringstrasse, a continuous avenue girdling the old medieval Vienna, was purely retrogressive in planning and completion. If a Baron Haussmann deserves credit for accommodating the magnificent heritage of Paris to the new industrial age by his engineering transformations, Francis Joseph and his experts also merit praise for their attempt to link the crowded old city with the more spacious suburbs. Before 1858 the Viennese were separated from these suburbs by a system of ramparts and moats known as the *Glacis-Gründe*, which was pierced at intervals by gateways and bridges that probably would not have surprised Richard the Lion-Heart's captors centuries earlier. To get a bit of fresh air during the warm season, the burghers and their families betook themselves to the summits of the ramparts, which were agreeably wide. Within the city proper, meanwhile, there was constant pressure placed upon the government to make room somehow for the developing offices of the bureaucracy and of the businessmen.[46]

Very late in 1857 imperial consent was secured for the destruction of the *Glacis-Gründe*, and in its place was planned the famous Ringstrasse, 150 feet wide (and so more spacious than the Parisian boulevards), with adequate room for a galaxy of new buildings. Seven men were identified with the planning of the most famous of the structures. For Hitler, the most richly gifted of the group was Theophilus Hansen, who "brought Athens to Vienna." His masterpiece was the Parliament Building, with its colossal pillars of red marble and walls of black and white marble. He also was responsible for the Greek-columned Bourse, the Musikvereinssaal, just off the Ring, the Lombardian Renaissance Academy of Fine Arts, and the Heinrichshof, a beautifully proportioned mansion opposite the Opera House. The new Rathaus, or City Hall, was delegated to Friedrich Schmidt, an adept in the Gothic style. Despite protests from the public, who wanted an edifice of Charles VI's baroque period, Schmidt persisted in a chilly Italianate Gothic style that was climaxed by a great tower 300 feet high. On the site of the ill-fated Ring Theater he was entrusted with planning the Franz-Josef Foundation, where he again played variations on a Gothic theme.

It was somewhat ironic that Schmidt lost out to H. V. Ferstel in the contest for the Votive Church, the largest of Viennese Gothic buildings. Ferstel also won the right to design the new University, which, with Schmidt's City Hall and Hansen's Parliament Building, dominated the incomparable Franzensring. He had been a member of the jury which considered the extension of the city, and his study of the colleges at Oxford supposedly influenced his winning sketches. The Austrian Museum for Art and Industry, inspired by the Italian Renaissance, also was his work. The Hofburg Theater and the Imperial Museums, also Renaissance in mood, were created by a team of architects, Semper and Hasenauer. The first building mentioned caused a mild stir in that its auditorium was shaped like a lyre. Here, one guesses, was touching tribute to the Greeks, but little comfort for the customers in the fourth gallery, who could not hear the lines. Eventually the less affluent patrons were pacified by a structural reformation. Hasenauer's superb stone stairways in the two museums and in the Hofburg Theater, however, won the unstinted applause of the Viennese from the beginning. Least appreciated of all of the Ringstrasse architects were Van der Nüll and Sicardsburg, whose French Renaissance Imperial Opera House was still "marvelously beautiful" to Hitler in 1942, though he cruelly gave credit for its beauty to Hasenauer. Their innate conservatism also was exhibited in the Sofiensaal, where one might hear a speech by Schönerer or a waltz by Johann Strauss.[47]

There is almost universal agreement that the Ringstrasse delighted and charmed the vast majority of the Viennese and the tourists who came to gape. Hitler was expressing a normal reaction in confessing that "the entire Ringstrasse affected me like a fairy tale out of the *Arabian Nights.*" [48] Less impression-

able observers of our day are likely at best to speak of the
Ring as "a shining circlet studded with semi-precious stones," [49]
or "a gorgeous chain of individual buildings entirely or almost
entirely unrelated to each other." [50] To a small minority of
sensitive artists in the 1890s the buildings on the Ring were
insolently guilty of two of the cardinal sins of the day. Their
architects not only steeped themselves in outworn ancient,
medieval, or Renaissance models; they also worshiped ornamentation for its own sake.

The leader of revolt against the traditional canons was Otto
Wagner, who was made professor of architecture at the Academy of Fine Arts in Vienna in 1894 because of his solid
reputation as a re-creator of Renaissance styles.[51] His inaugural
lecture warned of the necessity of harmonizing art forms with
the requirements of modern life, and he point-blank declared
that "nothing that is not practical can be beautiful." Like his
American contemporary, Frank Lloyd Wright, Wagner was
intensely interested in the machine and the consequences it
would have on the older ideas of design and ornamentation. He
sarcastically dismissed the possibility of winning official and
popular approval for his progressive notions, and it was not long
before he was called "a sensation-monger, a train-bearer of
fashion." Assigned the task of planning the Stadtbahn, the
metropolitan railway system which encircled the outskirts of
the city, Wagner revealed some of his new tendencies in designing the stations, particularly the one on the Karlsplatz (1894).
His ironwork and roof here were logical developments of his
century, but his outer walls were treated in most unorthodox
manner. They were thin marble slabs, simply secured and
carrying no load. A year later his *Moderne Architektur* spoke of
a future style which would stress "great simplicity and an
energetic exhibition of construction and materials."

A decade later Wagner was forcing real screams from Viennese conservatives with his extraordinary Postal Savings Building, right on the Ringstrasse. Sigfried Giedion calls its interior
"without doubt one of the most uncompromising rooms of the
first years of the twentieth century," with its "astonishing purity

of design." In this inspiration Wagner again treated the wall as a plane surface, used aluminum bolts to secure his marble slabs, and provided the interior with severely beautiful glass and iron vaulting. Poor Wagner attracted too much controversy with this simplified and rationalized structure, and his later career was restricted for the most part to drafting projects that were never accepted. He was especially concerned with problems of city planning and traffic regulation, for he vehemently denounced the expansion of the big city at the hands of "blind chance" and "detestable usury." If personally unable to force a wholehearted response from the state or public, Wagner at any rate did inspire talented followers or supporters in the architectural guild.

One of his most famous students was Josef Maria Olbrich,[52] who played a leading part in the formation of the Vienna *Sezession* in April, 1897.[53] This "secession" was the withdrawal of nineteen young artists from the Academy of Fine Arts, which they felt was completely out of step with the needs of their generation. These young artists revealed a degree of affinity with the faddish *l'Art Nouveau*, which stressed curves rather than straight lines and valued a bulge rather than a straight wall in the façade of a building. They also were influenced by Charles Rennie Mackintosh, a Glasgow designer who offered "lines of hesitant elegance" and "verticals everywhere." Gustav Klimt was their actual president, and he was already creating exotic figures with slender graceful lines that would finally eventuate in the lush and mannered ceiling paintings for the University. To secure a fitting place for exhibiting the works of such men as Rodin, Whistler, and Mackintosh, the *Sezession* group decided to build a haven all of their own. Olbrich was commissioned as architect, and by 1899 the women of the Naschmarkt were humorously talking of the "golden head of cabbage" which surmounted the structure. This metal cupola with its frizzled leaves was apt to blind conservative and radical alike in their estimate of the worth of the rest of Olbrich's design. The front view was boldly worked out in terms of three blocks that did true justice to Wagner's ideas on simplicity, even if the market women were aesthetically astute in deriding the needless ornamentation of the gilded ball on top. Olbrich's mature work, save for some villas in Hietzing, was done in Germany, where he seemingly escaped the worst of the *Sezession* stylistic affectations and developed a substantial feeling for structural qualities. Americans had a good chance to measure his merits in 1904, when he created the German pavilion at the St. Louis Exposition. Olbrich died at the comparatively early age of forty-one in 1908, leaving to Wagner's other great student, Josef Hoffmann, the duty of carrying on the revolt.[54]

Hoffmann's first great work paradoxically was his most uncompromisingly functional work. Twelve kilometers from Vienna, in the Wienerwald country, he completed at Purkersdorf in 1904 a Convalescent Home of astonishing modernity. Here were completely flat roofs, windows without moldings, and that true harbinger of things to come, the high, upright staircase window. A year later Hoffmann was designing a mansion for M. Stoclet in Brussels that was more in tune with the elegant fancy of the *Sezession*. There was a high staircase window, to be sure, and much reliance on square forms, but the edges of the latter were emphasized by black beading in the *Sezession* manner, and the general impression was one of chic comfort, even warmth. Hoffmann went on to design equally smart pavilions and buildings for his country's exhibits at international expositions, and he always was careful to balance the monumental with the decorative. His name was globally famous for perfect adjustments and sophisticated proportioning, and his great standing in Austria itself was a formidable rebuttal of Hitler's opinion that the new architecture could not be successful there.

Hoffmann's expert adaptation of the best of Wagner and of the *Sezession* tended to hide almost completely the work and thought of the fourth great Austrian architect of the period, Adolf Loos, a Viennese who had been trained in Germany and in the United States.[55] Returning to Vienna in 1896, Loos was happy to find that Wagner's *Moderne Architektur* coincided with many of his own dicta, but then he was shocked by the wide notoriety achieved by the *Sezession*. To him, the rebels were merely exchanging the futility of dull academic routine for an equally sterile exercise in aimless ornamentation. In articles appearing in the press in 1897–98 he bewailed the manufacture of showy articles which had no basic utility and generally proclaimed himself a believer in the purely functional. Culture, he insisted, now came from the engineers; the plumber was its quartermaster.

Loos found it difficult to get commissions bigger than the decoration of shops and private homes for some time. In these endeavors he distinguished himself by choice of materials and by rigid exclusion of fussy detail. In 1910 he built the Steiner house in Vienna, which ranks with Hoffmann's Convalescent Home in its amazing prefiguration of future styles. Pevsner particularly stresses Loos's "unmitigated contrast of receding center and projecting wings, the unbroken line of the roofs, the small openings in the attic, the horizontal windows with their large undivided panes." A few advanced souls appreciated Loos's house and the direction in which he was headed, but Hoffmann was the apparent success. In 1913 Paul Stefan eloquently lamented the destruction of many of the homes of the Inner City and their replacement by frightfully ugly and uncomfortable edifices. He regretted that the baleful influence of a benighted city father kept the Municipal Board of Public Works from commissioning new works similar to Loos's house.[56] Lethargy and active hostility did indeed play havoc with utilization of Loos's brilliance, but it is noteworthy that the German Empire had not reversed Austria's neglect of "one of the greatest creators in modern architecture." The new architecture had to battle for its creeds everywhere, and Hitler was unfair in attributing to Austria a particular lack of appreciation for the novel modes.

The Vagabond's Return

ON March 12, 1938, Vienna was occupied by the German Army as a result of the failure of the British, French, or Italians to aid Schuschnigg in his country's hour of travail. On the afternoon of the fateful day, Hitler himself drove into Braunau, where he had been born, and subsequently was heartily welcomed in Linz by his most famous fifth columnist in Austria, Dr. Seyss-Inquart. Next morning he visited his parents' graveyard in Leonding and started on a triumphal progress to Vienna. Swastikas and the rest of the Nazi paraphernalia celebrated his coming, and Vienna accorded him a welcome that he recalled with great pleasure and some embarrassment in later years. The "Heils" predicted by Schönerer echoed resoundingly up and down the Ringstrasse, while from the beloved spire of St. Stephen's floated the swastika, emblem of the triumph of the vagabond turned folk-hero.

It is not difficult to imagine the previously ignored conqueror's thoughts. Did the moth-eaten Habsburgs ever receive such hysterical screams of approval from the mob? Did Lueger at the top of his form really comprehend the ease with which a master could control the crowd? Did Schönerer with his sophomores and perfect Wagnerites have any inkling of the way a once-inconsequential nobody could accomplish the sacred *Anschluss?* Had Adler, dying in the debris of November, 1918, perceived ever so faintly that the claims of "blood" would triumph over his eminently logical and stunningly dull theories of human betterment? Did the Jews still believe that antisemitism was merely a constant but ineffectual part of the

Austrian scene? Let them pay the penalty of their complacency and their greed in trying to monopolize the products of German inspiration. It would be just retribution to begin with Freud, that pernicious old man with the nasty notions, but foreign opinion could not be completely flouted for a while yet. Were there fools about who cherished dreams of Otto of Habsburg's coronation—a return to the "good old days" when a real folk-genius nearly starved in the gutters? Let them be driven into the dust, to join their idols in the Capuchin Crypt.

No hero, leader, or dictator of the first half of this century was ever so marked and molded by a modern city as was Hitler. His youthful dreams of glorious achievement in artistic creativity dissolved with the cold rejection of his talents and credentials by the gentlemen of the Academy. His pride in his "race" was challenged by dull Socialist clods who seemed to have no aversion to being part of a faceless mob which they called the proletariat. The possible admiration he might have had for the Habsburgs and their empire was poisoned by his conviction that they prostituted German interests for the sake of Slavs and Magyars, using parliaments to mask their callousness. The cultural promise of Vienna was to him no more than a mélange of whimpering Jewish obscenities and internationalist dry rot. Lueger and Schönerer were for Hitler the only vital men on the scene, but the former actually misunderstood the Jewish "menace" and failed to work for the holy German race, while the latter forgot his earthy ancestry and cut himself off from the pulsating masses.

Vienna was the most international of the great European cities in the decade before Sarajevo, and the collision of its worldly and somewhat tired culture with the mounting insecurity young Hitler felt was of enormous portent for the future. The Habsburgs had explicitly represented the ancient system of disparate lands linked only by a common master, and for some generations their approach to the problems of dominion had been German, save for dynastic ties with other states and for the inevitable conditioning that derived from loyalty to Rome. The nineteenth century brutally disarrayed these preconceptions, so that the Austria and Vienna of Hitler's early years were alive with challenge and questioning.

In Metternich's quieter day migrants in moderate numbers came in to minister to the needs of Biedermeier society in Vienna, but by 1890 the rapid industrialization and extension of transportation made Vienna the true hub of a most heterogeneous empire. The Viennese of 1890 who manifested neither shame nor particular elation over a Croatian grandmother or an Italian grandfather was beginning to resent the flood of new dwellers who admittedly were needed to take care of the new burdens, while economic depressions and the housing shortage added to his tensions.

After 1867 German Liberalism had deified a maximum of economic freedom, including the right of the individual to move about as he pleased. While speaking much of the brotherhood of man, German Liberalism paradoxically attempted to perpetuate the German control of Austria, often with language and actions that were the acme of self-righteousness. In the confusion of opinion which marked the apogee of German Liberalism and its period of grumbling opposition, three major tendencies contended for the support of the new voters or for the old voters who had lost faith with the doctrines of Liberalism.

The Pan-Germans at first wanted to revamp the empire or even to cast part of it adrift, virtually, in order to maintain German supremacy. Later they were ostensibly willing to solve the future of German Austria by joining the Hohenzollern Empire and by espousing Lutheranism. The Christian Socialists appealed to the squeezed little man, whether peasant, artisan, or tradesman, simultaneously calling for a return to decency in family life. The Marxian Social Democrats, moving slowly but steadily to a position of impressive strength, predicted the wonders of the classless society as they paused momentarily to debate hours, wages, and the problems of national self-determination.

Any young German Austrian of average intelligence would have been interested in 1907 by the choices offered, and Hitler,

with unending time to read the newspapers of the day, evinced interest in the ideas or techniques of all three parties. One had the right idea about blood and "race," the second knew how to uphold the virtues of old, while the third, even if utterly damned by a faulty analysis of human drives, had learned much of the art of propagandizing the masses.

Hitler selected the strands he wanted for the future and gradually evolved while in Vienna the fundamental principles of National Socialism. Bumping into Czechs, Italians, and Slovenes intensified his devotion to Germandom. Reading the stereotyped denunciations of Jews and the "Jewish spirit" seemed to offer an explanation of his own footless existence. The sight of well-disciplined Christian Social meetings or of the Social Democrats marching with pride along the Ringstrasse on May Day excited his dreams of the regimented *Volk* of the future. The tonal splendors of the Wagnerian music-dramas, whose very creation rivaled in time the coming of the Second Reich, offered proof of the endless fecundity of the German genius. The stink of the creatures who haunted the charitable establishments and the gloom of the tenements in which the workers swarmed and bred roused in his mind an understandable passion for a better society.

Somehow the principles he worked out suffered moral ship-wreck. In reacting violently against international Vienna and the Habsburgs, who seemed so cold and remote in the sprawling Hofburg, he developed a contempt for non-Germans which was limited only by his ambivalent appreciation of what they were doing to destroy the empire. If Czechs and Slovenes gained his contempt, the Jews became the object of his searing hatred. To him, they contaminated German culture, they exploited the worthy but helpless Germans of Austria, and they plotted a Marxist commonwealth to complete their vengeance upon "Aryans." Hunger and misery, though the result of Hitler's own shiftlessness and quirks of temperament, intensified the gro-tesqueness of his fearful analysis and energized the fanaticism which he would demonstrate consistently in the future.

Out of the complex of the experiences in Vienna emerged

the world-shaker of the post-Versailles generation. His ideas, such as they were, were fixed before the war came, though the techniques of propagation were perfected only with time. The generation of middle-class Germans which was dazed by inflation and worried by Communism after 1919 did not succumb to his poisons until the capitalistic world reeled under the impact of the depression of 1929. Then, at last, the mesmerizing mannerisms and the keening note came into their own. What had been learned in Vienna and sharpened by war and by a thousand false starts in postwar Germany exerted its evil attraction. The frantic middle class found a hero whose apprenticeship went back many years.

"Vienna was and remained for me the hardest, but also the most thorough, school of my life."

Notes

INTRODUCTION

1. The quotation appears in Peter Gay, *The Dilemma of Democratic Socialism* (New York, 1952), p. 203. It is evidently a translation from Eduard Bernstein, *Die Voraussetzungen des Sozialismus und die Aufgaben der Sozialdemokratie* (Stuttgart, 1920).

VOICES OF SPRING: VIENNA, *1906*

1. August Kubizek, *The Young Hitler I Knew*, trans. E. V. Anderson (Boston, 1955), p. 102.
2. Konrad Heiden, *Der Fuehrer*, trans. Ralph Manheim (Boston, 1944), pp. 44–52; Kubizek, *The Young Hitler I Knew*, pp. 8–55. Franz Jetzinger, *Hitlers Jugend* (Vienna, 1956), pp. 304–5, asserts that Hitler left the Steyr Realschule for good in June, 1905.
3. Kubizek, *The Young Hitler I Knew*, pp. 103, 111.
4. The programs of the Imperial Opera are kept in the *Musik-sammlung* of the Austrian National Library in Vienna.
5. Albert Zoller, *Hitler Privat* (Düsseldorf, 1949), p. 58.
6. Kubizek, *The Young Hitler I Knew*, p. 105.
7. As drawn from the issues of the *Neue Freie Presse* of May and June, 1906.

"THE MOST MISERABLE TIME OF MY LIFE"

1. August Kubizek, *The Young Hitler I Knew*, trans. E. V. Anderson (Boston, 1955), p. 111.
2. *Mein Kampf*, p. 27. All quotations from *Mein Kampf* are taken from the English edition published by Reynal and Hitchcock and Houghton Mifflin Company, New York, 1939.

3. Kubizek, *The Young Hitler I Knew*, pp. 143–49; Walter Görlitz and Herbert A. Quint, *Adolf Hitler* (Stuttgart, 1952), p. 44.
4. Josef Greiner, *Das Ende des Hitler-Mythos* (Zurich, Leipzig, and Vienna, 1947), pp. 9–30.
5. *Männerheim (Wien XX. Bezirk, Meldemannstrasse Nr. 27)* (Vienna, 1905).
6. Emil Kläger, *Durch die Wiener Quartiere des Elends und Verbrechens* (Vienna, 1908).
7. The kreuzer was worth one-half an American cent of the period.
8. Kläger, *Durch die Wiener Quartiere*, pp. 75–78.
9. Greiner, *Das Ende des Hitler-Mythos*, pp. 13–14.
10. *Ibid.*, pp. 20–22.   11. *Ibid.*, p. 30.
12. *Ibid.*, pp. 110–11; Franz Jetzinger, *Hitlers Jugend* (Vienna, 1956), p. 224.
13. Greiner, *Das Ende des Hitler-Mythos*, p. 16.
14. *Ibid.*, p. 11; Görlitz and Quint, *Adolf Hitler*, p. 49.
15. *Die Wohltätigkeits-Vereine der k.k. Reichshaupt- und Residenzstadt Wien*, 2d ed. (Vienna, 1905), p. 383; *Statistisches Jahrbuch der Stadt Wien für das Jahr 1911* (Vienna, 1913), p. 886.
16. Raimund Fürlinger, *Obdachlosigkeit und Obdachlosen-Fürsorge* (Vienna, 1916), p. 4.
17. *Wohltätigkeits-Vereine*, p. 397.
18. Kläger, *Durch die Wiener Quartiere*, p. 31.
19. *Wohltätigkeits-Vereine*, p. 398.
20. Kläger, *Durch die Wiener Quartiere*, p. 96.
21. Max Winter, *Im dunkelsten Wien* (Vienna and Leipzig, 1904), pp. 33–34.
22. Hermann Drawe, *Unter Vagabunden* (Vienna, 1910), pp. 27–40.
23. Kläger, *Durch die Wiener Quartiere*, pp. 146–55.
24. *Ibid.*, pp. 43–68.
25. Greiner, *Das Ende des Hitler-Mythos*, p. 111.
26. *Mein Kampf*, p. 33.
27. Heinrich Goldemund, *Die Wiener Wohnungs-Verhältnisse und Vorschläge zur Verbesserung derselben* (Vienna, 1910), pp. 4–7, 15, 23; Friedrich Funder, *Vom Gestern ins Heute*, 2d ed. (Vienna, 1953), pp. 257–58.
28. Reinhard E. Petermann, *Wien im Zeitalter Kaiser Franz Josephs I* (Vienna, 1908), pp. 141, 144, 147.

29. M. Willfort, *Zur Wohnungsnot in Wien* (Vienna, 1911), pp. 5–6.
30. *Mein Kampf*. p. 38.

LUEGER AND THE COMMON MAN

1. *Mein Kampf* (New York, 1939), pp. 128, 158.
2. The most valuable works on Lueger are: Rudolf Kuppe, *Karl Lueger und seine Zeit* (Vienna, 1933) and *Dr. Karl Lueger: Persönlichkeit und Wirken* (Vienna, 1947); Kurt Skalnik, *Dr. Karl Lueger: Der Mann zwischen den Zeiten* (Vienna and Munich, 1954).
3. For Lueger's early political activities, see Hugo Hantsch, *Die Geschichte Österreichs* (Graz and Vienna, n.d.), II, 411–12.
4. The gulden was worth 48.2 cents.
5. Arthur J. May, *The Hapsburg Monarchy* (Cambridge, Mass., 1951), pp. 223–24; Hantsch, *Die Geschichte Österreichs*, II, 440–41.
6. For Vogelsang, see Joseph Schwalber, *Vogelsang und die moderne christlich-soziale Politik* (Munich, 1927); Joh. Christoph Allmayer-Beck, *Vogelsang: Vom Feudalismus zur Volksbewegung* (Vienna, 1952); Wiard Klopp, *Die sozialen Lehren des Freiherrn Karl von Vogelsang* (St. Pölten, 1894), a selection of Vogelsang's writings; Hans Rizzi, "Karl von Vogelsang," *Neue österreichische Biographie, 1815–1918* (Vienna, 1923–35), II, 186–95.
7. See below, pp. 133–36.
8. Richard Charmatz, *Lebensbilder aus der Geschichte Oesterreichs* (Vienna, c.1947), pp. 114–16; Francesco S. Nitti, *Catholic Socialism* (London, 1908), pp. 202–15.
9. Schwalber, *Vogelsang*, pp. 51–52.
10. Hantsch, *Die Geschichte Österreichs*, II, 444–45.
11. Friedrich Funder, *Vom Gestern ins Heute*, 2d ed. (Vienna, 1953), pp. 128–48.
12. Gustav Kolmer, *Parlament und Verfassung in Österreich* (Vienna and Leipzig, 1902–14), IV, 160.
13. Richard Charmatz, *Vom Kaiserreich zur Republik* (Vienna, c.1947), p. 88.
14. Kuppe, *Karl Lueger und seine Zeit*, pp. 207, 210–13, 215–17.
15. *Stenographische Protokolle über die Sitzungen des Hauses der*

Abgeordneten des Reichsrates, XVII Session, VII–VIII, 7044, Oct. 22, 1901. Hereafter references to the stenographic reports of the Lower House will be abbreviated *S.P.A.*, with the appropriate volume, pages, and date.

16. *S.P.A.*, X Session, VII, 7788–92, April 20, 1888.
17. *Ibid.*, XI Session, III, 2811, Oct. 30, 1891.
18. *Ibid.*, XI Session, VII, 7812, Nov. 5, 1892.
19. *Ibid.*, XI Session, XVIII, 22219, Dec. 18, 1895.
20. *Mein Kampf*, p. 158.
21. A typical speech of this tenor can be found in *S.P.A.*, XI Session, XI, 13180, April 18, 1894.
22. For the march to the mayoralty, see Kolmer, *Parlament und Verfassung*, VI, 37–46; Hantsch, *Die Geschichte Österreichs*, II, 458–59; Skalnik, *Dr. Karl Lueger*, pp. 86–113.
23. Kuppe, *Karl Lueger und seine Zeit*, p. 445.
24. *Ibid.*, pp. 448–51.   25. *Mein Kampf*, p. 129.
26. Maria Hornor Lansdale, *Vienna and the Viennese* (Philadelphia, 1902), p. 113.
27. For the best short account of Lueger's achievements for Vienna, see Kuppe, *Dr. Karl Lueger: Persönlichkeit und Wirken*, pp. 93–131.
28. Funder, *Vom Gestern ins Heute*, p. 451.
29. *Ibid.*, pp. 322–23, 331.   30. *Ibid.*, pp. 234–37.
31. *Ibid.*, pp. 267–70, 273.
32. Kuppe, *Karl Lueger und seine Zeit*, p. 472.
33. *S.P.A.*, XVII Session, XXI–XXII, 18334–35, Feb. 18, 1903.
34. Kuppe, *Karl Lueger und seine Zeit*, p. 515.
35. Otto Friedlaender, *Letzter Glanz der Märchenstadt* (Vienna, c.1949), p. 162.
36. Kuppe, *Karl Lueger und seine Zeit*, p. 517.
37. *Ibid.*, p. 518.   38. *Ibid.*, p. 519.
39. Felix Salten, *Das österreichische Antlitz* (Berlin, 1909), pp. 130–32.

"DEUTSCHLAND, DEUTSCHLAND ÜBER ALLES"

1. *Mein Kampf* (New York, 1939), pp. 124–25.
2. *Ibid.*, p. 126.
3. See Walter C. Langsam, *The Napoleonic Wars and German Nationalism in Austria* (New York, 1930); André Robert, *L'Idée*

Nationale Autrichienne et les Guerres de Napoléon (Paris, 1933).
4. Paul Molisch, *Politische Geschichte der deutschen Hochschulen in Österreich von 1848 bis 1918* (Vienna and Leipzig, 1939), pp. 32–37. Hereafter cited as *Hochschulen*.
5. Paul Molisch, *Geschichte der deutschnationalen Bewegung in Oesterreich* (Jena, 1926), pp. 63–64. Hereafter cited as *Bewegung*. Also Adam Wandruszka in *Geschichte der Republik Österreich*, ed. Heinrich Benedikt (Munich, 1954), pp. 370–74.
6. Molisch, *Bewegung*, pp. 70–73, 78–79.
7. *Ibid.*, pp. 80–85. 8. *Ibid.*, p. 86.
9. The most comprehensive study for Schönerer is Eduard Pichl, *Georg Schönerer* (Oldenburg and Berlin, 1939), a revision of his *Georg Schönerer und die Entwicklung des Alldeutschthums in der Ostmark* (Vienna, 1912–23). Equally favorable to Schönerer are Viktor Bibl, *Georg von Schönerer* (Leipzig, 1942); Erwin Mayer-Löwenschwerdt, *Schönerer, der Vorkämpfer* (Vienna and Leipzig, 1938); Fritz A. Neuschäfer, *Georg Ritter von Schönerer* (Hamburg, 1935); Heinrich Schnee, *Georg Ritter von Schönerer* (Reichenberg, 1943). Richard Charmatz, *Lebensbilder aus der Geschichte Oesterreichs* (Vienna, 1947), pp. 141–52, and Oscar Karbach, "The Founder of Modern Political Antisemitism: George von Schönerer," *Jewish Social Studies*, VII (1945), 3–30, offer much more balanced estimates. A thoroughly stimulating evaluation is offered by Wandruszka, *Geschichte*, pp. 289–97, 374–82.
10. For a lengthy survey of Schönerer's first term, see Pichl, *Georg Schönerer*, I, 27–81.
11. Speech of Feb. 21, 1876, reprinted in *ibid.*, III, 21–25.
12. Speech of Dec. 18, 1878, reprinted in *ibid.*, III, 45–47.
13. Speech of March 7, 1878, reprinted in abbreviated form in *ibid.*, III, 40–45.
14. *Ibid.*, II, 4. 15. *Ibid.*, I, 84–87.
16. Molisch, *Bewegung*, pp. 106–10.
17. For a survey of their parliamentary activities in 1879–85, see Pichl, *Georg Schönerer*, I, 119–250.
18. Text of Linz Program in Gustav Kolmer, *Parlament und Verfassung in Österreich* (Vienna and Leipzig, 1902–14), III, 212–14.
19. Pichl, *Georg Schönerer*, I, 162. 20. *Ibid.*, II, 59.
21. *Ibid.*, I, 228, 232. 22. *Ibid.*, I, 243. 23. *Ibid.*, I, 115.

24. R. A. Kann, "German-speaking Jewry during Austria-Hungary's Constitutional Era (1867–1918)," *Jewish Social Studies*, X (1948), 239–56.
25. Pichl, *Georg Schönerer*, I, 200–6.
26. *Ibid.*, I, 195–99.   27. *Ibid.*, I, 183–93.
28. For a summary of his parliamentary activities in 1885–88, see *ibid.*, I, 267–332.   29. *Ibid.*, I, 282.
30. Reprinted in *ibid.*, III, 332–51.
31. *Ibid.*, I, 321–25.   32. *Ibid.*, I, 189–92.
33. Molisch, *Bewegung*, pp. 135–40; Pichl, *Georg Schönerer*, II, 271–96.
34. Pichl, *Georg Schönerer*, II, 25–43.
35. *Ibid.*, II, 73–110.   36. *Ibid.*, II, 59–67.
37. Molisch, *Hochschulen*, pp. 101–5, 125–26.
38. Hermann Bahr, *Selbstbildnis* (Berlin, 1923), p. 143.
39. Pichl, *Georg Schönerer*, II, 379–85.
40. Verwaltungsarchiv (Staatsarchiv des Innern und der Justiz). Österreichische Ministerratsprotokolle, No. 35, April 16, 1885.
41. Pichl, *Georg Schönerer*, II, 434–85.
42. Molisch, *Bewegung*, pp. 176–79.
43. Margarete Jakob, "Das Deutsche Volksblatt und seine politische Geschichte in den Jahren 1889/99" (unpubl. diss., Vienna, 1937), pp. 17–23.
44. Pichl, *Georg Schönerer*, IV, 8.   45. *Ibid.*, IV, 87–94.
46. *Ibid.*, IV, 27–55.   47. *Ibid.*, IV, 113; V, 1.
48. Richard Charmatz, *Österreichs innere Geschichte von 1848 bis 1907* (Berlin, 1911), II, 106–17.
49. Pichl, *Georg Schönerer*, V, 41.   50. *Ibid.*, VI, 383–84.
51. *Ibid.*, VI, 385.   52. *Ibid.*, VI, 389.
53. Reichsrat speech of Nov. 5, 1898, *ibid.*, V, 60–61.
54. Reichsrat speech of March 23, 1898, *ibid.*, V, 47.
55. *Ibid.*, V, 63–64.   56. *Ibid.*, V, 74–75.   57. *Ibid.*, V, 372.
58. *Ibid.*, V, 367.   59. *Ibid.*, VI, 164–69.
60. For Schönerer's parliamentary activity in 1901–7, see *ibid.*, V, 123–227.   61. *Ibid.*, V, 133, 186, 196.
62. *Ibid.*, V, 187, 191–92.   63. *Ibid.*, V, 165–66.
64. William A. Jenks, *The Austrian Electoral Reform of 1907* (New York, 1950), pp. 179–87.
65. Pichl, *Georg Schönerer*, V, 236–45.   66. *Ibid.*, VI, 73–77.
67. *Mein Kampf*, p. 126.   68. *Ibid.*, pp. 129–53.

THE JEWS IN AUSTRIA

1. His identity was revealed by the *Neue Freie Presse*, June 19, 1882, p. 3.
2. Ludwig, Freiherr von Oppenheimer, *Austriaca* (Leipzig, 1882), pp. 187, 190–91, 195–96, 199, 202–4, 211, 220–21, 235, 242–44.
3. See below, pp. 133–36.
4. *Das Vaterland*, May 27, 1882; June 15, 1882.
5. *Neue Freie Presse, Morgenblatt*, April 6, 1882.
6. Leo Goldhammer, *Die Juden Wiens* (Vienna and Leipzig, 1927).
7. *Ibid.*, p. 9.
8. *Ibid.*, p. 10. Figures are taken from the census of 1910.
9. *Ibid.*, p. 18.   10. *Ibid.*, p. 25.
11. *Ibid.*, pp. 35, 37.   12. *Ibid.*, pp. 39–40.
13. *Ibid.*, pp. 41–43.   14. *Ibid.*, pp. 45–48.
15. *Mein Kampf* (New York, 1939), p. 78.
16. H. Montane, *Die Prostitution in Wien* (Hamburg, Leipzig, and Vienna, 1925).
17. August Kubizek, *The Young Hitler I Knew*, trans. E. V. Anderson (Boston, 1955), pp. 235–36.
18. Montane, *Die Prostitution in Wien*, pp. 60–74.
19. *Ibid.*, p. 78.   20. *Ibid.*, p. 92.
21. *Ibid.*, pp. 82–83.   22. *Ibid.*, p. 171.
23. Kubizek, *The Young Hitler I Knew*, p. 253.
24. *Mein Kampf*, pp. 67–71.
25. Margarete Jakob, "Das Deutsche Volksblatt und seine politische Geschichte in den Jahren 1889/99" (unpubl. diss., Vienna, 1937), p. 37.
26. *Deutsches Volksblatt, Morgenblatt*, Oct. 20, 1907. Future references always will refer to the *Morgenblatt*, or morning edition, unless otherwise stated.   27. *Ibid.*, Oct. 11, 1907.
28. *Ibid.*, Oct. 23, 1907.   29. *Ibid.*, Nov. 22, 1907.
30. *Ibid.*, Nov. 5, 1907.   31. *Ibid.*, *Abendblatt*.
32. *Ibid.*, Nov. 13, 1907.   33. *Ibid.*, Dec. 14, 1907.
34. *Ibid.*, Oct. 9, 1907.   35. *Ibid.*, Oct. 27, 1907.
36. *Ibid.*, Oct. 30, 1907.   37. *Ibid.*, Oct. 20, 1907.
38. *Ibid.*, Nov. 5, 1907.   39. *Ibid.*, Nov. 8, 1907.
40. Kurt Skalnik, *Dr. Karl Lueger: Der Mann zwischen den Zeiten* (Vienna and Munich, 1954), p. 149.   41. *Ibid.*, p. 156.

42. *Deutsches Volksblatt,* Nov. 23, 1907.

43. *Ibid.,* Dec. 3, 1907.   44. *Ibid.,* Oct. 19, 1907.

45. *Alldeutsches Tagblatt,* Oct. 20, 1907.

46. *Deutsches Volksblatt,* Nov. 27, 1907.

47. Josef Greiner, *Das Ende des Hitler-Mythos* (Zurich, Leipzig, and Vienna, 1947), pp. 70–71, argues that Hitler might well have been engaged as a chorus-boy by Karczag had he owned a tuxedo and other sartorial prerequisites.

48. *Deutsches Volksblatt,* Nov. 10, 1907.

49. *Ibid.,* Nov. 23, 1907.   50. *Ibid.,* Dec. 15, 1907.

51. *Ibid.,* Oct. 30, 1907.   52. *Ibid.,* Oct. 19, 1907.

53. *Ibid.,* Nov. 19, 1907.

54. *Das Vaterland,* June 20, 1879.   55. *Ibid.,* Dec. 23, 1879.

56. *Ibid.,* Jan. 23, 1880.   57. *Ibid.,* March 3, 1880.

58. *Ibid.,* May 8, 1880.   59. *Ibid.,* April 17, 1882.

60. *Ibid.,* Nov. 25, 1880.   61. *Ibid.,* Oct. 18, 1907.

62. *Ibid.,* Oct. 30, 1907.   63. *Ibid.,* Oct. 20, 1907.

64. *Ibid.,* Nov. 23, 1907.   65. *Ibid.,* Nov. 24, 1907.

66. *Alldeutsches Tagblatt,* Dec. 20, 1907.

67. *Ibid.,* Oct. 27, 1907.   68. *Ibid.,* Nov. 10, 1907.

69. *Ibid.,* Nov. 28, 1907.   70. *Ibid.,* Nov. 21, 1907.

71. *Ibid.,* Oct. 1, 1907.   72. *Ibid.,* Oct. 11, 1907.

73. Kubizek, *The Young Hitler I Knew,* pp. 80–81.

74. *Mein Kampf,* p. 151.

75. *Alldeutsches Tagblatt,* Oct. 20, 1907.

76. *Ibid.,* Dec. 3, 1907.   77. *Ibid.,* Dec. 28, 1907.

78. *Ibid.,* Nov. 24, 1907.

"THIS BABYLONIAN REALM"

1. *Mein Kampf* (New York, 1939), p. 160.

2. *Ibid.,* p. 51 and p. 160.

3. *Neue Freie Presse, Morgenblatt,* Oct. 24, 1907. Future references will always refer to the *Morgenblatt,* or morning edition, unless otherwise stated.

4. *Ibid., Nachmittagsblatt,* Nov. 11, 1907; *Abendblatt,* Nov. 12, 1907.

5. *Mein Kampf,* pp. 167–68.

6. *Neue Freie Presse, Nachmittagsblatt,* April 13, 1908; Arthur J. May, *The Hapsburg Monarchy* (Cambridge, Mass., 1951), pp. 341–42.

7. *Neue Freie Presse, Abendblatt,* Sept. 19, 1908; May, *The Haps-burg Monarchy,* p. 426.
8. *Neue Freie Presse,* Oct. 8, 1908.
9. *Ibid., Abendblatt,* Oct. 8, 1908.
10. *Ibid.,* Oct. 10, 1908.   11. *Ibid.,* Oct. 16, 1908.
12. *Ibid., Nachmittagsblatt,* Oct. 19, 1908.
13. May, *The Hapsburg Monarchy,* pp. 432–33.
14. *Mein Kampf,* pp. 206–7.
15. Hugo Hantsch, *Die Geschichte Österreichs* (Graz and Vienna, n.d.), II, 598.
16. For summaries of the Agram and Friedjung trials, see May, *The Hapsburg Monarchy,* pp. 383–85; Viktor Bibl, *Geschichte Oesterreichs im XX Jahrhundert* (Leipzig, Vienna, and Berlin, n.d.), pp. 54–55; Hantsch, *Die Geschichte Österreichs,* II, 520.
17. *Neue Freie Presse, Abendblatt,* May 29, 1913.
18. *Ibid.,* May 30, 1913.   19. *Ibid., Abendblatt,* May 30, 1913.
20. *Ibid.,* May 31, 1913.   21. *Ibid., Abendblatt,* May 31, 1913.
22. *Ibid.,* June 1, 1913.   23. *Ibid.,* June 4, 1913.
24. *Ibid.,* June 5, 1913.   25. *Ibid., Abendblatt,* June 5, 1913.
26. Summarized in the *Literary Digest,* Oct. 6, 1928.
27. *Mein Kampf,* p. 119.   28. *Ibid.,* p. 94.

"THE GRINNING, UGLY FACE OF MARXISM"

1. *Mein Kampf* (New York, 1939), p. 51.   2. *Ibid.,* p. 52.
3. *Ibid.,* p. 52–54.   4. *Ibid.,* p. 55.   5. *Ibid.,* p. 59.
6. *Ibid.,* p 66.   7. *Ibid.,* p. 80.
8. Max Ermers, *Victor Adler* (Vienna and Leipzig, 1932), p. 16.
9. Ludwig Brügel, *Geschichte der österreichischen Sozialdemokratie* (Vienna, 1922–25), I, 141.
10. Ermers, *Victor Adler,* p. 47.
11. Julius Deutsch, *Geschichte der österreichischen Arbeiter-bewegung,* 3d ed. (Vienna, 1947), pp. 20–21.
12. Ermers, *Victor Adler,* pp. 49–50.
13. *Ibid.,* pp. 69–70; Richard Charmatz, *Lebensbilder aus der Geschichte Oesterreichs* (Vienna, c.1947), pp. 95–111.
14. Hugo Hantsch, *Die Geschichte Österreichs* (Graz and Vienna, n.d.), II, 418.
15. Brügel, *Geschichte,* II, 84–87; III, 92.
16. Ermers, *Victor Adler,* p. 120.

17. Deutsch, *Geschichte*, pp. 26–27.
18. *Ibid.*, p. 27; Ermers, *Victor Adler*, p. 125.
19. Brügel, *Geschichte*, III, 263–67.
20. *Neue Freie Presse, Morgenblatt*, May 1, 1883.
21. Ermers, *Victor Adler*, pp. 130–31.
22. Richard Charmatz, *Österreichs innere Geschichte von 1848 bis 1907* (Berlin, 1911), II, 32–34.
23. Ermers, *Victor Adler*, pp. 19–20.
24. *Grosse Gestalten des Sozialismus, I. Band: Victor Adler aus seinen Reden und Schriften*, ed. Anton Tesarek (Vienna, 1947), p. 16. Hereafter cited as *Reden und Schriften*.
25. Ermers, *Victor Adler*, p. 150.
26. Brügel, *Geschichte*, III, 382–83.   27. *Ibid.*, III, 390.
28. Hantsch, *Die Geschichte Österreichs*, II, 448–49.
29. *Reden und Schriften*, pp. 199–213.
30. Ermers, *Victor Adler*, p. 198.
31. *Reden und Schriften*, pp. 72–88.
32. Charmatz, *Lebensbilder aus der Geschichte Oesterreichs*, pp. 182–83.
33. Brügel, *Geschichte*, IV, 43–48.   34. *Ibid.*, IV, 80–83.
35. *Ibid.*, IV, 163.   36. *Ibid.*, IV, 149–50, 171, 177–78.
37. *Ibid.*, IV, 232–33, 267–73.
38. *Reden und Schriften*, pp. 139–42.
39. Hantsch, *Die Geschichte Österreichs*, II, 471.
40. Quoted by Maria Hornor Lansdale, *Vienna and the Viennese* (Philadelphia, 1902), pp. 65–66.
41. Brügel, *Geschichte*, IV, 311, 316.
42. Robert A. Kann, *The Multinational Empire: Nationalism and National Reform in the Habsburg Monarchy, 1848–1918* (New York, 1950), II, 155–57; Charmatz, *Österreichs innere Geschichte*, II, 134.
43. Hantsch, *Die Geschichte Österreichs*, II, 472.
44. Brügel, *Geschichte*, IV, 345–47.
45. William A. Jenks, *The Austrian Electoral Reform of 1907* (New York, 1950) pp. 30–33, 40–44.   46. *Ibid.*, p. 87.
47. G. D. H. Cole, *The Second International, 1889–1914*, Part II (London and New York, 1956), p. 531.
48. Brügel, *Geschichte*, IV, 165.   49. *Ibid.*, V, 40.
50. Wilhelm Kosch, *Die Deutschen in Österreich und ihr Ausgleich mit den Tschechen* (Leipzig, 1909), p. 64.

51. Brügel, *Geschichte*, V, 51–52.   52. *Ibid.*, V, 81–89.
53. *Ibid.*, V, 91–101.   54. *Ibid.*, V, 105–6.
55. *Ibid.*, V, 100–1.
56. For discussions of Renner, Bauer, and Social Democratic theorizing about nationalism, see Hugo Hantsch, *Die Nationalitätenfrage im alten Österreich* (Vienna, 1953), pp. 69–80; Kann, *The Multinational Empire*, II, 154–78; Cole, *The Second International*, pp. 551–57; Albert Fuchs, *Geistige Strömungen in Österreich, 1867–1918* (Vienna, 1949), pp. 122–27; Oscar Jászi, *The Dissolution of the Habsburg Monarchy* (Chicago, 1929), pp. 177–84.
57. Brügel, *Geschichte*, V, 65–66.
58. *Reden und Schriften*, pp. 252–57.   59. *Ibid.*, pp. 257–59.
60. Brügel, *Geschichte*, V, 120–21, 125.
61. *Reden und Schriften*, pp. 213–18.
62. Brügel, *Geschichte*, V, 112.
63. Jenks, *Austrian Electoral Reform*, p. 73.
64. Brügel, *Geschichte*, V, 170–76.   65. *Ibid.*, V, 179–81.
66. Adam Wandruszka in *Geschichte der Republik Österreich*, ed. Heinrich Benedikt (Munich, 1954), p. 426.
67. Charmatz, *Lebensbilder aus der Geschichte Oesterreichs*, pp. 200–1.

"SYMPTOMS OF DEBILITY"

1. *Mein Kampf* (New York, 1939), p. 29.   2. *Ibid.*, p. 159.
3. *Hitler's Secret Conversations* (New York, 1953), pp. 270–71.
4. Maria Hornor Lansdale, *Vienna and the Viennese* (Philadelphia, 1902), pp. 94–97.
5. *Hitler's Secret Conversations*, p. 552.
6. August Kubizek, *The Young Hitler I Knew*, trans. E. V. Anderson (Boston, 1955), pp. 185–92, gives a fine picture of his opera-going with Hitler.
7. Max Graf, *Legend of a Musical City* (New York, 1945), pp. 210–11.   8. *Ibid.*, p. 208.
9. Robert Haas, *Die Wiener Oper* (Vienna and Budapest, 1926), pp. 64–66.
10. David and Frederic Ewen, *Musical Vienna* (New York and London, 1939), p. 288.
11. Felix Weingartner, *Buffets and Rewards* (London, 1937), p. 255.
12. *Ibid.*, pp. 258–59.

13. Paul Stefan, *Das Grab in Wien* (Berlin, 1913), pp. 96–99.
14. Weingartner, *Buffets and Rewards,* p. 268; Haas, *Die Wiener Oper,* p. 67.
15. Graf, *Legend of a Musical City,* p. 206.
16. Haas, *Die Wiener Oper,* pp. 67–68.
17. Paul Stefan, *Die Wiener Oper* (Vienna and Leipzig, 1922), pp. 106–7.
18. Haas, *Die Wiener Oper,* p. 68.
19. *Ibid.,* pp. 66–67; Wilhelm Wymetal, *Marie Jeritza* (Vienna and Leipzig, 1922), p. 11.
20. Wymetal, *Marie Jeritza,* pp. 26–27.
21. Maria Jeritza, *Sunlight and Song* (New York, 1924), p. 17.
22. Graf, *Legend of a Musical City,* p. 228.
23. Ernest Newman, *The Life of Richard Wagner* (New York, 1941), III, 138–40.   24. *Ibid.,* pp. 196–200.
25. Graf, *Legend of a Musical City,* pp. 156–57.
26. Alois Przistaupinsky, *50 Jahre Wiener Operntheater* (Vienna, 1919), Tables 92–99.
27. Bruno Walter, *Theme and Variations* (New York, 1946), p. 169.
28. Nicolas Slonimsky, *Music since 1900* (New York, 1949), p. 49.
29. David Ewen, *The Complete Book of 20th Century Music* (New York, 1952), p. 351; Slonimsky, *Music since 1900,* p. 133.
30. Slonimsky, *Music since 1900,* p. 135.
31. *Ibid.,* pp. 363, 366, 368.
32. Kubizek, *The Young Hitler I Knew,* p. 162.
33. *Mein Kampf,* pp. 75–77.
34. Valuable discussions in English of Viennese literary activity between 1890 and 1914 are: Jethro Bithell, *Modern German Literature, 1880–1938* (London, 1946); Victor Lange, *Modern German Literature* (Ithaca, 1945); Arthur Eloesser, *Modern German Literature* (New York, 1933).
35. Bithell, *Modern German Literature,* p. 98.
36. *Ibid.,* pp. 173–74; Eloesser, *Modern German Literature,* p. 189.
37. Eloesser, *Modern German Literature,* p. 171.
38. Felix Salten, *Geister der Zeit* (Berlin, Vienna, and Leipzig, 1924), pp. 15–27; Eloesser, *Modern German Literature,* pp. 178–80; Bithell, *Modern German Literature,* pp. 102–3.
39. On Hugo von Hofmannsthal, see Bithell, *Modern German Literature,* pp. 236–55; Lange, *Modern German Literature,* pp. 40–43; Eloesser, *Modern German Literature,* pp. 180–89.

40. Bithell, *Modern German Literature*, pp. 100–2.
41. On Schnitzler, see Sol Liptzin, *Arthur Schnitzler* (New York, 1932); Eloesser, *Modern German Literature*, pp. 171–76; Bithell, *Modern German Literature*, pp. 257–65.
42. Ernest Jones, *The Life and Work of Sigmund Freud* (New York, 1953–57), I, 292–93, 330; II, 261.
43. *Mein Kampf*, p. 45.   44. *Ibid.*, p. 159.
45. *Hitler's Secret Conversations*, p. 169.
46. Lansdale, *Vienna and the Viennese*, pp. 3–5.
47. A. S. Levetus, *Imperial Vienna* (London and New York, 1905), pp. 214–28.   48. *Mein Kampf*, p. 27.
49. Edward Crankshaw, *Vienna: The Image of a Culture in Decline* (New York, 1938), p. 7.
50. Nikolaus Pevsner, *Pioneers of Modern Design* (New York, 1949), p. 107.
51. On Wagner, see Sigfried Giedion, *Space, Time, and Architecture* (Cambridge, Mass., 1949), pp. 250–55, 570–71; Pevsner, *Pioneers of Modern Design*, pp. 12, 14; Sheldon Cheney, *The New World Architecture* (London, New York, Toronto, 1930), pp. 181–82.
52. On Olbrich, see Cheney, *New World Architecture*, pp. 183–85; Pevsner, *Pioneers of Modern Design*, pp. 119–21.
53. On the *Sezession*, see Cheney, *New World Architecture*, pp. 181–84; Pevsner, *Pioneers of Modern Design*, pp. 104–5, 119–21; Levetus, *Imperial Vienna*, pp. 261–65.
54. On Hoffmann, see Cheney, *New World Architecture*, pp. 185–92; Pevsner, *Pioneers of Modern Design*, pp. 121–23.
55. On Loos, see Pevsner, *Pioneers of Modern Design*, pp. 12, 14, 123–24; Gustav Adolf Platz, *Die Baukunst der neuesten Zeit* (Berlin, 1930), pp. 24–25.
56. Stefan, *Das Grab in Wien*, p. 12.

Bibliography

OFFICIAL SOURCES

Haus der Abgeordneten des österreichischen Reichsrates. Stenographische Protokolle über die Sitzungen des Hauses der Abgeordneten des Reichsrates. X Session, 1888. XI Session, 1891, 1892, 1894, 1895. XII Session, 1901.

Männerheim (Wien XX. Bezirk, Meldemannstrasse Nr. 27). Vienna, 1905.

Österreichische Ministerratsprotokolle, 1885.

Statistisches Jahrbuch der Stadt Wien für das Jahr 1911. Vienna, 1913.

Die Wohltätigkeits-Vereine der k.k. Reichshaupt- und Residenzstadt Wien. 2d ed. Vienna, 1905.

OTHER SOURCES

Allmayer-Beck, Joh. Christoph. Vogelsang: Vom Feudalismus zur Volksbewegung. Vienna, 1952.

Bahr, Hermann. Selbstbildnis. Berlin, 1923.

Benedikt, Heinrich, ed. Geschichte der Republik Österreich. Munich, 1954.

Bibl, Viktor. Georg von Schönerer. Leipzig, 1942.

—— Geschichte Oesterreichs im XX Jahrhundert. Leipzig, Vienna, and Berlin, n.d.

Bithell, Jethro. Modern German Literature, 1880–1938. London, 1946.

Brügel, Ludwig. Geschichte der österreichischen Sozialdemokratie. Vienna, 1922–25.

Charmatz, Richard. Deutsch-österreichische Politik. Leipzig, 1907.

—— Lebensbilder aus der Geschichte Oesterreichs. Vienna, c. 1947.

—— Österreichs innere Geschichte von 1848 bis 1907. Leipzig, 1911.

Charmatz, Richard (*Continued*)
—— Vom Kaiserreich zur Republik. Vienna, c. 1947.

Cheney, Sheldon. The New World Architecture. London, New York, and Toronto, 1930.

Cole, George D. H. The Second International, 1889–1914, Part II. London and New York, 1956.

Crankshaw, Edward. Vienna: The Image of a Culture in Decline. New York, 1938.

Deutsch, Julius. Geschichte der österreichischen Arbeiterbewegung. 3d ed. Vienna, 1947.

Drawe, Hermann. Unter Vagabunden. Vienna, 1910.

Eloesser, Arthur. Modern German Literature. New York, 1933.

Ermers, Max. Victor Adler. Vienna and Leipzig, 1932.

Ewen, David. The Complete Book of 20th Century Music. New York, 1952.

Ewen, David, and Frederic Ewen. Musical Vienna. New York and London, 1939.

Friedlaender, Otto. Letzter Glanz der Märchenstadt. Vienna, c. 1949.

Fuchs, Albert. Geistige Strömungen in Österreich, 1867–1918. Vienna, 1949.

Funder, Friedrich. Vom Gestern ins Heute. 2d ed. Vienna, 1953.

Fürlinger, Raimund. Obdachlosigkeit und Obdachlosen-Fürsorge. Vienna, 1916.

Gay, Peter. The Dilemma of Democratic Socialism. New York, 1952.

Giedion, Sigfried. Space, Time, and Architecture. Cambridge, Mass., 1949.

Goldemund, Heinrich. Die Wiener Wohnungs-Verhältnisse und Vorschläge zur Verbesserung derselben. Vienna, 1910.

Goldhammer, Leo. Die Juden Wiens. Vienna and Leipzig, 1927.

Görlitz, Walter, and Herbert A. Quint. Adolf Hitler. Stuttgart, 1952.

Graf, Max. Legend of a Musical City. New York, 1945.

Greiner, Josef. Das Ende des Hitler-Mythos. Zurich, Leipzig, and Vienna, 1947.

Haas, Robert. Die Wiener Oper. Vienna and Budapest, 1926.

Hantsch, Hugo. Die Geschichte Österreichs. Graz and Vienna, 1947–50.

—— Die Nationalitätenfrage im alten Österreich. Vienna, 1953.

Heiden, Konrad. Der Fuehrer. Trans. Ralph Manheim. Boston, 1944.

Hitler, Adolf. Mein Kampf (Reynal and Hitchcock–Houghton Mifflin edition). New York, 1939.
—— Secret Conversations, 1941–1944. Trans. Norman Cameron and R. H. Stevens. New York, 1953.
Jakob, Margarete. "Das Deutsche Volksblatt und seine politische Geschichte in den Jahren 1889/99." Unpublished dissertation, Vienna, 1937.
Jászi, Oscar. The Dissolution of the Habsburg Monarchy. Chicago, 1929.
Jenks, William A. The Austrian Electoral Reform of 1907. New York, 1950.
Jeritza, Maria. Sunlight and Song. New York, 1924.
Jetzinger, Franz. Hitlers Jugend. Vienna, 1956.
Jones, Ernest. The Life and Work of Sigmund Freud. New York, 1953–57.
Kann, Robert A. "German-speaking Jewry during Austria-Hungary's Constitutional Era (1867–1918)," *Jewish Social Studies*, X (1948), 239–56.
—— The Multinational Empire: Nationalism and National Reform in the Habsburg Monarchy, 1848–1918. New York, 1950.
Karbach, Oscar. "The Founder of Modern Political Antisemitism: George von Schönerer," *Jewish Social Studies*, VII (1945), 3–30.
Kläger, Emil. Durch die Wiener Quartiere des Elends und Verbrechens. Vienna, 1908.
Klopp, Wiard, ed. Die sozialen Lehren des Freiherrn Karl von Vogelsang. St. Pölten, 1894.
Kolmer, Gustav. Parlament und Verfassung in Österreich. Vienna and Leipzig, 1902–11.
Kosch, Wilhelm. Die Deutschen in Österreich und ihr Ausgleich mit den Tschechen. Leipzig, 1909.
Kubizek, August. The Young Hitler I Knew. Trans. E. V. Anderson. Boston, 1955.
Kuppe, Rudolf. Dr. Karl Lueger: Persönlichkeit und Wirken. Vienna, 1947.
—— Karl Lueger und seine Zeit. Vienna, 1933.
Lange, Victor. Modern German Literature. Ithaca, 1945.
Lansdale, Maria Hornor. Vienna and the Viennese. Philadelphia, 1902.
Levetus, A. S. Imperial Vienna. London and New York, 1905.
Liptzin, Sol. Arthur Schnitzler. New York, 1932.

May, Arthur J. The Hapsburg Monarchy. Cambridge, Mass., 1951.
Mayer-Löwenschwerdt, Erwin. Schönerer, der Vorkämpfer. Vienna and Leipzig, 1938.
Molisch, Paul. Geschichte der deutschnationalen Bewegung in Oesterreich. Jena, 1926.
—— Politische Geschichte der deutschen Hochschulen in Österreich von 1848 bis 1918. Vienna and Leipzig, 1939.
Montane, H. Die Prostitution in Wien. Hamburg, Leipzig, and Vienna, 1925.
Neuschäfer, Fritz A. Georg Ritter von Schönerer. Hamburg, 1935.
Newman, Ernest. The Life of Richard Wagner. New York, 1937–41.
Nitti, Francesco S. Catholic Socialism. London, 1908.
Oppenheimer, Ludwig, Freiherr von. Austriaca. Leipzig, 1882.
Petermann, Reinhard E. Wien im Zeitalter Kaiser Franz Josephs I. Vienna, 1908.
Pevsner, Nikolaus. Pioneers of Modern Design. New York, 1949.
Pichl, Eduard. Georg Schönerer. Oldenburg and Berlin, 1938.
Platz, Gustav Adolf. Die Baukunst der neuesten Zeit. Berlin, 1930.
Przistaupinsky, Alois. 50 Jahre Wiener Operntheater. Vienna, 1919.
Rizzi, Hans. "Karl von Vogelsang," Neue österreichische Biographie, 1815–1918, II, 186–95. Vienna, 1925.
Salten, Felix. Geister der Zeit. Berlin, Vienna, and Leipzig, 1924.
—— Das österreichische Antlitz. Berlin, 1909.
Schnee, Heinrich. Georg Ritter von Schönerer. Reichenberg, 1943.
Schwalber, Joseph. Vogelsang und die moderne christlich-soziale Politik. Munich, 1927.
Skalnik, Kurt. Dr. Karl Lueger: Der Mann zwischen den Zeiten. Vienna and Munich, 1954.
Slonimsky, Nicolas. Music since 1900. New York, 1949.
Stefan, Paul. Das Grab in Wien. Berlin, 1913.
—— Die Wiener Oper. Vienna and Leipzig, 1922.
Tesarek, Anton, ed. Grosse Gestalten des Sozialismus, I. Band: Victor Adler aus seinen Reden und Schriften. Vienna, 1947.
Walter, Bruno. Theme and Variations. New York, 1946.
Weingartner, Felix. Buffets and Rewards. London, 1937.
Willfort, M. Zur Wohnungsnot in Wien. Vienna, 1911.
Winter, Max. Im dunkelsten Wien. Vienna and Leipzig, 1904.
Wymetal, Wilhelm. Marie Jeritza. Vienna and Leipzig, 1922.
Zoller, Albert. Hitler Privat. Düsseldorf, 1949.

NEWSPAPERS

Alldeutsches Tagblatt. October, November, December, 1907.
Deutsches Volksblatt. October, November, December, 1907.
Neue Freie Presse. April, 1882. May, 1883. May, June, 1906. October, November, 1907. April, September, October, 1908. May, June, 1913.
Das Vaterland. June, December, 1879. January, March, May, November, 1880. April, May, June, 1882. October, November, December, 1907.

Index